Y0-BRO-701

The Random House Series in Money and Banking
EDITOR: HARLAN M. SMITH, *University of Minnesota*

THE ESSENTIALS OF MONEY AND BANKING
by Harlan M. Smith
University of Minnesota
A Core Volume (clothbound)

INTERNATIONAL MONETARY RELATIONS
by Delbert Snider
Miami University, Oxford, Ohio
(paperback)

FINANCIAL INSTITUTIONS
by Raymond W. Goldsmith
Yale University
(paperback)

ELEMENTS OF MONETARY POLICY
by Thomas Mayer
University of California at Davis
(paperback)

ELEMENTARY MONETARY THEORY
by Harlan M. Smith
University of Minnesota
(paperback)

COMMERCIAL BANKING IN THE ECONOMY
by Paul Nadler
New York University
(paperback)

the essentials of money and banking

HARLAN M. SMITH · UNIVERSITY OF MINNESOTA

THE *essentials*

OF *money* AND

banking

 random house • new york

preface to the series

by Harlan M. Smith

This series of books in money and banking has two primary purposes. First, it provides users of existing textbooks in the field with appropriate supplementary material in areas to which they may wish to devote additional attention. Second, in conjunction with the "core" volume (*The Essentials of Money and Banking* by Harlan M. Smith), this series makes it possible for each instructor and student in the field to put together a collection of books that will best suit his needs in terms of the amount of reading involved and the proportion of the course to be devoted to the different segments of the field. The core volume makes it possible to ensure that a basic minimum is covered in each of the areas traditionally included in money and banking courses. The "satellite" books may then be used to supplement the basic text in desired areas. The series thus provides a maximum degree of flexibility in selecting textbook materials for money and banking courses.

These books can serve other purposes as well, for each one is written in such a manner that it can be used independently, or in any desired combination, by anyone possessing an interest in its subject. The books provide, in every case, systematic expositions of their subjects, yet each is short enough to serve as supplementary text material in various courses as well as in the standard money and banking courses.

preface

This small volume represents a selection from the field of money and banking of the information and analysis that is most essential for a college course in the subject. All the areas traditionally covered in such a course are included, but they are not all treated in as much detail as in the usual lengthy textbook. Attention is focussed on the fundamentals in each area. With respect to these, however, enough explanatory material is provided to enable the student to obtain a real understanding of the essentials. For example, the illustration of the credit expansion process is developed with great care so that the student is well grounded in this basic topic. Similarly, the student is taught to work out the effects of various monetary and fiscal transactions so that he can fully grasp the analysis of factors determining the money supply and the operation of policy instruments. Understanding of policy problems is further augmented by analysis of the historical development of policy. The treatment presents money and commercial banking within a framework of monetary assets and financial institutions.

The brevity of this volume is intended to make it possible for a college course to employ supplementary material to develop selected portions of the subject more fully. The book is designed to be supplemented by any or all of the paperbacks in the Random House Series in Money and Banking. Taken together, the entire set provides extensive coverage of every part of the field. For courses that are not long enough to permit use of the entire set, some supplementary volumes may be optional reading or may be omitted entirely with knowledge that the present "core" volume provides the most essential material in each part of the field. The instructor is thus in a position to hold to a minimum the reading assigned for any areas he chooses and to assign further reading in the areas that he wishes to treat more extensively. This "core" volume is, then, a true "introduction" to money and banking.

Harlan M. Smith

Minneapolis, Minnesota
September, 1967

contents

tables

figures

the essentials of money and banking

money and liquid assets

EVERYBODY IS AFFECTED BY THE WAY OUR MONE-
tary economy works. Everybody should accordingly benefit by learn-
ing about the monetary system. And any study of money requires us
to develop some understanding of banking and its economic role. It
is the purpose of this book to set forth in a relatively brief exposition
the basic essentials of money and banking.

We shall learn how the monetary and banking system can facilitate the operation of the entire economy. We shall note what economic
disturbances can arise in the system and what effects these may have.
We shall also consider the possibilities of using policies in the sphere
of money and banking to deal with some types of economic problems
even when they arise outside that sphere.

We begin in this chapter by looking at the functions of money
and at the various forms of money. This will lead us to regard some
assets as though they were "near money." Additional key ideas will
be developed as we proceed.

economic role of money

An economy of self-sufficient economic units would have no use for money, and an exchange economy could work without money. In an exchange economy people buy and sell goods or services. Such transactions could be effected by barter, but bartering has inherent difficulties that practically preclude the development of a high degree of specialization and exchange. To obtain a desired commodity or service, one must be able to offer in return a commodity or service wanted by the supplier. Stated briefly, a double coincidence of wants is necessary. While such fortuitous circumstances do occasionally occur, few if any of us today could directly exchange the services we sell to make our living for all the goods and services we consume. True, the exchange might be achieved indirectly through a series of exchanges, but an exorbitant amount of time would likely be consumed just in the bartering process. Moreover, the process would be complicated tremendously by the indivisibility of some of the units in which goods are available. Since exchange ratios among all goods are not one for one, suppliers of some goods will always find themselves embarrassed because they cannot divide their product into pieces equal in value to the amount of something else that they wish to acquire. They do not really want the task of having to dispose of a surplus of something that they have acquired. Imagine a hatter acquiring ten dozen fresh eggs in exchange for a hat for the farmer's wife.

Money is an economic catalyst. It overcomes the disadvantages of barter and facilitates exchange. It is essential for the development of a high degree of specialization and interdependence of economic units. A monetary system may be said to be composed of (1) a common standard of value or unit of account (in terms of which the value of everything else is expressed) and (2) a commonly accepted medium of exchange (by payment of which debts are discharged). Money as a medium of exchange provides its possessor with "generalized" purchasing power, or command over goods and services in general.

forms of money

Money may be defined as anything that functions as a commonly accepted medium of exchange. Many different things have served as money in different times and places.[1] The wampum of the American Indians is familiar to every school child in this country. One does not need to study economics to learn that other countries use a currency different from our own. Not everything is equally suitable as a medium of exchange. The widespread use of metal coins probably stems from their physical properties—such as portability and durability—from the ease with which they lend themselves to attempts at standardization, and from their high value per unit of weight. Standardization itself produces economies and introduces safeguards in the process of exchange. Standard coins make it possible to count money in simple fashion and obviate the need of weighing and assaying metal pieces.

The development of a satisfactory coinage was not without difficulties, as any historical study of the subject can attest. Debasement of the coinage, by clipping coins or otherwise, resulted in coins of higher metallic value being hoarded (sometimes melted down for bullion) and disappearing from circulation while the debased coins were passed on in trade. The proposition that "bad money" drives out "good money" is known as Gresham's Law. Private enterprise in coinage is not consistent with the development of a coinage that is uniform and otherwise satisfactory. However, the usual government monopoly of coinage in each country has not of itself ensured such a coinage. Governments have debased coins for their own purposes, only to have them decline in value. More recent history has seen the widespread use of "token" coins (the value of whose commodity content is known to be less than the face value of the coins) instead of "full-bodied" coins. But this is only one aspect of more fundamental changes in the nature of money.

Convenience has probably been the key to the development and use of more sophisticated forms of money and credit. Carrying substantial amounts of commodity money is often inconvenient. This has been remedied by the rise of other forms of money—for example, "representative money," each piece of which represents a certain amount of the commodity money, such as the $1 silver certificate that was our common dollar bill for many years. Convertibility into the commodity or commodity money may give representative money

[1] See Sir Norman Angell, *The Story of Money* (New York: Frederick A. Stokes Company, 1929); A. R. Burns, *Money and Monetary Policy in Early Times* (New York: Knopf, 1927); Paul Einzig, *Primitive Money* (London: Eyre & Spottiswoode, 1949); William H. Furness III, *The Island of Stone Money* (Philadelphia: Lippincott, 1910).

general acceptability, though it may become and remain generally acceptable without regard to convertibility.

Even more significantly, most money now takes the form of a debt (or a claim, when regarded from the viewpoint of the holder of the money rather than of the issuer). As paper money came into widespread use, it took the form of a debt of the bank or government issuing it. The issuer promised to pay to the bearer a specified sum of generally acceptable money. When too much money was issued and the issuer could not meet demands for redemption, the issuer's notes depreciated or ceased to be generally acceptable. In this country we had a long history of problems associated with developing a satisfactory paper money. At first paper money was issued by private banks chartered by the states and then by banks chartered by the federal government. But it was not until the issuance of paper money was centralized in the Federal Reserve System that the country had a satisfactory paper money. The solution of the problem of over-issue fostered general acceptability of notes without redeemability in other money, especially as Federal Reserve notes were made legal tender for all debts public and private.

The important role of government in developing a satisfactory money should not lead one into mistakenly thinking that government sanction of a "money" (for example, by itself issuing the money or by making it legal tender) is either a necessary or a sufficient condition to achieve general acceptability. What has circulated as money has often been created by private interests, from the merchants of old to the banks of more modern times. And government sanction has sometimes been unable to maintain the acceptability of a money, as during the German hyperinflation of 1923. Overissue of any money, relative to the amount needed to carry on the ordinary business of the economy at a reasonably stable price level, seems to result generally in the depreciation of the money; if carried too far, general acceptability may be destroyed. Limitation of issue is thus of first importance, not government sanction.

It is possible, of course, for money to be in too limited supply. The development of a primitive exchange economy is hampered if people sometimes have to resort to barter because not enough money is in circulation to be used for all transactions. Although it is easy to see the consequences for a monetary economy of far too little money and of far too much money, it is not so easy to determine the "optimum" amount of money in any given situation. We shall give more attention to criteria for regulating the money supply later;

suffice it to assert here that the development of a satisfactory money depends fundamentally upon the volume of the money relative to the need for it. The most important respect, then, in which government may promote "sound money" is through control of the amount of money created.

United States money supply

The forms of money in widespread use in the United States today, are given in Table 1.1. (Students should consult the most recent issue of the *Federal Reserve Bulletin* to update the statistics.) The money

Table 1.1 Principal Forms of Money in the United States, January, 1967
(*millions of dollars*)

Coins		4,461
Standard silver dollars	482	
Fractional coin	3,979	
Silver certificates		553
Federal Reserve notes		37,962
Currency (total of above)*		42,976
Demand deposits held by the public		153,250

* Figures exclude over $3.5 billion held by the Federal Reserve but include over $4.5 billion held by commercial banks.

SOURCE: *Federal Reserve Bulletin* (March, 1967), p. 405, 408.

stock has been simplified by the fact that general issuance of some older forms of money for public use has ceased. These include the Civil War greenbacks (United States notes), Treasury notes of 1890, gold coins and gold certificates, bank notes of banks chartered by the states, national bank notes, and some others. The process is now proceeding to its limit with the replacement of silver certificates by Federal Reserve notes. (A rise in the market value of silver has resulted in the private purchase of silver from the Treasury. The use of silver for nonmonetary purposes has also been a major factor in the rise of its market value. Thus there has been a reduction in the stock of silver against which the Treasury can issue silver certificates.)

It is noteworthy that demand deposits (checking accounts) are included in Table 1.1 as part of the money supply. The justification for this is that payments by check vastly exceed payments by coin or paper currency, and accordingly it must be recognized that demand deposits constitute the largest part of the actual medium of exchange. Changes in the total money supply are chargeable largely to those factors that determine the supply of demand deposits.

Our money, then, consists of currency (coin and paper money), which we shall call "pocketbook money," and demand deposits, which we shall call "checkbook money."

near money

The common distinction between money and nonmonetary assets is made by calling anything "money" if it is a generally accepted medium of exchange. For anything to be generally acceptable as a medium of exchange it normally has to have a relatively stable value. The particular item of exchange will not serve well if one does not know from one day to the next how much one can buy with it. Indeed, the greater the stability over time, the more satisfactory it is as a medium of exchange. Stability of value (purchasing power) over time also enables a monetary asset to serve as a temporary "store of value." One can hold some of his wealth in money form until such time as he chooses to spend the money in some way. Alternatively, one can store his wealth in various other forms, but if he puts it in some forms, he may have some difficulty converting it into money without any loss should he need to do so. Assets can be classified with regard to the ease with which they can be converted into money without substantial risk of capital loss. Those easily converted are called "liquid assets;" those at the other end of the scale are called "illiquid assets." The most highly liquid assets are thought of as "near money" or good "money substitutes."

The volume of good money substitutes that people possess may have an influence on their behavior comparable, to some degree, to that of their stock of money. Consequently, information about the money supply needs to be supplemented by information about the total supply of close money substitutes. And significance can be expected to attach to changes in the public's desires with respect to their liquidity in general, or more specifically to the proportions they wish to maintain between their holdings of money and various forms of near money.

Securities of various kinds provide attractive alternatives to holding more money (of any kind) than is required to handle expected transactions because securities are earning assets. There is in general, however, an inverse relationship between earnings and liquidity. The most liquid securities have relatively low yields; the higher yields are obtainable only by investing in less liquid assets. While money is the embodiment of generalized purchasing power, a security involves a highly specific set of relationships between the owner and the issuer. Broadly speaking, a purchaser of a security is either a lender or a purchaser of certain specified rights of ownership with respect to the property and earnings of the issuer of the security. A bondholder is a lender to whom the sum specified on the face of the bond is payable at the due date of the bond and to whom interest payments of specified size are to be made meanwhile. If the bond nominally carries a 3 percent coupon or interest rate, the actual yield on a purchaser's investment will vary inversely with the amount he invested in his purchase of the bond. It will be greater than 3 percent if the purchaser bought the bond for less than its "par," or face, amount and less than 3 percent if he bought the bond at a "premium" instead of at a "discount." A purchaser of a share of corporate stock, on the other hand, has purchased part ownership in the firm; there is no loan repayment involved. If the purchaser wants his money back at any time, he must sell the stock to someone else. Meanwhile his earnings depend upon the earnings of the company and its dividend policy. If the company fails, bondholders and other creditors will be paid off first, the stockholders having only a residual claim on the assets. Stockholders are thus riskbearers to a greater degree than bondholders, and equities (shares of stock) are generally considered less liquid than bonds, other things being the same. A comparable distinction crops up elsewhere with less effect on liquidity. For example, depositing money in a savings account in a commercial bank is in form making a loan to the bank, while putting the same money into a savings and loan association is purchasing a share of ownership. Legally the bank must pay you upon thirty days' notice if you want to withdraw your funds from a savings account, while the savings and loan association need not pay until it has funds enough not tied up in its own lending operations. In practice both institutions commonly return your funds upon demand. The difference in rate of return in the two instances derives in part from differing regulation of the two institutions. There is some debate over the merits of the different regulations.

Table 1.2 shows public holdings of liquid assets of types com-

Table 1.2   Selected Liquid Assets Held by the Public*
(billions of dollars)

	DECEMBER, 1966
Total	599.6
Demand deposits and currency	168.5
Time deposits	
Commercial banks	158.4
Mutual savings banks	54.8
Postal savings system	.1
Savings and loan shares	113.2
U. S. government savings bonds	50.9
U. S. government securities maturing within one year	53.6

* Excludes amounts owned by the United States government, the Federal Re
serve, domestic banks, and savings and loan associations.
SOURCE: *Economic Report of the President*, 90th Congress, First Session, Trans-
mitted to the Congress January, 1967, p. 269, Table B-47. Figures are seasonally
adjusted.

monly regarded as money substitutes and hence alternatives to holding some wealth in money form. Savings deposits in banks are in
practice so readily transferable to checking accounts or "pocketbook
money" that some economists contend it does not matter to the individual what portion of his assets are in the one form or the other.
Therefore, they add time accounts to checking accounts in computing
what they consider to be the appropriate total for the money supply.[2]
If we go beyond this, even though other liquid assets may also be
readily convertible into money and their possession may affect the
holder like the possession of more money, one gets into the difficult
question of where to draw the line between what to include and
what to exclude from the total that acts like money in respects other
than making payments directly. For example, United States Treasury
bills are short-term securities (typically payable in three months
from date of issue) that involve as little risk as any security and that

[2] Savings deposits are included in Table 1.2 as part of the time deposit figures.
Strictly speaking, it is mainly the passbook savings accounts that are readily
withdrawable; recent figures show that these comprise about 60 percent of the
time deposits for member banks of the Federal Reserve System. Various savings
certificates, on the other hand, can be cashed only at specified times. However,
negotiable certificates of deposit issued in large denominations have been developed as a relatively new type of liquid instrument used by big business. A breakdown of the time deposit figures in Table 1.2 by these categories is not available.

have an established market in which resale is easy. Many banks and some business firms invest temporarily idle cash in such bills rather than hold the cash idle until needed. But a longer-term security that is near the redemption date may be as liquid under some circumstances as the short-term security.[3] The wide variety of securities, proximities to due dates, and so forth, make somewhat arbitrary any decision as to what to count as though it were almost money, and as economic conditions change over time, the dividing line would need to be shifted.

Therefore, it is simplest to define money as confined to that which serves directly as a medium of exchange (currency and demand deposits) and to treat highly liquid financial assets as near money or money substitutes. In Chapter Eight there will be further discussion of the issuance and handling of various types of financial assets by financial institutions other than commercial banks. Individuals do, of course, make decisions as to whether their distribution of their wealth among various assets leaves them liquid enough, and economists have to take into account any changes that affect people's liquidity and study the effects of people's decisions about liquidity.

We have now seen that for the holders of securities such assets are an alternative to money as a way of storing wealth. The allocation of wealth by individuals among various possible forms is determined by the relative importance that they attach to such factors as safety, liquidity, and earnings of the assets. And the amount of their wealth —especially in relatively liquid form—influences, along with their current income, the volume of their spending.

In the acquisition of securities the investor transfers money to the seller, thus giving him generalized purchasing power in addition to whatever he previously possessed. Where this transaction takes the form of a loan, a debt is created that the borrower is obligated to repay. In general, people voluntarily assume debts because the immediate use for which they borrow money is worth enough to them that they are willing to pay interest for the privilege of borrowing. Thus, people are willing to pay interest on a mortgage loan in order that they may acquire ownership of a house before they would otherwise be able to do so. Or a business firm is able, by virtue of borrowing someone's savings, to purchase productive equipment that enables it to produce more goods and thereby to earn more than enough to repay the loan and the interest on it. Debtor and creditor both gain,

[3] Table 1.2 shows public holdings of securities maturing within a year; of this total, it is estimated that Treasury bills constitute about $40 billion.

the latter by earning interest while deferring the use of savings until he wants to spend them and the former by being able to earn from the use of the funds or by being able to enjoy something at present instead of in the future. The economist would say that the loan transaction results in increased production, that is, increased want satisfaction. It has done so by putting the money of the saver to use. Use of a security (a debt instrument) as a store of value thus results in money being spent rather than lying idle. In other words, the velocity of circulation of money has been increased. Thus debt creation provides alternative stores of value, affects the use of money, and affects production. Those to whom the term "debt" has a negative connotation might better appreciate its role if they remember that debt and credit are two sides of the same thing and involve the transfer of a claim or purchasing power.

This brief introduction has served to make us aware that money as a medium of exchange helps "make the wheels go round" in the economy. If we are to understand the functioning of our economy, we must heed the role of money substitutes. As we pursue our field of study, we shall note that an increase or decrease of money or of liquid assets or debts and also a shifting from one to another of these affect the economy. Therefore, it is necessary to know (1) the factors affecting money and credit, (2) what controls can be applied to them, and (3) the role of financial institutions in the economy. To understand the role of such institutions, it is best to start with an examination of commercial banks.

questions

1. *What characteristics are desirable in money if it is to perform its several functions satisfactorily?*
2. *Should time deposits be considered part of the money supply?*
3. *Upon what does the liquidity of an asset depend?*
4. *How can money be a debt?*
5. *Define and give illustrations of "near money."*

· T W O ·

bank assets and liabilities

THE TWO MOST OBVIOUS FUNCTIONS OF BANKS are as storehouses for one's money and as places where money can be borrowed. But how do banks affect the economy at large? This chapter will begin our exploration of that question. We shall consider the significance of the banks' handling of near money and other financial assets as well as their handling of money.

An economy can get along without banks, as it can without money; but as money greases the wheels of the economic machine, so does the banking system. It is a great convenience. As we already noted in the first chapter, the demand deposits of banks constitute the largest part of the money supply today. Most payments are made by drawing checks on such deposits. The commercial banks, that is, banks that hold checking accounts (demand deposits), perform the mechanical job of handling the vast number of checks—subtracting the proper amounts from the accounts of depositors who write the checks and adding to the accounts of those who deposit checks.

Of course, they also make possible a shift from deposits to pocketbook money or vice versa. In addition, banks enable people who wish to earn interest on some of their money to convert it into a form of near money, namely savings (time) deposits rather than demand deposits. Increasingly popular in recent years are various other forms of time deposits. Such deposits usually carry a higher rate of interest in exchange for making the deposit specified non-withdrawable for a period of time, such as three months, six months, or one year. In these cases one receives a certificate of deposit that is automatically renewable or cashable at the end of the specified period.

Thus, people as bank depositors even within the operations of a single bank can choose between liquidity and earnings. They can, of course, withdraw money from the bank and invest it elsewhere if they wish. A bank has the same sort of choice between liquidity and earnings; how it chooses will be influenced strongly by the behavior of the bank's depositors. The bank is motivated by its desire for profit in whatever situation it finds itself.

How banks operate in various situations has important implications for the whole economics system and so we need to examine these operations. Let us turn next, then, to an investigation of banking with particular attention to bank dealings in money, near money, and other financial instruments.

banking as a business

A commercial bank is obviously a business. Its income is earned primarily by making loans, for which interest is charged. The initial source of funds for lending is the capital raised when the bank is established. Raising capital usually involves the issuance and sale of bank stock. The purchaser of the stock is purchasing part ownership of the bank. He is risking the money he has invested in the stock in the expectation of gain from the earnings of the bank. If capital were the sole source of a bank's funds for lending, the bank would not have much business. Additional funds are obtained by attracting the public to deposit in the bank as a safe, convenient, and desirable place to keep some of its money. The interest paid on savings deposits and other time deposits attracts funds that are likely to remain for longer periods of time than funds deposited in a checking account. But substantial sums are deposited in checking accounts because depositors find payment by check to be so convenient and safe. All funds (demand and time) deposited by the public in a bank enable the bank to make loans because not all deposits are likely to be withdrawn at the same time. Competition among banks for deposits by the public is competition for funds to lend. The funds deposited in a bank do not always represent a diminution in the physical amount of coin or paper money held by depositors; it may, and more frequently does, represent a check drawn upon another bank. When someone receives such a check and deposits it in his bank, the receiving bank obtains funds as soon as the check is cleared.[1] Such funds are not different in function for the receiving bank from those received when the public deposits currency. All funds can be held as a reserve behind deposits or can be put to other use as we shall note. Ordinarily a bank owns the building in which it conducts its business. The bank building and the currency or other reserves, whether obtained from the sale of stock or from deposits of the public, are assets of the bank.

Of course, when someone deposits in a bank, the bank owes him that much cash, and it may have to pay any or all of it to him (or for him, if in a checking account) at some time. Although the cash received (by direct deposit or indirectly through clearing a check drawn on another bank) is an asset for the bank, the bank has a liability of equal amount that it may sometime have to meet. Banking as we know it has developed because normally depositors do not all demand the return of their money at the same time. Thus, the bank does not need to keep a reserve equal to more than a small fraction of its total deposit liability at any one time. In the past a common cause of bank failures was an insufficiency of cash reserves on hand at the bank to satisfy the demands of the depositors for cash funds. Therefore, banks have been required by law to maintain a certain minimum reserve. A common requirement has specified that cash reserves be no less than 10 percent of deposits.

The fact that only a fraction of funds deposited need be kept on hand enables a bank to make loans. This can lead to an expansion of the money supply as banks create additional demand deposits for the borrowers.

balance sheet

It is time now to sketch the picture of the assets and liabilities of banks more systematically and in a little more detail. The assets

---

[1] The clearing of checks is described later in this chapter.

are the items of value that the bank owns. Liabilities are the amounts that the bank owes others. Or, as usually stated, they represent the claims of others against the bank and hence against its assets. The term "net worth" is used to designate the difference between the assets of a business and its liabilities. Residual claimants of the bank's assets are, of course, the owners of the bank; if stock has been issued, these are the stockholders. The "capital accounts" represent their interest in the bank. Because the stockholders have a claim on any assets not offset by liabilities, the sum of liabilities and capital accounts equals the assets of the business. The financial statement that shows assets, liabilities, and capital accounts is called a "balance sheet."

Like other businesses, banks may set up several capital accounts. Together these represent net worth. The par value of outstanding capital stock of the bank is listed in one account. As the bank earns net income, this may be entered into an account for undivided profit. From this dividends are paid, or portions of the profit are retained permanently in the business and listed in an account called "surplus." Some profits may be represented in special "reserve accounts" against which subsequent losses may be charged. The size of the capital accounts in the aggregate for a bank is important to bank depositors because it indicates the extent to which the bank could absorb losses in value of assets without becoming insolvent, that is, without having liabilities in excess of the value of the assets.

assets

Table 2.1 shows the principal assets and liabilities, in the aggregate, for all commercial banks in the United States. Some of the items merit a few words of explanation. The item "reserves with Federal Reserve banks" refers to the funds that banks have deposited in the twelve Federal Reserve banks. Banks that are members of the Federal Reserve System were required when that system was established to deposit sufficient funds with their district Federal Reserve banks to meet their reserve requirement, and they still carry the bulk of their legal reserves as a deposit in the district banks. This is safe and relatively convenient since a bank can most easily meet adverse clearing house balances by writing checks on its deposit at a Federal Reserve bank. In addition, many banks, especially small banks, keep some funds on deposit in banks in other

Table 2.1 Commercial Bank Assets, Liabilities, and Capital Accounts,
June 30, 1966
(*millions of dollars*)

Total assets			385,393
Cash assets		60,013	
Reserves with Federal Reserve banks	18,094		
Currency and coin	5,234		
Balance with domestic banks	13,548		
Cash items in process of collection	23,137		
Loans		211,980	
Commercial and industrial	77,245		
Agriculture	8,488		
For purchase or carrying securities	8,633		
To financial institutions	15,904		
Real estate	51,899		
Other (to individuals)	47,682		
Miscellaneous	5,227		
Investments		102,258	
U.S. government securities*	53,503		
Bills 9,095			
Notes 12,306			
Bonds 32,102			
State and local government securities	40,612		
Other securities	8,142		
Other assets (including bank premises)		11,142	
Total liabilities			354,084
Total deposits		338,004	
Demand deposits	181,877		
Time deposits	156,127		
Borrowings		4,353	
Other liabilities		11,727	
Total capital accounts			31,309

* The breakdown is not available from the Federal Reserve; estimated by the author.

SOURCE: *Federal Reserve Bulletin* (March, 1967), pp. 408, 412, 413.

cities, especially in financial centers or nearby large cities. These funds appear in Table 2.1 under the heading "balance with domestic banks." The large "correspondent banks," as they are called, perform a number of services for the banks depositing funds with them. They provide a facility for the small bank to make payments easily to or from the deposit account in the area of the larger bank. This is especially important for banks that are not members of the Federal Reserve System. The larger bank is apt to have more experience and information about business conditions in a wider area because it is often sought out by the smaller banks for advice on business and credit conditions and banking policy. The balance sheet item "balance with domestic banks" cannot then reflect more than one dimension of the relationship among correspondent banks. "Cash items in process of collection" refers to checks deposited in a bank but not yet collected from the banks on which they are drawn.

Normally the largest item on the assets side of the balance sheet is termed "loans" or "loans and discounts." The latter are merely loans that were discounted; that is, the interest payable on the loan was subtracted from the face amount of the loan (the amount to be repaid) and the difference is what was actually available to the borrower to use. Banks make loans (including those discounted) to various classes of borrowers. The most important are business firms in the fields of commerce or industry. The loans help finance the production or marketing of goods. Other loans are made to household consumers, to farmers, or to other financial institutions, including banks.

When a bank makes a loan, it not only requires the borrower to sign a note that constitutes a legal promise to repay by the due date, but it may also require the borrower to pledge collateral for the loan. This takes the form of assets whose value the bank expects will be at least equal to the size of the debt to the bank. If the borrower does not pay the bank as agreed, the bank may go through legal proceedings to obtain possession of the assets pledged as collateral for the loan and may sell the assets to recover the amount lent. Loans may be classified on the basis of the form of security behind the loan. Commercial loans may have an inventory of marketable goods as collateral. Real estate loans are generally secured by mortgages on the real estate; the standard joke that "I don't own my house, the bank does" is testimony to the fact that people commonly sign a mortgage when they buy a home, and banks are among those that furnish the money initially and then hold the mortgage. Installment purchases of household durables, especially automobiles, are often financed directly or indirectly by bank credit (indirectly when the bank lends some of the funds to the finance company or other initial lender).

Direct loans to consumers fall largely in the category "other (to individuals)" in Table 2.1. The automobile or other consumer good pledged as collateral is ordinarily the security for these consumer loans and can be sold by the lender if the borrower defaults on the loan repayments. Securities, such as stocks or bonds, may be pledged as collateral for loans at times. When the bank accepts securities or a claim on real estate as its protection against default by the borrower, it needs to hedge against the possibility that the value of the securities or real estate may decline before the loan is repaid. It hedges against such a decline by "margining" the loan, that is, by lending less than the full market value of the collateral at the time of the loan. Banks frequently refuse to lend more than 60 percent of the current market value of real estate on a conventional mortgage loan. These practices protect the banks against losses that might otherwise occur. Regulations of the Federal Reserve Board of Governors fix the margin requirements that limit the amount that banks or others may lend anyone to purchase securities when the securities themselves are the collateral on which the lender relies in case of default by the borrower. This is to prevent bank credit from being used too extensively to finance a speculative stock market boom.

Loans may also be classified by duration. Since a bank has so many liabilities that it may be required to meet upon demand, it prefers that most of its funds not be tied up for long periods. The normal three-month commercial loan has traditionally been a favorite of bankers as a consequence. Consumer loans, which have become an important part of bank lending only in the last few decades, are mostly installment loans on which monthly repayments are made, even though the full amount of a given loan may not be paid off for as much as three years. Mortgages are also generally amortized monthly now; this represents a great improvement over conditions in the days when the funds were tied up until repayment time, for then the borrower was often unable to meet the large obligation all at once. A movement in the other direction is the increase in recent years in the number of "term loans" made by banks. These are loans made for longer than a year and frequently for as much as three to five years. Typically, repayment is made in installments at intervals over the term of the loan. Small businesses that do not have ready access to intermediate-term capital markets frequently avail themselves of this type of bank loan to finance such things as the purchase of new equipment.

Other financial institutions find that they sometimes need to supplement their loanable funds by borrowing from commercial banks. Banks also borrow from each other at times to meet temporary needs for additional funds.

Banks invest some of their funds in obligations of federal, state, or local government units and in high-grade marketable corporate bonds. The rate of return on these is generally less than on the loans made by the banks, but the marketability of the securities provides a way to obtain more cash when needed. The shorter term the securities, or the closer the due date of the securities, the less risk the bank takes with respect to the possible drop in market price of the security at the time the bank might need to sell it. Consequently, banks generally try to include in their portfolio some securities that mature soon. It will be noted in Table 2.1 that not all the funds that banks invest in United States government securities are invested in the higher yield long-term bonds. Some funds are invested in shorter-term notes and in ninety-day Treasury bills. The active market in bills makes it very easy for banks to sell some of them if they need funds quickly or want to invest funds in them temporarily.

The risk of default of interest or principal by the issuer of the securities is reduced partly by diversification—that is, investing in securities of a variety of issuers—and by legal prohibition of investment in speculative issues or investment of more than 10 percent of a bank's capital and surplus in securities of any one private issuer. Banks are not permitted to buy common stock (except of other banks). Investment in United States government obligations is also a way of avoiding default risks. Since 1933 commercial banks have been forbidden to engage in what is essentially investment banking business, that is, the purchase or underwriting of new issues of corporate securities for the purpose of profit from their resale. The purpose of such regulation is to prevent a repetition of the heavy losses that occurred in the early 1930's when commercial banks were caught with too much of their funds tied up in such operations, just when the securities markets were in bad shape.

liabilities

The principal liabilities of commercial banks are what they owe their depositors—the amounts that depositors are entitled to withdraw. Demand deposits are drawn upon by the depositor writing checks that are payable on demand. Time deposits need not be paid out by the bank until the end of a defined period; however, the usual savings account is withdrawable upon presentation of a withdrawal slip, without the nominally required thirty-day notice. Time certificates of deposit, however, can be converted back to cash only after a specified length of time. Recently businesses with temporary excess funds have been purchasing bank certificates of deposit. Some of these are negotiable, thus allowing a business to transfer these certificates to another party should it need the funds invested before the maturation date of the certificates. Table 2.2 shows the typical picture of deposit ownership among different classes of depositors.

When a bank makes a payment on its own behalf, as for example when it makes a payment to meet banking expenses, it writes a check signed by a bank officer. The holder of such a check has the same sort of claim on the bank as does the holder of a deposit account; thus, officers' checks are listed with demand deposits as bank liabilities. The same is true of certified checks, which guarantee the recipient of these checks that the writers of the checks do indeed have sufficient funds on deposit at the bank to cover the checks. When a check is certified, the bank reduces the writer's deposit by the amount of the certified check, and the bank's liability for the latter takes the place of the liability for that amount of demand deposits.

Since 1933 banks have been prohibited from paying interest on demand deposits, and the Federal Reserve System has regulated maximum interest rates payable by member banks on time deposits. The intent was to avoid costly interest rate competition among banks, which it was thought might force banks into more risky loan and investment policies in search for high enough rates of return to meet rising interest on their own deposit accounts. The lower rate of turnover of time deposits compared to demand deposits has provided the rationale for requiring a smaller cash reserve behind the former and permitting interest to be paid on them. The experience of recent years attests to the vigor of competition among banks and between banks and other financial institutions seeking to attract the deposit of funds

Table 2.2   Ownership of Bank Deposits, December, 1963
              (*billions of dollars*)

Demand deposits and currency*	163.7
Consumers and nonprofit organizations	77.0
Farm business	5.5
Nonfarm noncorporate business	12.5
Corporate business	30.8
U. S. government	7.9
State and local governments	13.2
Savings institutions	4.0
Insurance companies	3.9
Finance, n.e.c.	4.5
Rest of the world	4.4
Time deposits and savings accounts	112.4
Consumers and nonprofit organizations	89.8
Corporate business	10.3
U. S. government	.3
State and local governments	8.1
Savings institutions	.2
Rest of the world	3.7

* Figures are not available that show demand deposit holdings alone. The currency component of the total is about $33 billion, or about 20 percent.
SOURCE: "Table 5, Flow of Funds," *Federal Reserve Bulletin* (April, 1964), p. 517.

with them to increase their loan potential. The competition is partly in the form of interest rate competition, within the recently increased limits.

The bulk of the public's contact with commercial banks is chiefly through the services provided in connection with checking accounts or savings accounts. Today banks typically levy service charges on these accounts in one form or another to help meet the cost of these services.

check clearance

The handling of checks written on demand deposits is the most time-consuming task of the banks. Automation now helps with some of the mechanical operations required. Cities with a substantial number of banks have established clearing houses to simplify the process of handling checks that each bank receives and that are drawn upon the other banks within the city. Each day the banks in the clearing house exchange checks drawn on each other. Computations may be made as to the total sums payable to each bank and from each bank as a consequence. Various methods may be used to effect the settlement. If on net balance a bank owes more than is owed to it, it may pay the difference to the clearing house itself, perhaps by a check on its Federal Reserve deposit. This provides the clearing house with funds with which to pay the net amounts owed to other banks in the clearing house. The check-clearing process becomes more complicated with respect to checks drawn on banks in other cities. This is where the clearing function of the Federal Reserve banks enters the picture directly for member banks and indirectly for nonmember banks (usually through their having correspondent relationships with some member bank). The Federal Reserve banks act as clearing houses for banks in different localities in their districts. There is also an inter-district settlement fund for the twelve Reserve banks. This fund helps to take care of clearings involving payments from banks in one Federal Reserve district to those in another.

behavior of the bank's depositors

The activity of the different deposit accounts is a matter of concern to the bank. The more frequently checks are drawn on a deposit account of any given average size, the higher is the cost of servicing the account. Some banks graduate their service charges according to the frequency of withdrawals and deposits in accounts. More important to the bank is the size and suddenness of withdrawals from accounts (chiefly checks drawn against accounts that the bank must honor in the clearings with other banks). It is easier for a bank to meet the demands on it of a depositor whose account does not vary widely from its average level than it is to adjust to large fluctuations in the size of the account of another depositor. As Table 2.2 shows, a large portion of demand deposits are owned by household consumers and nonprofit organizations. In the aggregate these accounts represent a larger portion of the liabilities of the banking system than the accounts of other financial institutions or of governments. Consumer accounts are typically subject to numerous small transactions rather than to sudden large reductions. The average consumer is probably not able to, nor would it pay him to, try to "economize" in the carrying of noninterest-bearing demand deposits even though there is a wide range of interest-bearing assets that could be a temporary repository for funds. By contrast, business firms, especially the larger ones, may be quite conscious of the "cost" of carrying demand deposits that earn nothing and try to economize in the holding of such deposits. They invest temporarily in other financial assets (including time certificates of deposit) funds that they may be accumulating for some large planned expenditure. When such outlays are made, even the bank's time deposits may accordingly be sharply reduced by a firm's action. Ordinarily, of course, the time and savings deposits are considered to be much less volatile than demand deposits. Business deposits of any type, then, may be subject to larger variations, as well as being individually larger on the average, than consumer bank deposits. Financial institutions hold demand deposits to take care of such discrepancies as may arise between receipts and necessary disbursements, but this does not entail planned large and sudden reductions in deposits. Government deposits are increased by tax collections and the sale of securities, and they are reduced by government expenditure. State and local governments vary in how much they try to earn interest on funds in their possession. The federal government typically transfers its deposits in commercial banks to Federal Reserve banks before disbursing the money. Such shifts of funds out of a bank make it necessary for the bank to regard United States government deposits as quite volatile. A bank must judge then the nature and behavior of its depositor accounts, and it must be prepared to adjust to the change in its reserves brought about by the actions of its depositors. The most profitable customers for the bank are, of course, those whose minimum deposit balances are relatively large and whose accounts can be serviced at relatively low cost. Since the bank wishes to keep any profitable depositor account, it will ordinarily be quite anxious to meet loan requests of such depositors.

bank reactions to change

The banking business is not simply a matter of obtaining some capital, attracting some depositors, and then investing the funds in a set of loans and securities. It is a matter of continuously adjusting to changing circumstances. We have just seen that the accounts of the bank's depositors change in various degrees. The ups and downs of individual accounts do not always offset one another. Sometimes the checks drawn on the deposit accounts in a bank are less than the checks deposited in such accounts; then the bank has additional funds that it may wish to lend or invest to increase its earnings. At other times it may face an adverse clearing house drain; checks drawn on its deposit accounts and paid to people who deposit them in other banks exceed the checks deposited in the bank in question. The bank must adjust to this in some fashion. Sometimes the bank is hard pressed to satisfy the demands of those who wish to borrow from the bank, while at other times there is a dearth of good loan applications. The volume of reserves of the whole banking system, hence the amount each bank (on the average) can use, is altered from time to time by the actions of monetary authorities or the government. Thus, there are changes in the volume of funds a bank has, or needs, or wants.

A bank cannot in general attract substantial deposits just when it may want or need funds. In order to have funds available when it needs them, it may, therefore, keep some funds idle. Reserves, over and above those required, are a good protection whenever the bank fears that it may need to be more liquid than usual. For example, just before seasonal cash withdrawals in December a bank might try to keep some excess reserves. If it needs funds at a time when it has no excess reserves, it may be able to borrow funds temporarily from other banks or from the Federal Reserve. Borrowing possibilities, of course, are not unlimited. To obtain the funds it needs to make desired loans or to cover adverse clearing house balances, a bank may sell some of its holdings of securities. It usually keeps some short-term securities for just such situations. When business conditions are good or improving, a bank is likely to have an increasing number of good loan applications. To increase its loans, it may use its excess reserves, sell some of its holdings of securities, and perhaps borrow additional funds for a time. When business conditions are bad or worsening, the number of good loan applications is likely to decline. In such circumstances a bank may allow loans to be paid off without replacing them by other loans, may pay off its own borrowings from other banks or the Federal Reserve, may invest funds in additional securities (probably highly liquid ones), or may build up excess reserves.

In these ways a bank adjusts to changes in its reserves, brought about by the actions of its depositors or the actions of others (including the Federal Reserve) and to changes in business conditions. Banking is then partly a matter of attracting funds to conduct normal banking operations and partly a matter of responding to changes that impinge upon them.

bank examination

Banks, in making decisions on how to conduct their business, must operate within a framework of legal regulations designed to preserve the soundness of the banks and to protect the depositors. Under the law banks are subject to periodic examination by authorities called "bank examiners." The examiners have a substantial influence upon the conduct of banking. They not only audit the books of a bank and check for legal violations; they also bring pressure to bear upon banks that are making what they consider to be questionable loans, buying risky securities, or otherwise engaging in practices that might weaken the bank. The individual banker generally does not know on what day the bank examiner will call at his bank. Accordingly, he finds it desirable to conform to the examiner's notions of what constitutes sound banking practice.

The legal basis for bank examination presents a picture of overlapping jurisdictions. All national banks are subject to examination by the office of the Comptroller of the Currency. Member banks in the Federal Reserve System are subject to examination by Federal Reserve examiners. The Federal Deposit Insurance Corporation (FDIC) is authorized to examine all the banks it insures. And banks chartered by states are subject to examination by the appropriate state bank examiners. A bank could thus be faced with conflicting requirements, stemming from examination by different authorities. In practice the situation is not so bad as it might appear. Discussion of bank examination standards reduces potential conflict. Sometimes two authorities combine in examining a bank; for example, a state member bank may be examined jointly by state and Federal Reserve examiners. Duplication is avoided in other cases by the acceptance by one authority of the report of another; for example the Federal Reserve tends to accept the reports on national banks from the Comptroller of the Currency.

economic effects of banks

Banks compete with one another to attract depositors because the funds deposited enable them to make loans or invest in securities from which their earnings derive. As we have seen, their banking operations involve decisions that must be made in the light of banking legislation, the behavior of depositors, the prospects of the loan applications presented to them, the state of the securities market, and more broadly, their own forecast of business conditions in the nation and in the local community. In the aggregate the actions of banks have significant effects on the economy. They affect the allocation of the nation's productive resources. The borrowers to whom bank credit is available obtain command over resources that are thereby unavailable to those to whom bank credit was denied. There are other sources of loanable funds (and we shall examine these in Chapter Eight), but there is no denying the impact of commercial banks on the allocation of economic resources too. Earlier in this chapter we noted the amounts of bank credit made available to various classes of borrowers. The allocation even within classes is important to those involved, for the banks decide in effect which firms or individuals will have a specific loan and which will be turned down. Since different borrowers would put resources to different uses in many cases, who gets funds does affect what some resources are allocated to producing.

The other primary effect of the banking system is on the money supply. This is so important that we shall examine it in detail later in this volume. For the present we shall consider the relation between borrower and lending bank.

debt and credit

When a person or firm borrows from a bank, he promises to repay. His promise, which may take the form of a promissory note, is a debt for the borrower and an asset for the lending bank. In granting the loan, the bank makes available to the borrower a certain sum, and the borrower may, for example, have the funds put in a deposit account (checking account). The deposit is a liability, that is, a debt of the bank, but clearly it is an asset of the borrower. The bank has extended credit to the borrower, which in our example takes the form of a new demand deposit. This deposit is new money created by the bank. The promissory note of the borrower would not be generally accepted by others to whom he might wish to make a payment, and even if accepted by someone, it would not likely be transferable to a third party. In short, the borrower's debt will not serve as money. But the bank exchanges debts with him, taking his promissory note and giving in return its own debt to him—namely, a deposit account in the bank. And the bank's debt, the deposit, does circulate as money. Checks written on the deposit are the normal way for the borrower to make payments. We say that the bank has "monetized" private debt. It has, thereby, made the borrower, and the community, more liquid by this extension of its own credit. Similarly, banks can monetize public debt, purchasing government securities by creating a bank deposit (or increasing a deposit) for the seller. In place of a government security the seller then has a new bank debt that serves as money. Most of our money supply is created by bank monetization of the debts of others through the basic process as here stated.

That it is profitable for banks to engage in this process gives some assurance that the economic system's need for money to operate effectively will likely be met if the banks have sufficient reserves. At the same time it raises the possibility that too much bank credit might be generated at times for economic stability. We must accordingly look into the techniques available to control bank reserves and bank credit in the public interest. Subsequent chapters will be concerned with these matters.[2]

questions

1. *Draw up and explain a typical bank's balance sheet.*
2. *Explain the process of check clearance.*
3. *How do banks affect resource allocation?*
4. *What is meant by saying that banks monetize debt, and what is its significance?*
5. *What is involved in the compromise between liquidity and earnings for a commercial bank?*

---

[2] A fuller treatment of other aspects of the banking business is given in a supplementary volume in this set. See Paul S. Nadler, *Commercial Banking in the Economy* (New York: Random House, to be published in 1968).

the development of

our banking

system

OUR MONETARY SYSTEM AND OUR BANKING SYS-
tem are the result of a slow evolution. How they evolved and all the
problems encountered in the process make a long story. To better
understand the requirements for the satisfactory functioning of a
monetary and banking system, we shall present a brief survey of the
highlights of that story. It is necessary at the start to outline the principal functions performed by a monetary and banking system.

functions performed and interests involved

In our monetary system the unit of account is the dollar. We make
comparisons of economic values in terms of dollars' worth. The
various forms of our money are also denominated in terms of dollars
or fractions thereof. The principal function of the money, in whatever form, is to serve as a medium of exchange. It provides a relatively simple means of settling claims against others or against us

arising out of economic transactions of all sorts, and thus it facilitates the operation of the economic system and the development of a complex economy. Money also serves as a store of value, but it is not at all unique in this respect since many other assets perform this function also. Wealth to be retained for later use may be kept in the form of money or of other durable assets. In the latter case it may need to be transformed into money again at the time of use.

We have indicated that commercial banks perform four major functions. To recapitulate: (1) They offer a means for the safekeeping of funds. When money is deposited in a bank account, safety is normally one of the objectives. And this is probably the most common way of seeking such safety now. (2) Banks provide an important part of the payments mechanism. It is estimated that about 90 percent of all money payments are made by the use of bank checks. What is called a commercial bank can be identified by its provision of bank accounts on which checks can be written. Handling the checks drawn on these demand deposits is a major portion of a bank's activity. It is a unique service performed by commercial banks. (3) Banks make loans. In this they are not unique, but they are a very important source of loans. They, therefore, play a significant role in determining the allocation of loanable funds. (4) Banks alter the money supply directly by certain of their actions. We shall see later the extent to which they can do so and the extent to which we rely on them to provide the growth of our money supply. Clearly, the money-creating function is one of great importance to the economy. The nature of our banking system is such that the lending and the money-creating functions are linked together. However, these should be recognized as distinct and indeed separable functions. Banks do create money by expanding loans. It would be quite possible to restrict the creation of money to government while leaving the lending function to private enterprise.[1]

Our banks do not restrict themselves entirely to the performance of these four functions. They do provide a variety of additional services, which will not be discussed here as they are of less concern for our present study.[2] An example of an additional service is that of the trust department of a bank relating to the administration of funds of the estate of a deceased person.

[1] Money creation by banks will be explained in detail in Chapter Five. The possibility of separating money creation and lending functions will be discussed in Chapter Fourteen in connection with 100 percent reserve banking.

[2] For a fuller analysis of the business done by banks, see a volume in this series by Paul Nadler, entitled, *Commercial Banking in the Economy* (New York: Random House, in preparation).

Let us ask what would be considered satisfactory performance of each of the major functions outlined. In a sense, it might be argued that how well any part of the monetary and banking system performs its functions may be gauged by the degree of reliance upon it; but this presumes the existence of alternatives that are themselves satisfactory. When such alternatives are lacking, the extent of use of any part of the monetary and banking system tells nothing of its adequacy. We must then be more specific about the objectives in the performance of the functions that we have enumerated.

From the discussion in Chapter One we can conclude that for any type of money to serve well as a medium of exchange implies ease and convenience of use, at the least. It must also be available in sufficient volume for the transactions people wish to conduct. Its use should entail no risk of its depreciation in value in terms of the unit of account. To serve as a satisfactory store of value, money must, in addition, be at least relatively stable in terms of purchasing power. Ideally, its purchasing power would be perfectly stable.

For banks to perform well their function of safekeeping of funds implies very low deposit losses. It implies also the ability of the depositor to get his funds back upon demand in the case of demand deposits and at the designated time in the case of other deposits. We can measure the performance of the banks' role in the payments process in part by the speed and cost of the check clearance mechanism. Since currency payment is a readily available alternative, the extent of use of checks by preference is indicative of how well banks serve the payment function by comparison with currency. It is more difficult to state generally accepted criteria for performance of the lending function by banks. Economists are wont to talk in terms of effects on the efficiency of the allocation of resources in the economy, but it is difficult to measure the impact of bank lending on the efficiency of resource allocation. Equity concepts are also relevant. Although people do not always agree on what is equitable, they become quite disturbed when they feel that banks are not fair. Usually some idea of equality of treatment lies at the root of the idea of what is fair. For the money-creating function to be performed well, the growth of the money supply must be kept within certain limits. This will be discussed at greater length later. Suffice it here to say, first, that the money supply needs to grow fast enough to avoid impeding economic growth and, second, that it should not grow so rapidly as to produce serious price inflation.

The satisfactory performance of these functions is a matter of concern to everybody, directly or indirectly through their consequences for the whole economic system. We can look, however, beyond this general interest when we consider banks as a particular type of social institution. As such, banks involve a number of different groups, each having their own interest in the way the banks function. The depositors have a direct interest in the safety of their deposits, and hence in the solvency of their banks. Those depositors holding checking accounts have perhaps the greatest interest in the liquidity of the banks as well. They also have an interest in the speed, cost, and efficiency of the check clearance mechanism. People holding savings deposits or time deposits have an interest in their own earnings on the deposits, and hence in the earnings of the banks. Borrowers and potential borrowers from banks have an interest in the availability of loans, in the fairness of the lender, and, more specifically, in the terms on which loans are available. In earlier days when banks issued their own bank notes as money, those who possessed the notes had an interest in their soundness, that is, in their stability of value in terms of the unit of account. This included their redeemability (at least by the bank) in terms of other, preferably standard, money.

A bank itself may be thought of as composed of owners, managers, and employees. Owners, of course, are interested primarily in the opportunity to earn profit in the banking business, and they are inevitably concerned if there is mismanagement of their bank. Bank management, in turn, wants a favorable environment in which to operate and has a stake in the profitability of the business. Bank employees in general have an interest in the success of their bank and, beyond that, in fair treatment for themselves. The public at large has a general interest, as we have indicated, in the satisfactory performance of all the functions of banks. While there is some conflict of interest among these groups, clearly the mutual interest in a healthy banking system is the overriding concern of all.

We would expect that as our economy has developed from small beginnings, has grown in size and complexity, and has industrialized, its monetary and banking needs would have undergone change. It is not surprising, therefore, that the monetary and banking system has both grown and changed over the years, nor that the problems faced in connection with the system have changed. The unifying thread through the history lies in the fact that the same functions were to be performed, by one means or another, in the changing setting and the same interests were concerned with how well the functions were performed. Our interest today is primarily in the conditions that must be met for the satisfactory performance of these functions.

United States monetary history

We are ready to consider briefly United States monetary and banking history, the problems faced, and how they are handled. In the colonial period there was no uniform monetary system and no commercial banks such as we know today. Although much of the economy consisted of relatively self-sufficient farms, there was need for money both for the townspeople and for such trade as took place between farm and town. There were small amounts of various kinds of money in circulation, mostly European coins brought by settlers or obtained for exports. The most common were Spanish "pieces of eight" and English coins, and the English pound was the usual unit of account. But there were not enough coins for the business to be conducted, and the shortage was made worse by the continuous loss of coins to pay for needed imports. The result was that various commodities had to serve from time to time as a medium of exchange, and the disadvantages of barter were a not uncommon experience. What coins there were were not uniform in weight, so confusion as to their value was common.

The resort to paper money in such a situation should not be surprising. Paper money has advantages of its own, particularly that of convenience where substantial payments are involved. The first colony to issue paper money was Massachusetts when faced with the need to pay troops for a military expedition in 1690 against the French in Canada. The notes were subsequently redeemed out of tax proceeds. But the temptation was great, and Massachusetts issued more, followed by other colonies, to meet other governmental expenditures. In time the issues so exceeded what could be redeemed by tax proceeds that the notes depreciated, some very seriously, from their face value. A similar fate befell the private issue of notes as private lenders printed notes. Though it was common to collateral such notes with land, this did not make them redeemable. Printing money became a "game" that the issuers of paper money could continuously win. Therefore, the game continued. The uncertainty and the losses arising from the depreciation of such money was a serious handicap to the normal course of business. Another chapter of monetary history of the same sort was written when the Continental Congress resorted to printing money to finance the Revolutionary War. So much was issued that in the end it became worthless, and "not worth a Continental" has become a synonym for worthless.

Thus we see a shortage and an excess of money are both unsatisfactory. A new effort to resolve the problem of a satisfactory medium of exchange and store of value began with the constitutional prohibition of money creation by the states and with the standardization of coinage by the federal government. In 1792 the first coinage law resulted in gold and silver coins of standard weight being minted from any gold or silver taken to the mint. Thus gold and silver and gold and silver coins became interchangeable. The number of grains of silver per dollar was fifteen times the number of grains per dollar of gold in the standard coins. This bimetallic standard was, however, doomed from the start because the relative value of these metals in the market fluctuated and did not tend to equal their relative value at the mint. The first trouble appeared with the market price of gold being more than fifteen times the market price of silver and silver being worth more at the mint than in the market. Consequently, no one took gold to be minted but sold it for silver, which was minted. Silver replaced gold in circulation. Subsequent changes in the mint ratio did not solve the problem because market and mint ratios always tended to diverge in one direction or the other. One metal or the other tended to dominate the coinage as the other metal tended to flow out in payment for imports or otherwise disappear from circulation. A generalization from this experience, called Gresham's Law, points out that bad money (that is, money made of a metal overvalued at the mint) drives out good money.

This problem was not resolved very quickly, for changes in ratios could not resolve it. Indeed, it played a very important role in political controversy in the last quarter of the nineteenth century. The politically inspired phrase "the crime of '73" referred to the dropping of coinage of the standard silver dollar. Silver interests, trying to offset a decline in the price of silver, combined with those adversely affected by the business cycle and general decline in the price level to press for free coinage of silver. Their pleas and the clamor for the restoration of bimetallism failed, but such efforts were successful in requiring the government to purchase a large quantity of silver and to mint token coins. This came to an end with the defeat of William Jennings Bryan in the presidential campaign of 1896 and the legal adoption of the gold standard in 1900. To be sure, a silver purchase program was again inaugurated in the 1930's with more benefit to silver interests than to the volume of money. As noted in Chapter One, the recent rise in the market value of silver has now reversed the process of silver accumulation by the Treasury. The role that gold has played since

1900 in the domestic monetary system will be examined in detail in Chapter Eleven.

The federal government did not issue much paper money until the Civil War[3] when it became necessary to help pay for the war. The Civil War "greenbacks" (United States notes) were issued in such volume that their purchasing power dropped more than 50 percent. The operation of Gresham's Law resulted in the disappearance of gold and silver coins from circulation and hence a shortage of fractional currency. People resorted to the use of postage stamps in lieu of small coins, and later fractional Treasury notes had to be issued. The flood of paper money continued and was augmented by privately issued notes which came to be called "shinplasters." After the Civil War there was much vacillation over retirement of the greenbacks as the political strength of forces opposing deflation grew.

The principal government paper money[4] over the years has consisted of gold certificates, issued since 1883, and silver certificates, issued since 1878. These are representative paper moneys, backed to the full value by the metals they represent, but being more convenient than coins except for small sums. No further problems need be noted here with respect to these notes. To round out the story of the evolution of our medium of exchange, we need to turn to the note issues of commercial banks.[5] This can be done as part of a more general discussion of the evolution of our banking system.

United States banking history

The history of banking in the United States is not a very even success story. The course of development of a sound banking structure was marked by a long struggle to overcome weaknesses in the system, and involved a major national banking crisis as recently as 1933. We shall review some of the main developments until the establishment of the Federal Reserve System.[6]

[3] Some circulating notes were issued earlier, chiefly during the War of 1812, but these were interest-bearing notes unlike normal currency.

[4] Space does not permit discussion of certain other note issues, which were of minor importance. The change in 1933 in the role of gold certificates is indicated in Chapter Eleven.

[5] How Federal Reserve notes fit into the picture is presented in Chapter Four.

[6] For a more extensive treatment of monetary and banking history, see the volume in this series by Blyn, *The History of Money in the United States* (New York: Random House, in preparation). See also Arthur Nussbaum, *A History of the Dollar* (New York: Columbia University Press, 1957).

Private banks and state chartered banks sprang up rapidly after the Revolutionary War. Their major function appears to have been money creation, as witness the fact that they were sometimes called banks of issue. The notes that they issued were lent to borrowers at interest, which was the source of their profit. The inherent danger of overissue of the paper money is thus readily evident. Actually, the tendency was kept in check to a substantial degree for a time by the first two banks chartered by the federal government.

The First Bank of the United States was chartered in 1791 to serve as a fiscal agent of the federal government, to make private loans, and to issue notes. The capital came primarily from private sources. Its headquarters was in Philadelphia, and there were branches in major cities throughout the country. Its size was such that it dominated the financial picture. When it expanded loans, some of the money flowed into other banks and augmented their reserves, at other times money was drained off from the system to retire loans at the First Bank. The bank made a practice of demanding specie redemption by other banks of the notes these other banks had issued. This placed a severe brake upon the volume of notes that they could issue. The opposition to this practice by the banks was probably an important factor in Congress' refusal to renew the First Bank's charter when it expired in 1811. In the next few years the number of banks multiplied rapidly. The War of 1812 was too much for many of these, but the paper money issue grew rapidly anyhow. With the money supply and the number of banks growing, Congress chartered the Second Bank of the United States in 1816 for a twenty-year period. In its early years its record was marred by incompetent and dishonest management, but this was cured before Nicholas Biddle became its president in 1823. The bank thereafter functioned very successfully and with a generally salutary effect upon the financial situation. But again it aroused much opposition from the other banks. To this was added opposition on various grounds from other sources, most notably President Jackson. The conflicts of interest, outlook, and personality (Jackson vs. Biddle) involved, spelled political disaster for the Second Bank, and its charter was not renewed by Congress. It did obtain a state charter, but unsound operation, begun before the switch and continued afterward, led to its failure in 1841.

Until 1837, except for some private banks, most banks were established under charters issued by the states. At first these charters tended to be granted like special privileges by special acts of the legislatures. The objections to this led to what was called "free banking," a system whereby anyone or any group meeting certain requirements set forth in state law would be entitled to a charter to establish a bank. The requirements were not very stringent, however, so banks proliferated without much relation to the needs of different communities, the competence of the bank managers, or the general soundness of the banks. Many banks had inadequate capital. Loans were frequently of a highly speculative nature or had inadequate security behind them to protect the bank. There were so many different types of bank notes issued in making the loans that it became impossible for the public to know whether a note was counterfeit or not, whether the issuing bank redeemed its notes in specie (gold), whether the notes were circulating at a discount, or even whether the issuing bank was still in existence. Paper money was issued to excess in some periods, and some bank notes depreciated to worthlessness, defrauding their holders. In some periods the total volume of notes outstanding contracted sharply, indicating also a reduced volume of bank loans. For example bank notes expanded 56 percent from 1834 to 1837, contracted by 60 percent from 1837 to 1843, then expanded by 119 percent from 1843 to 1848.[7] The effect on the volume of economic activity could not help but be unstabilizing. This, in turn, was hard on the banks. As a result of the combination of factors, bank failures were numerous, inflicting severe losses on depositors. It can be argued that the economic development of the nation proceeded more rapidly, albeit unevenly, by virtue of the banks' creating purchasing power for business substantially in excess of what current saving could have financed. This, of course, hardly constitutes adequate justification for our early chaotic banking system.

The unsatisfactoriness of the system was not unrecognized at the time, and several efforts were made to deal with parts of the problem. These were not comprehensive enough and had only limited success. Most notable were the Suffolk Banking System and the New York Safety Fund System. The Suffolk Bank of Boston presented notes to the bank of issuance for redemption but undertook to redeem such notes of other banks if they kept a redemption fund with it. Thus the redeemability of notes could be readily tested, and this tended to make banks more cautious and issue fewer notes than otherwise. New York State established a Safety Fund by assessing banks and used this to insure bank depositors and note holders against loss through bank failure. But the Fund had no power to check overexpansion nor to

[7] Lester V. Chandler, *The Economics of Money and Banking*, 4th ed. (New York: Harper & Row, 1964).

prevent bank failure. Lacking the power to deal with the causes of trouble, the Fund proved inadequate.

The federal government's handling of its own funds, after the demise of the Second Bank of the United States, presented some problems of its own. Indeed before its demise, President Andrew Jackson had withdrawn government funds from the Second Bank and deposited them in selected banks, which came to be known as "pet banks." Losses were suffered when some of these failed during the depression of 1837. Subsequently the Independent Treasury System was established to enable the federal government to be independent of the banks. Tax proceeds were held in nine subtreasuries around the country, and government disbursements were made from them. The receipts and disbursements were made in specie. Actually government securities could be accepted in payment of taxes, but bank notes were not accepted by the government. The effect of this system was to drain reserves from the banking system during seasons when tax collections were running higher than government expenditures and to increase bank reserves as the government drew down its Treasury balances. When the federal budget was relatively small this was not very serious, but as the budget grew, it became a potentially disturbing factor.

During the Civil War a major change was introduced into our banking system. The National Banking Act sought to establish a system of federally chartered banks, partly to help finance the war and partly to remedy the defects we have been discussing. The act created the office of Comptroller of the Currency in the Treasury Department. This office was empowered to charter and supervise national banks. More adequate capital was required to obtain a charter than was typically required by state banking legislation. To provide further protection of bank creditors, the bank stock of national banks was subject to double liability. Further safety was provided by placing a ceiling on the size of loan, in relation to its capital, that a bank could lend to any one borrower (10 percent).

The law made an attempt to vary the reserve requirements in accordance with the liquidity needs of banks, which, in turn, were partly the result of provisions regarding the form in which reserves could be kept. Banks were classified as country banks, reserve city banks, or central reserve city banks. Country banks could keep up to three-fifths of their required reserve as deposits in the other banks, and reserve city banks could keep up to one-half of their required reserve in central reserve city banks. The reserve required behind notes and deposits (later deposits only) were 15 percent for country banks and

25 percent for the others. In addition, government bond purchases equal to a portion of a bank's capital were required, reflecting one of the motives for establishing the system, namely to help finance the war. The new banks were empowered to accept government deposits and did so, although the Independent Treasury System continued to be used as well.

The national banks were authorized to issue their own bank notes, but these were printed for them by the Bureau of Engraving and Printing, thus making the currency more uniform in appearance. Great pains were taken in the law to ensure that these notes would be safe. The volume of notes was limited in several ways, and the attempt was made to provide for acceptability and redeemability. A bank's note issue was limited by its capital stock, by a collateral requirement (note issue could not exceed 90 percent of the value of United States government bonds that the bank deposited with the Comptroller of the Currency), and initially (until 1874), by a reserve requirement. There was even a ceiling on the total note circulation, but this was removed after 1875. Each national bank had to accept other national bank notes at par. And each bank maintained a 5 percent redemption fund with the Comptroller of the Currency to help ensure that they would redeem their notes in lawful money. The notes were not made full legal tender, but they were accepted by the federal government and used in making most payments.

The expectation was that the state banks would generally obtain national charters, but this expectation was not fulfilled. In order to bring pressure upon these banks to join the system, Congress in 1866 levied a 10 percent tax on bank notes issued by state banks. This made their issuance unprofitable, and they disappeared from circulation. State banks that retained their state charters, as many did, found it necessary to make their loans in the form of deposits against which the borrower could write checks. This provided a great stimulus to the use of checking accounts, the advantages of which were increasing anyhow as the speed of transportation and communication increased. Although the number of state banks did at first decline substantially after the tax, there was a subsequent increase again, and state banks became more numerous than national banks. This left us with a dual banking system. The state banks remain generally among the smaller banks, although there are some exceptions, some are large. National banks hold the major portion of the nation's bank deposits today.

The establishment of the national banking system and the elimination of the state bank notes removed some of the earlier problems.

In particular, the country was no longer flooded with a vast variety of depreciating bank notes, and the capital required for national banks represented a gain over the conditions of many earlier banks. However, the National Banking System was still not without serious problems. Experience with the system led people to the conclusion that the aggregate supply of bank notes had been made too inelastic to meet adequately the needs of an expanding economy. Not only was adequate growth not ensured, but the variation in seasonal needs was not being met, and there was no way to expand note issue in a crisis. We had gone too far in our anxiety to solve the problem of note overissue. The development of checking facilities was a gain, but there was no system to facilitate clearance of checks on a nationwide basis. And the reserve system had serious defects. The large number of independent banks had no way of drawing upon excess reserves in some areas to cover temporary deficiencies in others. The banks were thus individually more vulnerable in the face of local economic problems than if the system consisted of fewer but larger banks with branches extended over wide areas. The special weakness of the reserve system came from the pyramiding of reserves. Banks typically deposited as many reserves as the law would allow at reserve city banks and central reserve city banks where they earned interest. When the banks needed to withdraw some of these deposits, it put severe pressure for liquidation upon the banks in the financial centers (the reserve city and central reserve city banks) since they kept only a fractional reserve behind these deposits. Successive panics and depressions made clear the need for further improvements in the banking system of the country, but it was not until the panic of 1907 that Congressional interest in reform initiated a study from which fundamental changes emerged. Earlier changes in the National Bank Act had been relatively minor. The National Monetary Commission established by Congress analyzed the problem and made suggestions that led to the creation of the Federal Reserve System.

questions

1. *Identify the main functions of commercial banks. How is the economy as a whole affected by the manner in which these functions are performed?*

2. *Which functions proved easier and which functions harder to get satisfactorily performed?*

3. *What particular interests do different groups have in banking?*

4. *Define the proper performance of the functions of money and of banking.*

5. *Why might it be easier or harder for monetary authorities to regulate money creation by the banking system when the money created took the form of bank deposits than when it had taken the form of bank notes?*

6. *Why did we abandon the attempt to make bimetallism work?*

7. *What interests, if any, gained at the expense of others from the weaknesses of our financial system?*

8. *What do you regard as the most important lesson to be learned from this brief review of monetary and banking history?*

·FOUR·

the structure of the

federal reserve

system

ON DECEMBER 23, 1913, CONGRESS PASSED AN ACT
that, according to its preamble was "An Act to provide for the establishment of Federal Reserve banks, to furnish an elastic currency, to
afford means of rediscounting commercial paper, to establish a more
effective supervision of banking in the United States, and for other
purposes." The panics of 1893 and 1907 had produced a great deal
of agitation for banking reforms. Following the 1907 panic, a Congressional committee, called the National Monetary Commission, undertook a thorough study of banking at home and abroad. Its report,
published in 1910, pointed to serious defects in the banking system
and made recommendations that were debated extensively. The result
of the investigation and debate was the passage of the Federal Reserve
Act.

National bank notes had provided the country with a more uniform and safe paper currency than before, but in time defects in the
system of note issue had become apparent. Banks were limited in note

issue by their total capital and by the amount that they were prepared to invest in United States government bonds (since the notes had to be secured 100 percent by such bonds). But neither of these factors fluctuated with the need of the economy for currency. Fluctuations in bond prices acted at times as a further deterrent to meeting the needs for currency.

provisions of the federal reserve act

These limitations the new system proposed to remedy. The twelve Federal Reserve Banks were empowered to issue notes on a basis that was expected to increase the supply in response to need and still avoid overissue. The notes were required to have a 40 percent gold certificate reserve behind them, and they were to be redeemable on demand in "lawful money." In addition, the issuing bank was to furnish collateral security equal in amount to the note issue. The collateral was to be "paper" rediscounted for commercial banks[1] or "bankers' acceptances"[2] purchased in the open market. In lieu of these, additional gold certificates could be furnished or, with some limitations, government securities might be used. It was expected that periods when more currency would be needed would be periods in which banks would be rediscounting more paper at the Federal Reserve and more bankers' acceptances would be offered. Thus the Federal Reserve's supply of collateral would rise to meet the need for more notes.

The provision of rediscount facilities was the solution offered to another problem, namely, how to enable the banking system to provide better accommodation for the needs of commerce and industry. Not only was the currency supply held to be too inelastic, so was the total supply of bank credit. In the new Federal Reserve banks the member banks were to find a source of additional reserves to meet the legitimate needs of business. Safeguards against overextension of credit were provided in the form of restrictions upon the rediscounting privilege. To be eligible for rediscount, paper of the banks had

[1] "Paper" refers to the promissory notes of those who borrowed from the commercial banks; these notes the banks could turn over to the Federal Reserve System in return for loans of reserve funds. The term "rediscount" implies that the note was originally discounted when the bank made the loan, then discounted again when used by the bank to borrow from the Federal Reserve.

[2] A banker's acceptance is a type of negotiable credit instrument that is in effect an obligation a bank has accepted to pay a proper holder a specified sum of money at a specified time.

to meet certain tests of maturity and purpose. The loans were not to be for more than ninety days for commercial loans nor for more than nine months for agricultural loans. Further, the loans were to be self-liquidating in nature and for the purpose of financing the production, storage, or marketing of goods. Fixed capital loans were thus excluded. Thus the rise in Federal Reserve credit through rediscounts was to be geared to the expansion of production and of goods coming to market.

Business needs were accommodated in other ways also. The Federal Reserve banks were empowered to make commercial and industrial loans directly, but this was to be done only in exceptional circumstances when other accommodation was unavailable. In practice the granting of such loans never became of much importance. What became more important were the changes in law that empowered the member banks to accept drafts originating in foreign trade and the power given the Federal Reserve to purchase bankers' acceptances in the open market. With these changes our foreign trade ceased to be financed so largely in London; a New York market developed for the types of credit instruments used in financing foreign trade.

Prior to the establishment of the Federal Reserve System the process of clearing checks between banks in different cities and different sections of the country was very slow, cumbersome, and costly. A vast network of correspondent relationships had grown up to reduce the problem to manageable proportions, but the process was vastly simplified and improved when the Federal Reserve System provided clearing services for the member banks. In addition to providing a central clearing apparatus for the nation, supplemented by regional clearings in each Federal Reserve district, the Federal Reserve has succeeded in reducing the extent of "nonpar" clearing. This refers to the practice of some banks of discounting checks presented against them, rather than cashing them at par or face value.

a decentralized central bank

A fundamental improvement in the banking system of the nation brought about by the establishment of the Federal Reserve System involved the handling of the nation's bank reserves. Under the National Banking System reserves were so widely scattered throughout the system that there was no way to use excess reserves from one region to meet a stringency in other regions. This is one of the prices we paid for a system of independent unit banks instead of a system of large banks with widely scattered branches. At the same time there was a tendency for banks outside the financial centers to deposit funds to their accounts in banks in the financial centers. These funds were part of the reserves of the outlying banks, but the repository banks of the financial centers treated these funds as "normal" deposits and kept a fractional reserve behind them. Thus there was a pyramiding of reserves, which caused real financial stringency in the financial centers and throughout the country when the outlying banks tried to get their funds back. These twin problems of scattering and pyramiding of reserves were cured by the Federal Reserve structure, for it involved a pooling of reserves from all member banks. Pyramiding was eliminated by keeping most required reserves of member banks at the district Federal Reserve Bank. Thus what amounted to a common pool was built up, and the Federal Reserve was in a position to make funds available where needed.

For the Federal Reserve banks to have these funds readily available, they must not try to maximize their profits. It is necessary for them to make decisions in terms of the public interest and to function as what is today called a "central bank." At the time of passage of the Federal Reserve Act, however, there was widespread sentiment against much "centralization" of banking power and control. It was feared that a single central bank might wield too much power, and some felt it would be too largely dominated by big monied interests in our financial centers. Consequently, the structure of the Federal Reserve System is unique among central banks. It consists of twelve regional Federal Reserve banks. Figure 4.1 shows the twelve districts into which the country was divided and also the branches of the twelve district banks.

Each of the twelve banks has its own board of directors. To ensure that these represent various interests, there are three classes of directors for each Federal Reserve Bank. Class A directors are bankers, one each elected by large banks, middle-sized banks, and small banks in the district. Three Class B directors, similarly elected, may not be directors, officers, or employees of banks and must be engaged in industry, commerce, or agriculture. Three Class C directors are appointed by the Board of Governors of the System, and again excluded are bank directors, officers, and employees. Class C directors are supposed to represent the public at large. The stock of each Federal Reserve Bank is owned by the member banks in the district. To be a member a bank must subscribe to stock of the district Reserve Bank

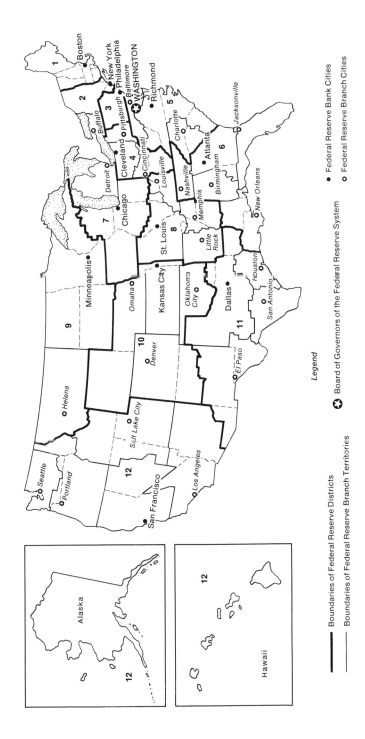

Figure 4.1. Boundaries of Federal Reserve Districts and Their Branch Territories

Legend

● Federal Reserve Bank Cities

○ Federal Reserve Branch Cities

✪ Board of Governors of the Federal Reserve System

— Boundaries of Federal Reserve Districts

— Boundaries of Federal Reserve Branch Territories

equal to 6 percent (no more and no less permitted) of the member bank's capital and surplus, but only half of this amount is paid in. On the paid-in amount the bank receives a 6 percent annual dividend. These ownership and control provisions were designed to ensure that the Reserve banks would be responsive to the needs of their district and aware of local credit and business conditions to a greater degree than a single central bank might be.

centralized decisions

To provide needed coordination, however, a central body was provided, and this has taken on increasing importance over the years. The Board of Governors of the Federal Reserve System consists of seven members, appointed by the President of the United States with the advice and consent of the Senate. The members are supposed to represent broadly financial, commercial, industrial, and agricultural interests, and no two can come from the same district. To give the Board of Governors some independence of current political pressures, the term of office is fourteen years, a member cannot be removed except for cause, and a member may not be reappointed. Members are also prohibited from having any connection (other than depositor) with any bank during their term on the board. The chairmanship and vice-chairmanship are filled from the board by the President every four years.

The Board of Governors is now the central policy-making body of the System, which, through its decisions, operates like a central bank. The twelve Reserve banks have to accommodate to decisions made by the Board of Governors. It is the board that determines what member-bank assets shall be acceptable for rediscount or as security for a loan, that exercises supervisory power over the member banks, and that determines monetary policy. Indeed the board examines the twelve Reserve banks and has considerable power over them.

This is quite a departure from the original conception of the board as a loose coordinating body with little power. There are two other central bodies in the System. They have little significance today but were originally set up to serve as a check on the board. The Federal Advisory Council, composed of a representative, usually a banker, elected by each Federal Reserve Bank, was established as an advisory body to the board. Presumably by virtue of its membership the views of the banking community would be readily available to the board.

The Conference of Presidents of the Reserve Banks, also an advisory panel, was designed to bring the weight of Reserve Bank views to bear upon the board.

The most important body in the System in the operation of monetary policy is the Open-Market Committee. It is this committee that makes the main decisions pertaining to efforts to control bank credit in the country and hence control the money supply. The committee consists of twelve members, seven being the members of the Board of Governors and the other five being presidents of Reserve banks, selected so as to provide for some rotation. In practice, the twelve Reserve bank presidents attend the meetings of the committee, and all are heard before decisions on open-market policy are taken. The twelve district Federal Reserve banks are of unequal size and influence in determining System policy. The New York bank is the largest and most influential, its location gives it closest contact with the domestic money market and the foreign-exchange market.

balance sheet of the system

The various activities of the Federal Reserve banks are reflected in the consolidated balance sheet of the twelve banks, shown in Table 4.1. The nation's monetary gold stock is represented by the gold certificates deposited with the System by the United States Treasury; these certificates constitute the legal reserve of the Reserve banks. The "cash" item reflects the service that the Reserve banks provide member banks of making currency available to them when needed. It shows current stock of cash for that purpose; this can, of course, be supplemented at any time by issuance of more Federal Reserve notes. "Discounts and advances" are primarily loans of additional reserves to banks temporarily in need of them. The holdings of "bank acceptances" indicates the extent to which, at the date of this statement of financial condition, the money market had fallen back on the System for credit, discounting bankers' acceptances. A banker's acceptance is a credit instrument which involves a bank accepting an obligation to pay a certain sum at a certain date—a promise that becomes a negotiable credit instrument "as good as money" with the Reserve banks' willingness to buy them if the market for them weakens. The monetary policy of the Federal Reserve is reflected largely in the changes in the volume of "government securities" held, as will be shown in more detail later. Here we note that securities of various

Table 4.1 **Consolidated Balance Sheet, Twelve Federal Reserve Banks, End of February, 1967**
(*millions of dollars*)

Total assets	64,833		
Total gold certificate reserves		12,626	
Cash		356	
Discounts and advances		165	
Member-bank borrowing			165
Other			0
Acceptances		113	
U. S. government securities		43,971	
Cash items in process of collection		6,703	
Bank premises		107	
Other assets		792	
Denominated in foreign currencies			293
All other			499
Total liabilities	63,540		
Federal Reserve notes		38,283	
Deposits		19,879	
Member-bank reserves			18,916
U. S. Treasurer—general account			386
Foreign			145
Other			213
Deferred availability cash items		5,153	
Other liabilities		225	
Capital accounts	1,293		
Capital paid in		575	
Surplus		570	
Other capital accounts		148	
Total liabilities and capital accounts	64,833		

SOURCE: *Federal Reserve Bulletin* (March, 1967), p. 402.

maturities are held. "Cash items in process of collection" refers to checks to be collected and is partially offset by deferred availability cash items (listed under liabilities), the difference being termed the "float."

The "liabilities" of the Reserve banks consist chiefly of Federal Reserve notes (which serve as the principal part of our currency) and the deposit accounts of member banks and others. We have already noted that member bank deposits at the Federal Reserve are reserves for the member banks. Foreign banks also frequently keep some funds on deposit with our Reserve banks. And the Federal Reserve acts as fiscal agent for the United States government, keeping Treasury and other deposits and disbursing government funds. It replaced the independent subtreasury system in 1920 in these functions. It also performs other functions for the government, such as the handling of government security transactions. The capital of the Reserve banks has already been discussed.

The Reserve banks earn interest on their loans and investments that more than cover their costs. They are required to pay 6 percent dividends on the paid-in capital stock held by member banks. The law has been changed several times regarding the disposition of the remaining earnings, but the main disposition of them has been to build up surplus slowly while turning over substantial portions of net earnings to the United States Treasury.

nonmember banks

It was the hope of the founders of the System that all commercial banks would join the System, but only national banks were required to join. Less than half the nation's nearly 14,000 commercial banks are now members, but those that are members hold about 85 percent of total deposits. To join, a bank must subscribe to Federal Reserve Bank stock, keep reserves at the Federal Reserve, meet certain requirements as to size of its capital, be subject to examination by the Federal Reserve, and comply with the same regulations prescribed for national banks, including paying at par any checks presented against it. Unwillingness to do the latter and inability to meet capital requirements appear to be principal factors explaining the failure of many small banks to join the system. There are substantial advantages to membership, however. These include the free check-clearing facilities, the servicing of member currency needs, and especially the availability of loans to members on favorable terms. In addition, Federal Reserve banks are constantly engaged in research on banking and business conditions in their district and are available for counsel and advice. The Board of Governors also has an excellent research staff and publishes useful statistical data. Nonmember banks can obtain some of these services by maintaining correspondent relationship with member banks. The small state banks outside the system do not entirely escape control of central monetary authorities, however, because credit control affects them and many are insured and examined by the Federal Deposit Insurance Corporation.

questions

1. *What were the principal objectives of the Federal Reserve Act?*

2. *Why were twelve Federal Reserve banks established instead of a single central bank?*

3. *What is the logic of the provisions regarding ownership and control of the Federal Reserve System?*

4. *How important are nonmember banks? Are there any reasons why they have not become members?*

5. *What is the principal way that the Federal Reserve serves the objective of "providing accommodation of commerce and business"?*

·FIVE·

bank credit expansion and contraction

IT HAS BEEN INDICATED IN EARLIER CHAPTERS that commercial banks can and do alter the money supply by their activities. It is the purpose of this chapter to explain more fully how they do so and to show the extent to which they can increase the money supply under given conditions today. The key to their ability to affect the money supply will be found in the fact that banks are required to keep reserves equal to only a fraction of their deposits.

how much can a bank lend?

How a bank alters the money supply can be most easily understood if we work through several simplified examples. The accompanying tabular accounts, numbered to correspond to the main steps involved in the examples, show the effects of each step on the balance sheets of the banks. Let us suppose that a 20 percent reserve is required behind all bank deposits and that all banks have exactly enough reserves to meet that requirement but no excess reserves. Let us look for a moment at the position of a single bank, Bank A. Bank A (1) has received a deposit of $1000 cash from John Doe because he has decided it is no longer safe hidden in his home. This gives the bank an additional $1000 cash reserve. Of this sum only $200 is needed to meet the legal reserve requirement; the other $800 is called "excess reserve."

Anytime banks have excess reserves they are able to increase their earnings by lending or investing in interest-bearing assets. Let us suppose, therefore, (2) that Bank A makes an $800 loan to a business firm. The firm will receive the funds in the form of a deposit in its checking account; it will proceed to use the funds for whatever purpose caused the firm to borrow, writing checks on the $800 deposit. It will be easiest to follow if we assume that the borrower spends the entire amount in a single transaction, writing an $800 check to cover it. Whoever receives this check will normally deposit it in his bank account, since we have no reason to suppose that his need of cash in pocket has increased by any such amount.

(1)		(2)	
Bank A		*Bank A*	
Assets	Liabilities	Assets	Liabilities
Cash reserves +$1000	Demand deposits +$1000	Loans +$800	Demand deposits +$800

What has happened to the money supply? The money supply has been defined to include currency plus demand deposits (that is, checking accounts). If we suppose that all the deposits in the preceeding paragraph were demand deposits, the matter is quite simple. John Doe still has $1000, in the form of a bank deposit, but this does not represent any change in the money supply because he previously held the money in cash form. However, somebody has had an additional $800 bank deposit ever since Bank A made the loan by creating an $800 deposit for the borrower. First the borrower had it; then the party to whom he wrote the $800 check. This $800 is the amount by which the money supply has increased. The currency in the hands of the public (outside of the banks) has decreased by $1000, but bank deposits held by the public have increased by $1800. Thus, the increase in the public's money stock is $800, the amount created by the bank loan. As long as the banks do not contract the total amount of their outstanding loans and investments, the money supply will not contract again. Indeed, there will be further expansion of the money supply within the banking system.

At this point it is desirable to raise the question whether Bank A could not have lent more than the $800 of the above example. After all a bank is required to keep only a 20 percent reserve behind its deposits. Therefore, an $800 excess reserve would appear to be able to back up $4000 of additional deposits; $4000 of new loans should be more profitable than only $800 of new loans if there were no shortage of good loan prospects. But the banker must pay attention not only to the reserve requirement but also to what tends to happen to the deposits he furnishes to the borrowers. He cannot expect that anyone will borrow from the bank and not use the funds borrowed. He can expect that checks will be drawn upon the new deposits. The pertinent question is whether he can count on the recipients of the checks being depositors in Bank A also. If they are depositors in his bank, his 20 percent reserve will be sufficient to back up the deposits as they transfer from one depositor's account to another. However, if the checks written on Bank A are paid to someone who deposits in Bank B, the check will be presented to Bank A, and payment of the full amount of the check will be demanded by Bank B. (The check is an order for the bank on which it is drawn, Bank A in this case, to pay the full face amount of the check to the person to whom it is written or, after that party endorses it, to the holder of the check.) But Bank A would have only $800 cash reserve to back the $4000 deposit it created, or to pay Bank B when it demands payment of the $4000 check. Clearly, it is not safe for Bank A to make a loan bigger than the amount of excess reserve it possessed if checks for the full amount of the loan may be written to parties who are not also depositors of Bank A.

What then are the chances that the checks drawn on deposits created by loans will circulate only among parties who keep their deposits at the same bank? In a city with a substantial number of competing banks it is obvious that the banker cannot count on this happening. This would be the case for most cities. But suppose the borrower is known by the banker to be borrowing to make a payment to another firm that also keeps its funds on deposit at Bank A; will bank A then be safe in lending a multiple of its excess reserves or not? Even if the borrower spends the funds thusly, the recipient may proceed to respend them by writing checks to parties who deposit with other banks. Indeed, even if Bank A could assume that no more than 10 percent of each respending of the funds created by the loan would go to depositors of other banks, it would merely take longer for the entire amount to be lost to Bank A. Even if Bank A were the only bank in the town, it could count on the loan creating an outflow of reserves, except if the town economy were completely isolated economically from the outside world. The consequences for a bank are serious if it creates a situation in which there is in due course a drain on reserves bigger than it can meet. Therefore, we can formulate the following rule: *When a bank comes into possession of new excess reserves, it can safely lend, at any one time, no more than an amount equal to those excess reserves.* This is a conservative rule, the reason for which we have now seen.

In the above example we assumed that Bank A made a loan to a business firm. An alternative use of its excess reserves would have been for Bank A to make what it would call an investment. That is, it could have purchased any security it was eligible to purchase, paying for it with a check on the bank itself. This check would normally be deposited by the recipient in some bank, and the same reasoning would apply as to the check written by the borrower in the above example. All the same conclusions would then follow. It is a matter of indifference whether the bank makes loans or investments insofar as magnitude of the operation and effect on the bank and on the money supply is concerned.

expansion by the whole banking system

The total effect of the $1000 deposited in Bank A has still not been ascertained. We have learned only that Bank A cannot itself safely lend or invest more than $800 as a result of receiving that initial deposit. But what of Bank B (3) which received a check for $800 drawn on Bank A when the borrower wrote such a check and paid it to one of Bank B's depositors? When Bank B presents the check to Bank A and A honors the check by paying Bank B the $800 cash, Bank A reduces the depositor's account by the amount of the check

(3)

Bank B		Bank A	
Assets	Liabilities	Assets	Liabilities
Cash reserve +$800	Demand deposits +$800	Cash reserve −$800	Demand deposits −$800

he wrote. Bank B now has more than enough to back the new $800 deposit. Bank B now has $640 excess reserve (since only $160 of the $800 cash is needed to provide a 20 percent reserve behind the $800 deposit in the customer's account). Hence, Bank B may lend or invest this excess reserve, like Bank A before it had done except that Bank B may lend only four-fifths as much as Bank A had lent.

(4)

Bank B

Assets	Liabilities
Loans + $640	Demand deposits + $640

Suppose (4) Bank B does lend a business firm $640. The process will work out as for Bank A, with the borrower (5) writing a check on his new deposit for $640 and paying it to someone who is a depositor in some other bank (or, if the funds do not leave Bank B directly, as indicated before, in due course they will be drawn off to other banks even if only a fraction goes outside Bank B at each respending of the $640). Consequently, we may suppose that Bank C receives deposit of the check or checks totaling $640 drawn on Bank B, and Bank B has to pay out the $640 to honor those checks. This puts Bank C in a position of having new deposits of $640, backed up by the required reserve in cash of $128 with excess reserves of $512 to lend. The process continues from bank to bank as long as there are

(5)

Bank C		Bank B	
Assets	Liabilities	Assets	Liabilities
Cash reserve + $640	Demand deposits + $640	Cash reserve − $640	Demand deposits − $640

excess reserves left anywhere in the system. All the excess reserves will have been used up only when $5 worth of new deposits have been created for each dollar of what was initially excess reserve. Since the initial excess reserve, which was all in Bank A to begin with, was $800, the deposit creation process will continue until five times that, or $4000 have been created, all of it new money that did not exist before. Total bank deposits in the system will be $5000 greater than before, but $1000 of it is merely a change from cash at home to a deposit in the bank for John Doe.

The magnitude of this multiple expansion of credit through bank loans or investments is clearly determined by the size of the required reserve ratio and the volume of excess reserves that appear in the banking system. The multiple of expansion per dollar of excess reserves is the reciprocal of the required reserve ratio; in the example above the required reserve ratio was 20 percent or one-fifth and the multiple was five. Thus it appears that the system of banks can do what the individual bank cannot do: expand the money supply by a multiple of any excess reserves. It might be supposed that the process could begin only if the amount of currency in circulation was reduced, but this is not correct. That bank deposits have not been created solely by this source of reserves is plain from the statistics on bank deposits, reserves, and currency. Table 5.1 shows that the total volume of bank reserves exceeds the volume of currency which banks hold

Table 5.1   Currency and Bank Reserves, June 30, 1966
(*millions of dollars*)

Total Federal Reserve and Treasury currency		46,322
Held by the Federal Reserve	3,768	
Held by commercial banks	5,234	
Held by the public	37,320	
Total commercial bank reserves		28,728
Member-bank reserves with		
a Federal Reserve Bank	18,094	
Commercial bank currency and coins	5,234	
Nonmember-bank commercial bank		
balance with domestic banks	5,400	
Total commercial bank demand deposits*		153,846

* Excludes interbank deposits and United States government deposits, but it does not exclude cash items in the process of collection.

SOURCE: *Federal Reserve Bulletin* (August, 1966), p. 1189 and (March, 1967), pp. 405 and 408.

plus what they could have deposited with the Federal Reserve. It is evident that banks have acquired reserves other than by the public depositing cash. What further sources of banks' reserve funds there may be will require a more extensive discussion. This will be provided in the next chapter along with examples of the effects of various monetary transactions.

some questions about the credit expansion process

Before we proceed with our discussion, it will be well to answer some queries about our description of credit expansion. What, it may be asked, if the initial deposit that started the process had been withdrawn at an early stage? Or, since withdrawals as well as deposits occur all the time, does the multiple expansion of credit really work as described? These are fair questions. In this volume we are attempting to describe how bank credit expansion occurs when it does occur. To do this we have begun with a simplified example. We started with the banking system fully "loaned up." That is, the volume of reserves was just adequate to meet the reserve requirement for the given value of deposits. In any real situation there would be a large number of cash deposits and withdrawals daily. These would tend roughly to offset one another much of the time. As long as they do offset, no net credit expansion can take place. Indeed, if our example of a new cash deposit is taken as representing just the net excess of deposits over withdrawals in some period, only a temporary expansion in the money supply could occur if the process were shortly reversed by a net cash withdrawal. But bank credit does sometimes expand to its limits on the basis of the addition of reserves that is more than temporary. Here we are illustrating the process that does occur under such circumstances. Our illustration could have supposed, equally well, that reserves were added to the system by other means: the choice of a net cash deposit was used only because of its simplicity and relative familiarity.

Another question is whether recipients of some of the checks might not have taken cash (pocketbook money) instead of depositing the checks in their banks. Would this not alter the outcome materially? To be sure, this may happen, and allowance would have to be made for any permanent withdrawal of part of the initial added reserves. However, there is nothing about the transactions described that would be likely to cause the recipient of any of the checks involved to want to increase permanently the amount of his pocketbook money by the amount of the check received. It is indeed safe to assume that even if some of the checks were initially cashed and pocketbook money obtained, that money would likely be spent and deposited in the banks by other recipients. We shall show subsequently how to take into account any net increase in pocketbook money that might result. The argument here is only that the magnitude will at most be minor and hence cannot be taken as halting or reversing the whole process of expansion described.

There is one more troublesome consideration. In our illustration of credit expansion we justified the assumption that the deposits created by bank lending would leave the bank that did the lending, but we implicitly assumed that deposits received by a bank in other ways stayed in the bank. We call the first type of deposits "derivative deposits" because they are derived from the bank's own lending activities. The other type is called "primary deposits." They come to the bank from outside. Is there warrant for treating the two types differently, and is not the outcome dependent upon having done so? Let us suppose that the recipients of one of the checks in our illustration deposits the check and then writes a check against the deposit to a depositor in another bank. In such a case the first of these two banks would not be able to expand its credit upon the basis of the new primary deposit, but the second bank would. It doesn't matter for our illustration of expansion where in the banking system a primary deposit comes to rest; whatever it is, some bank will be able to expand on the basis of the excess reserves it brings with it. As long as the loan that led to a later primary deposit somewhere is outstanding, there will be a deposit and excess reserve somewhere in the system on which further expansion is possible by the bank possessing it. Thus, it makes no difference whether the expansion is by the first recipient bank or some other bank. But this does raise the question of when or whether any bank can itself count on holding the deposit long enough to warrant making an additional loan. One answer might be that any individual bank would be well advised to wait a while until it could see that the average level of its deposits was remaining higher than before, and then put the added reserves to work. At most this would imply that our credit expansion process would proceed with some lags. Actually this is not the only answer, for a bank can, if it chooses to do so, put excess reserves to work quite promptly. If it fears the reserves may be quite temporary, it can lend at very short term at first. For example, it may lend for twenty-four hours to another bank, or it may buy securities maturing in a short time. If it should be caught by the deposit disappearing before that time, it may cover its needs by then borrowing for a short time itself. If instead it finds its average level of deposits permanently higher, it may slowly shift from shorter- to longer-term investments or loans. The potential mobility of primary deposits does affect the speed of credit expansion or the liquidity of the assets on which the expansion takes place, but it does not prevent bank credit expansion.

Nor does the repayment of some of the loans made during the expansion process cause us to modify our conclusions. When a loan is repaid, the bank is in a position to renew or replace the loan with another. As long as the additional reserves that initiated expansion remain within the system, the expanded volume of bank credit and money can be supported.

simultaneous expansion

We can now consider an example of credit expansion that is not as simple. It would be more realistic to start with a situation in which many banks possess excess reserves, of different amounts, instead of one bank alone having an excess. We shall not investigate now the sources of the excess reserves. Rather we shall inquire into the extent to which the process of credit expansion changes when many banks, rather than just one, have excess reserves. The chief difference for any individual bank comes from the fact that when it expands its loans it may not lose so many of its reserves to other banks. For other banks are likely to be expanding their loans simultaneously, and the upshot will be that checks drawn on the deposits created by other banks will be deposited partly in Bank A, even while checks drawn on Bank A are deposited in other banks. In the clearing house these checks may partially offset, and Bank A may not lose all its excess reserves by virtue of its own lending operations. But this does not mean, even if all banks had equal amounts of excess reserves, that any one bank could safely expand a multiple of its excess reserves at once. If they all did so simultaneously, to be sure, they would create a situation in which each was fully "loaned up," and if checks drawn against each bank's newly created deposits were exactly offset by the deposit in the bank of checks drawn on the newly created deposits of other banks, no reserves would flow from one bank to another and the situation would be stabilized.

No bank can count on the distribution of reserves among the different banks remaining the same at the end of the credit expansion process as at the beginning. Consequently, it cannot be said that even in the end each bank will have expanded to the full multiple of its initial excess reserves, especially if the size of excess reserves was not initially the same in every bank. Ordinarily they would not be of the same size in all banks. No bank is, therefore, safe if it assumes it can expand at once by the multiple of its excess reserves given by the reciprocal of the required reserve ratio, even though other banks are expanding simultaneously. What it may indeed learn by sad experience is that if it gets out of step with the rest of the system, expanding faster than other banks whose actions, in turn, affect its reserve position, it may be forced to slow up the rate at which it is expanding credit. Adverse clearing house drains on its reserves will occur any time checks drawn on it by virtue of its new loans exceed checks deposited in it by virtue of the new loans of other banks.

The rule derived from our first example is still a good rule for conservative banking: it is safe to lend at any one time only an amount equal to the bank's excess reserves. In the first example, Bank A has nothing further to consider after making its $800 loan. But now we realize that if other banks are expanding loans simultaneously, Bank A will find itself losing less than $800 reserves after its loan and may be able to lend again. Bank A must be careful not to expand further more rapidly than other banks are expanding. The process will be a step-by-step process, similar to that we saw in the first example. Although we can calculate the total expansion in the system as the product of the total excess reserves that were in the system when expansion started and the reciprocal of the required reserve ratio, there is no way of calculating the total amount by which any single bank will have expanded.

size of the multiple

These examples have employed a very simple multiple to determine the limits of credit expansion for the system of banks. While the multiple we have used does give a simple estimate of the amount of credit expansion possible on excess reserves, other factors may reduce the potential expansion somewhat. These may be neglected for small changes, but when large changes are involved, they need to be taken into account. The formula that a bank must use to determine its reserve requirement at any time is more complicated than indicated, but for our purposes it is not necessary to consider it in detail. What we do need to consider is that people tend to vary the amount of money that they carry outside their bank accounts with variations in the amount of money in their bank accounts. Consequently, as the system expands loans and investments, increasing the total of bank deposits, we can expect the public to take some cash out of the banks.

This reduces the volume of excess reserves on which the system can expand. We may take this into account by adding to the reserve required behind deposits some percentage to allow for the added cash the public may want. The formula for the system multiple might then be written:

$$\frac{1}{\text{Required reserve ratio plus cash drain ratio}}$$

If the public held another $13 in cash for every increase in bank deposits of $100, the multiple would be approximately three if the required reserve ratio were 20 percent.

In practice the system multiple is still more difficult to estimate because the reserve requirement differs for different classes of banks and for different classes of deposits. Table 5.2 shows the range within

Table 5.2   Reserve Requirements for Member Banks of the Federal Reserve System

Net demand deposits	
Reserve city banks	10–22 percent
Country banks	7–14
Time deposits	
All member banks	3–10

SOURCE: *Federal Reserve Bulletin* (July, 1967), p. 1180.

which the Federal Reserve fixes the requirements for member banks. Requirements for banks chartered by the states are generally lower. One cannot be sure in advance how the new deposits would be finally distributed, starting with any given distribution of excess reserves. If the excess reserves were distributed in proportion to deposits, however, and the public could be expected to keep a constant ratio between savings deposits and checking accounts, a rough estimate might be made by using a weighted average of required reserve ratios.

credit contraction

Sometimes the money supply may be contracted by the actions of the banks. There are numerous similarities between bank credit expansion and credit contraction, but the differences are equally significant. It may be useful to start with as simple an example as possible of credit contraction and take up a more realistic example subsequently. We shall suppose, therefore, a situation in which all banks have reserves just equal to the reserves required for their given deposits, and we shall revert to the simple supposition that the reserve requirement is the same for all banks and all deposits.

Let us suppose that Mr. Jones withdraws $1000 in cash from his bank, Bank A, and holds the cash, or pays it to others who hold it, so that the public's pocketbook money has increased by $1000. At this point the money supply has not yet been changed because the public holds $1000 less money in the form of demand deposits. Bank A has reduced a depositor's account by the $1000, but it has had to pay $1000 cash out of its reserves. With $1000 less deposits to hold reserves behind, the reserve requirement for Bank A has dropped by $200 (assuming a 20 percent reserve requirement). But its reserves have been reduced by $1000. This leaves Bank A with a deficit in its reserves of $800. To meet its reserve requirement it must either acquire $800 more reserves or reduce its deposits by five times that ($4000) without any further loss in reserves. What can it do to accomplish either of these objectives and meet the reserve requirement?

There are several courses of action open to a bank when it finds itself with a shortage of reserves. It may borrow reserves from other banks if they have excess reserves to lend. If the bank borrows from banks that are members of the Federal Reserve System, it will obtain reserves on deposit at a Federal Reserve Bank. This is called borrowing federal funds, though it is not government money but money owned by a private bank. In our example other banks are fully loaned up so this source of funds is excluded. When there is a central bank such as our Federal Reserve, the bank might borrow directly from it. But the loan must later be paid off; therefore, borrowing is at best a temporary way to remedy the situation. Sooner or later, some assets must be reduced for the bank to solve its problem. If it borrowed until such time as its own borrowers repaid outstanding loans, the situation would probably work out as follows. The borrowers from the bank are likely to be depositors in the bank. At the time when they must repay the bank, they must have enough in their deposit accounts to meet what they are required to pay, unless the bank will extend the loan for a longer time. Loans falling due will then normally be repaid by checks drawn upon the accounts of depositors. From these checks the bank will receive no additional reserves; all it can do with the checks is to reduce the amounts credited to the accounts of the borrowers, return their canceled checks, and return the notes they signed promising to repay the original loans. This process adds nothing to bank reserves, but reduces the number of reserves the bank needs by reducing the total deposits owed to others. The total loans of the bank would have to be reduced by $4000 in this manner if the $800 deficit in reserves were to be wiped out. At the same time, this reduction of bank loans involves the public giving up $4000 in deposits which the bank had at one time created and lent to them. Total money supply is thus reduced by $4000. Here we have an illustration of how a reduction in reserves in the banking system reduces the money supply by a multiple of the reserve deficit. In this particular case we see the entire reduction could come about in a single bank. However, the bank normally could get out of its difficulties in a much less costly fashion. A reduction of $4000 in loans will result in it losing a lot of interest. Hence it will normally choose a remedy that is less costly and that may cover its deficit much more quickly.

Bank A, facing an $800 deficit in its reserves, may simply sell some asset for $800. To be sure, it will be no better off than in the preceding case if any assets it sells are bought by its own depositors, for they pay by writing checks on their deposits in Bank A. The bank would then have to sell $4000 in assets. But if Bank A sells government securities that it owns, it can sell them on the open market. This market is a national market in which it is very unlikely that the buyers will be its own depositors. A purchase of one of the securities sold by Bank A will then probably be paid for by a check written on some other bank, which we shall call Bank B. Bank A can present the check to Bank B for payment in the clearing house. Since we are supposing a net addition to the offsetting transactions involving the banks, Bank A will receive $800 in cash from Bank B and add this to its reserves. Bank A has now solved its problem, losing only $800 worth of assets instead of $4000. It has eliminated its initial $800 deficiency in reserves.

But Bank B now faces a deficit in its reserves of $640 because it has had to pay out $800 in honoring a check drawn upon it, written by one of its depositors. Bank B reduces his account by the $800 also, but this reduces the reserves the bank needs by only $160. A loss of $800 reserves in a transaction that reduces the reserve requirement only $160 leaves Bank B with a deficit of $640. It can best meet this deficit the same way that Bank A before it had done; it sells $640 of securities from its portfolio, and in an open-market sale receives the

$640 of reserves it needs. But it does so at the expense of some other bank, Bank C, whose depositor bought the security sold by Bank B. Bank C reduces the depositor's bank balance by $640, and honors the check by paying Bank B the $640 from its reserves. This transaction leaves it with a deficit of $512. The process continues from bank to bank, stage to stage, as long as any bank has a deficit in its reserves.

The deficit disappears from the system only when the public has given up $4000 in deposits to buy securities from the banks. The money supply has thus been reduced by a multiple of the original deficit in the system. The contraction process results in reserves moving from bank to bank, but there is no recovery of reserves for the system as a whole. The total decline in deposits is five times the original withdrawal of deposits. The multiple that applies to the original deposit withdrawal to get total deposit reduction, or to original reserve deficit to get total reduction in money supply is, as in the deposit expansion case, the reciprocal of the required reserve ratio.

simultaneous contraction

A more realistic example of credit contraction by the banking system would start from a position in which many banks were short of reserves, not one bank only, and the deficits differed in size from bank to bank. We need not concern ourselves at this point with the reason for the system being short of reserves. We shall only explore the results. Examine the position of Bank A trying to gain reserves by selling securities on the open market at the same time that other banks are doing the same. Under these circumstances depositors of Bank A will probably buy some securities, but it is less likely that the securities will be those sold by Bank A. Therefore, the checks to purchase them will be drawn on Bank A and will go to other banks. In the clearing house Bank A will have checks on other banks that may be partly or entirely offset by checks drawn on Bank A. Thus Bank A will not gain $800 of reserves from a sale of $800 worth of securities. It will have to sell more securities to make up its deficit in reserves. Other banks will be in a similar position, and all will have to continue selling securities until the public has parted with enough demand deposits to lower the reserve requirement to the actual level of reserves in the banking system. This will be the same multiple of the total deficit in the system as before. But again we cannot assert that each bank individually will have sold securities equal to the multiple of its original deficit, for we do not know whether reserves will be distributed in the end among banks in the system in proportion to their original deficits.

We can make an assertion, however, about the rate at which the contraction by an individual bank must proceed. When each bank finds that its initial sale of securities does not bring in reserves equal to the size of the deficit, it undertakes further sales. As each bank does so, it finds that it gains less reserves than if it alone had a deficit. The rate of contraction by one bank is affected by the rate of contraction of other banks. But this works very differently from the case of simultaneous expansion by all banks. During credit expansion a bank cannot surge too far ahead of other banks, for if it expands too rapidly in relation to the rest of the system, it would lose reserves. This would force it to reduce its rate of expansion. However, a bank can expand more slowly than the rest of the system without deleterious effects. Under such circumstances the result would be an accumulation of reserves. In the case of credit contraction by all banks together, the bank that moves too slowly in trying to make up its deficit may find the deficit growing; this will happen if its depositors buy securities faster than the bank is selling securities to depositors of other banks. Therefore, it must contract as fast as the other banks in general. If it should contract faster than others, the bank might temporarily gain excess reserves, but the pressure that this would put on other banks would produce more security sales on their part and would affect the first bank adversely in turn. Contracting faster than is necessary is not advantageous generally. Contracting more slowly than others worsens a bank's position and forces it to keep pace with others. Consequently, banks tend to keep in step with each other during contraction.

conclusion

In the preceding example we have seen that individual banks are caught in an undesirable situation if from a loaned-up position anything drains reserves from the system and forces them to contract their loans or investments. The contraction will necessarily have to be a multiple of the deficit in reserves in the system. Banks cannot avoid this, however good may be the assets that they must sell. The system of banks as a whole cannot get reserves just because they need them; they can only sell assets which reduces deposit liabilities and this reduces the need for reserves. This is one reason that stability in a fractional-reserve banking system requires a central bank that can add to the reserves of the banking system to make multiple-credit contraction unnecessary.

On the other hand, the existence of excess reserves in the system may make possible a greater expansion of the money supply than is at some times desirable from the point of view of the economy as a whole. There is nothing about the individual loan applications received by banks that gives an adequate indication of whether or not the situation is one in which money supply is expanding too much for general economic stability. The credit expansion multiple refers to the maximum possible expansion of deposits per dollar of excess reserves, but it does not indicate whether or not that much expansion will take place in any given instance. Banks may at times have excess reserves that they do not lend or invest. In a time of depression the banker may not consider loan applications worth the risk for the bank. If at the same time the banker's expectations for the future of security yields keeps him from expanding the bank's investments substantially, or if he fears that the bank may need to be more liquid than usual, he may decide not to expand on the excess reserves. In this case the actual expansion in the system may be far less than the potential expansion. Our examples gave only the upper limits of expansion, not a basis for prediction of the actual amount of expansion under all circumstances.

We have seen in these examples how a change in the reserves of the banking system may lead to a change in the money supply by a multiple of the change in such reserves, though the action of each individual bank tends to be of a magnitude equal to that of any deficit or excess reserve it faces. The nature of the process that produces that result, and the reasons for the magnitude of the reaction have been examined. The examples used have been simplified to lay bare the essentials of the process. Some factors that alter the magnitude were mentioned; these can be applied in other cases as well. We need to find out next what changes bank reserves, in addition to what our example showed. Taking these things together, we can see how the banks may be in a position where the money supply that they generate could be either insufficient for the needs of the economy or excessive.

questions

1. *Starting with a banking system fully loaned up, a required reserve ratio of 25 percent, and an initial deposit of $5000 in Bank A, trace the credit expansion process step by step through the first four banks in the series. Assume that the loans made by each bank result in the borrower writing checks on his deposit account that are paid to persons who bank with the next bank in the series. Compare each bank before its reserve position has been affected and after it has adjusted to the change in its reserves. In the latter case allow time for checks to have cleared against any new deposits it created. Compare for the System as a whole the reserves, deposits, and money supply before the expansion process started and after it concluded.*

2. *Suppose that instead of the above cause of credit expansion Bank A sold $5000 of securities to the Federal Reserve Bank, receiving $5000 reserves in payment, on the basis of which the individual bank expanded its loans. How much different would be the total expansion of the money supply in the entire system of many commercial banks?*

3. *Demonstrate why an individual bank cannot expect to be able to expand its loans by a multiple of any new excess reserves it possesses.*

4. *A banking system which is fully loaned up finds that the public withdraws $100 million dollars within a relatively short period. Explain the process of credit contraction. By how much will the nation's money supply shrink if the required reserve ratio is only 10 percent? How much if it is 33 1/3 percent? Assume in both cases that there is no central bank or no intervention by the central bank.*

determinants of the money supply

AS LONG AS OUR MONEY SUPPLY IS NOT CONFINED to a commodity that is scarce, it would be possible to order things so that the supply of money could be increased without limit. Obviously the result, since the volume of goods and services we can produce is not without limit, would be that the prices of goods and services would rise as more dollars chased the limited supply of them. Obviously, there can be too much money. It may not be quite so obvious, but there can also be too little money for the best functioning of the economy. The decline in the nation's money supply by about 25 percent from 1929 to 1933 certainly did not help promote recovery from the Great Depression. Though we may not be able to define the optimum money supply for the economy at any given time, we can identify the extremes that we should avoid. But if such are to be avoided, and any control exercised over the money supply, we must discover what factors tend to govern the money supply. Then we shall be able to consider to what extent various factors can be deliberately controlled.

We have already learned that the money supply consists of currency (which we called pocketbook money) and demand deposits (checkbook money). Now we must turn our attention to what determines the quantity of each type of money.

changes in the supply of currency

Since currency today consists chiefly of coins issued by the United States Treasury and paper money issued by the Federal Reserve, it may be supposed that the federal government and the Federal Reserve determine the supply of currency. In a sense they do, of course, for if they failed to issue the currency, there would be less of it. But the old fear of currency overissue, even by government, has become a misplaced fear. It is not that government may not follow an inflationary fiscal policy, but that overissue of the currency as such is no longer a problem. If more currency is issued than the public wishes to carry, the extra currency, if it gets into public hands at all, will merely be deposited in banks. Actually, the government and the Federal Reserve are passive in the matter of the supply of currency, issuing it only in response to the amount that the public tries to carry. And the public determines what portion of its total money supply it wishes to carry in pocketbook form and what portion in checkbook form. There are seasonal variations in the ratio between the two forms of money, more pocketbook money being required by the public at the Christmas season particularly. The amount of coin needed depends partly upon the extent of sales taxation, the extension of metered parking zones, and the like. In the past depressions often reduced confidence in the banks temporarily, leading to a shift in the direction of pocketbook money. The objective of government and Federal Reserve policy with respect to these desires is to try to enable people to realize their wishes for holding part of their money in pocketbook form. The amount needed for the purpose, though varying for reasons such as those indicated, tends also to rise and fall with changes in the total money supply. Other things being the same (or otherwise taken into account), the public tends to increase its holdings of currency in rough proportion to the increase in the total volume of demand deposits it holds. Thus the money supply is determined by the volume of demand deposits.

Before we examine what determines the volume of demand deposits, let us consider how new coins or new Federal Reserve notes actually get into circulation. As the above implies, the initiative comes from the public, which goes to banks and writes checks for cash. The banks furnish the United States coins and the paper money of the Federal Reserve directly to the public, and as their supplies need replenishing, they go to the Federal Reserve (if a member bank, otherwise to a correspondent bank that is a member) and similarly write checks for cash, taking it in the form they need. The Federal Reserve is a sort of storage depot for currency. It provides the banks the desired amounts in return for reducing the reserves of the banks (that is, the bank's deposits at the Federal Reserve Bank) by equal amounts. Should the Federal Reserve banks run low on their stock of their own notes, they can, of course, issue more and have them ready for further calls. They must meet the requirements for note issue, to be sure, but in the past this has not been a practical obstacle to meeting the requests of the banks and thence the public. Until 1965 the reserve required behind notes was the same or nearly the same as that behind the Federal Reserve's deposit liabilities.[1] When a bank got currency, it reduced its deposit at the Federal Reserve by the same amount as the cash it received. Even if the entire withdrawal took the form of notes, the Federal Reserve would find enough, or nearly enough, reserves released from backing the deposit to back the new notes. Shortage of collateral has not been a problem either since government securities could be used for the purpose.

To be ready to meet the request of banks for more coins, the Federal Reserve requests the Treasury to furnish certain amounts of new coin from time to time. In recent years the Treasury has had difficulty minting new coin of some denominations fast enough to keep up with the demand. When the coins are minted, the Treasury deposits the coins to its own account in the Federal Reserve. Thus the coin is no gift; the Federal Reserve has a deposit liability equal to the increase in its cash assets, but the government will not demand to withdraw its deposit in cash form. Therefore, the Federal Reserve can use the cash as required for member banks and still honor government checks drawn on the government account and payable to member banks. Such checks merely shift the deposit from the Treasury account to member bank accounts.

Thus the amount of currency adjusts to the actions of the public and in effect varies with the changes in the volume of demand deposits and certain other influences as suggested.

[1] Prior to 1945 the requirement was 40 percent behind notes and 35 percent behind deposits; since 1945 it has been 25 percent behind both.

changes in deposits and reserves

What then determines the volume of demand deposits? In Chapter Five we saw that changes in the total volume of demand deposits, and hence in the money supply, were brought about by changes in the aggregate volume of loans and investments made by the banking system as a whole. We illustrated the process by which the money supply can be expanded by supposing that the reserves of the banking system were expanded by the public's decision to carry less pocketbook money and to deposit some in a bank or banks. This illustration was selected as being the most readily understandable initially, but this is not in fact the principal source of the new reserves on which the nation's money supply has grown. Other factors are more important in altering bank reserves and lending power. We shall stress the way in which various actions of the Federal Reserve and the federal government affect bank lending power.

open-market operations

The main tool of the Federal Reserve in trying to control the variation of the money supply is open-market operations. When the Federal Reserve purchases government securities in the open market, it simply places orders with dealers in government securities for purchase of such securities as it may designate and on such terms as it may specify it is willing to buy. Here the Reserve is not buying new securities directly from the United States Treasury. It buys old issues of government securities from whomever happens to own them and is willing to sell on the terms available.

To get an understanding of the essential results of the transactions, we shall simplify the process by supposing the mechanics to be a little different from what they actually are. Our example will involve an individual who sells a marketable government security (one that can be sold from person to person, unlike the Series E Savings Bond that is better known among small savers). The seller will receive payment in the form of a check written by and drawn on a Federal Reserve Bank. This check the seller will normally deposit in his own bank, and his bank in turn will deposit it in its reserve account at its district Federal Reserve Bank. (The twelve Federal Reserve banks will be treated as a unit.) The Federal Reserve now has back the check it wrote and has in effect honored the check by increasing the deposit of the bank at the Federal Reserve. But that deposit increase is a reserve increase for the bank, equal in amount to the increase in the bank's own deposit liabilities. It, therefore, puts the bank in possession of excess reserves, the reserve requirement being satisfied by only a portion of the new reserves. Credit expansion by this bank may now proceed exactly as in the case presented in Chapter Five where someone deposited added cash in the bank. If the Federal Reserve should purchase (as it normally would when engaging in an open-market operation) a substantial bloc of securities, sold in all likelihood by a variety of holders who deposit their checks in a variety of banks, it is easy to see that simultaneous credit expansion by many banks may ensue and a general expansion of the money supply thus follow. It is, of course, possible that the banks may not expand at all, or may not expand to the limits permitted by the reserve requirement, if business conditions or the quality of loan applications make them hesitant to do so. Banks are generally reluctant to lend much in a depression, especially if business conditions in general are getting worse. But even if the banks do not utilize the excess reserves that result from the open-market purchases by the Federal Reserve, demand deposits of the public will have increased by the full amount of these purchases. People will have converted some of their assets from the form of government securities to the form of demand deposits.

If banks did want to expand their loans, they might themselves have been the ones to sell securities when the Federal Reserve was buying. In that case the banks would have received the checks of the Federal Reserve and their reserve accounts and excess reserves would have been increased by the full amount. They could thus expand their loans or investments whether or not there were other ready sellers of government securities. But our first example shows that the banks may benefit and gain reserves even without selling securities themselves if others sell when the Federal Reserve wants to buy.

The Federal Reserve can be sure of being able to buy or to sell government securities in the open market if its price is right. That is, there is always a price at which the transaction can be completed; in anything like normal circumstances that price need not be far from that prevailing in the market when the Federal Reserve enters to buy or sell. Bid and asked quotations give an indication of the state of the market.

Let us consider the effect of an open-market sale of government securities by the Federal Reserve. The buyer writes a check upon his bank, and the Federal Reserve collects by reducing the reserves (on deposit at the Federal Reserve) by the amount of the check. The bank reduces the purchaser's deposit at the bank by that amount, and the canceled check is returned at the end of the month in the depositor's bank statement. The effect has been a reduction in the money supply, demand deposits in a bank having been reduced by the amount of the security purchase. Moreover, the lending power of the banks have been reduced since bank reserves equal in value to the security sale have also been extinguished (the Federal Reserve reduced the reserves of the bank on which the check was drawn). If the banks were fully loaned up at the time the Federal Reserve sold securities on the open market, they could not have bought any of them, but the fact that bank depositors bought them would have reduced the reserves of banks as much as their deposits, caused a deficit in the reserves, and forced a multiple-credit contraction upon the system of banks. Such a contraction of credit is very seldom called for. Therefore, we may regard open-market sales by the Federal Reserve as a way of putting the brakes on a credit expansion process, forcing the banks to slow down or halt the increase in the money supply, rather than as a means of forcing large decreases in the money supply, for large decreases would be likely to have disastrous effects on the economy.

It is apparent from these examples of open-market operations that the Federal Reserve's power to buy and sell government securities in the open market gives it a powerful tool of credit control. It can add at will to the reserves of the banking system or subtract from them, thus changing the money supply directly by the amount of the transactions, and in addition changing by substantially more than that the lending power of the banking system. If the Federal Reserve's policy is to increase bank lending power, it is referred to as an "easy-money" policy; if to reduce bank lending power, it is called a "tight-money" policy.

changes in the required reserve ratio

Another tool that is quite powerful is the variation of the required reserve ratio. The Federal Reserve may vary the required reserve ratio for member banks within certain statutory limits (as shown in

Table 5.2, page 62). A reduction in the ratio releases many reserves for credit expansion and raises the multiple applicable to each dollar of excess reserves. An increase in the ratio reduces bank lending power by converting excess reserves into required reserves and by lowering the multiple (the amount of deposits that may be created by the System per dollar of excess reserves remaining in the system). The change in the requirement does not of itself change the money supply directly, and what the reaction to a change may be in any specific case depends upon circumstances. If the requirement is reduced, the amount of credit expansion will depend upon whether the banks want to expand credit or want to become more liquid. Contraction by the System to meet liquidity needs could presumably be halted by a sufficient reduction in the reserve requirement, however, so even if no expansion of credit follows the change, it is no proof that the change made no difference. What would have happened otherwise needs to be known.

An increase in the requirement, even if only to lock up excess reserves, may have a very uneven effect on different banks in the System since the excess reserves to be mopped up may be very unevenly distributed among banks. An increase in the requirement that still left many banks with substantial excess reserves may affect other banks severely if they had very few excess reserves. The contraction forced upon banks that were not carrying large excess reserves seems a heavy penalty to pay for not anticipating the change in requirement. Consequently, the requirement is changed infrequently, and when changed, it is not usually by very substantial amounts.

By contrast, the Federal Reserve is in the open market almost continuously, adjusting its actions to try to even out the impact on bank reserves of the numerous other factors influencing them. And there is less objection to the pressure to curtail bank lending resulting from general open-market sales by the Federal Reserve than there is to an increase in the reserve requirement.

Quite apart from changes in the reserve requirement, the stability of the money supply and the earning power of the banking system are affected by the average level of the required reserve ratio. A low ratio gives a high-credit-creation and -contraction multiple, as we saw in Chapter Five. Thus given changes in reserves in the banking system may lead to much bigger swings in the money supply than if the required reserve ratio were substantially higher. The lower the requirement, however, the more earning assets the banks may acquire per dollar of reserves and hence the higher the earnings of banks may be. The latter may be sufficient to explain the preference of bankers for low rather than high required reserve ratios.

variation of rediscount rates

In efforts to control credit the Federal Reserve banks may change their rediscount rates. Since the twelve banks change rates more or less together, we can simplify our discussion by speaking of a change in "the" rediscount rate. This is the rate of discount applied by the Federal Reserve when member banks sell to the Federal Reserve "paper" that meets certain requirements in order to obtain a temporary loan of some additional reserves. This "eligible paper," as it is called, is in the form of notes signed by customers who borrowed from the member bank. The purpose of changing the rediscount rate from time to time is presumably to change the readiness with which banks obtain additional funds from the Federal Reserve by rediscounting the promissory notes of their own customers. Since the rate is not customarily raised high enough to make such borrowing unprofitable, it is doubtful if it constitutes any penalty to the bank that borrows when the Federal Reserve is trying to put the brakes on credit expansion. Certainly a change in the rate does not of itself alter bank reserves or lending power. It may, nonetheless, have an indirect effect on credit even if there is no immediately visible effect on the volume of rediscounts for which banks apply. Generally, the rediscount rate alterations have been made along with changes in open-market policy, and they help call attention to the change in policy. A rise in the rate is a sort of signal to the member banks that the Federal Reserve is desirous of braking credit expansion, that the reserve position of the banks is likely to be tightened rather than loosened, and that it behooves them, therefore, not to overextend themselves in granting new loans. If an increase in the rediscount rate is accompanied by open-market sales, bank reserves are actually contracted.

Similarly, a reduction of the rediscount rate indicates that the Federal Reserve plans to make reserves more plentiful and encourages banks to be more liberal in granting loans. The actual change in the cost of temporary loans from the Federal Reserve is probably less important than this more general significance of the change. In recent years the rate has also been changed to keep more nearly in line with interest rates abroad. In particular the rate has been increased in an effort to influence short-term liquid capital to remain in this country rather than seek higher rates abroad.

Another possible influence of discount rate changes has been through the rates charged borrowers by member banks. It has been contended that a change in the rediscount rate will lead banks to change their rates for a loan and thus increase or reduce the volume of loans demanded of them. Consequently, less loans will be made when rates go up, more when they go down. Credit expansion can be dampened by an increase in rates or encouraged by a decrease in rates. This price mechanism appears to work very imperfectly, however, and sometimes shows no signs of working at all. Again, however, appearances may not tell the whole story; for even if banks do not change their customer loan rates when the rediscount rate changes, they may themselves be easier or tougher in dealing with loan applications. The effect may be through the supply of credit rather than through affecting the demand for credit.

If changing the rediscount rate has only an indirect effect, the rediscounting operations themselves have a more direct effect on bank lending power and hence potentially on the money supply. When a bank sells the Federal Reserve some paper that is eligible for rediscount, its reserves are augmented by the face amount of the note sold, minus the discount for the length of time the original note still has to run. Thus when rediscounts increase, the money supply the System can support is enlarged. Whether the actual money supply is enlarged is less obvious. The purpose of the rediscount privilege is to enable banks to cover temporary needs for reserves. Rediscounting was never intended as a source of expanding bank reserves generally. If it were used only to make up temporary deficits in reserves, a rise in total rediscounts would indicate only a cushioning of a contraction rather than a prospective rise in money supply. As it is, there are various circumstances in which rediscounts may rise. One is where banks are reluctant to turn down some of the loan applications for which their reserves are not quite adequate, and the rediscounts then do indicate credit expansion. Another is when the Federal Reserve is engaging in open-market sales of government securities, which appears to be offset at least partially by a rise in rediscounts. Banks that may be forced to rediscount to cover the deficits produced by the open-market sales of the Federal Reserve will not behave the same as though neither the Federal Reserve sales nor the rediscounts had taken place, even if the reserve position after the two is unchanged. Rediscounts are in effect only temporary loans, and as such they have to be repaid. Hence, a more conservative lending policy will be induced by the circumstances that we are considering. Let us look further to the actual process that occurs when the rediscounted paper matures. Both loans are then due—the loan by the Federal Reserve to the member bank and the loan by the bank to its customer. The Federal Reserve returns the rediscounted paper to the bank, whose reserves are then reduced by the face amount of the paper. The bank in turn collects from the original borrower, typically receiving a check on his deposit account in the same bank. Thus the bank finds its reserves and deposits reduced by equal amounts. If it is not to have a deficit in reserves when rediscounts mature, the bank must work itself out of its presumably temporary need of those additional reserves. This presumes that normally banks would have no outstanding rediscounts, but there have been periods when a certain volume of rediscounts was closer to "normal" and other times when a certain volume of excess reserves seemed to be normal. In the former situation it is the change in the actual level of rediscounts that is significant, as in the latter it is the change in the level of excess reserves that is to be watched. Regardless, the change in actual reserves brought about by rediscounts or their repayment is clear. More must be known about the circumstances to interpret the full implications for the money supply of any observed change.

potential monetary effects of government handling of its funds

The money supply is also affected by various transactions of the federal government. When the government collects taxes and deposits them in commercial banks, there is a shift in the ownership of bank deposits from taxpayers to the government. Whether to call this a change in the money supply depends upon whether one wishes to look at gross demand deposits, which are not changed, or at the statistical measure called "demand deposits adjusted," which excludes from the total the interbank and United States government deposits and cash items in process of collection. Demand deposits adjusted will be lower after taxes are collected and before they are spent by government. The federal government normally wishes to conduct its fiscal operations in such a manner that monetary conditions are not unduly disturbed by the timing of tax collections and government expenditures. But it is easy to show that it can exert quite a leverage on credit conditions if it chooses to do so just by the way it handles its bank balances. Suppose, for example, that the Treasury decides to transfer some of its funds from a commercial bank to the Federal Reserve. Since we are familiar with the use of checks we may imagine that this is done by the Treasury writing a check on its account in the commercial bank and depositing that check to its account at the Federal Reserve. The Federal Reserve will then obtain payment of the check from the bank on which it is drawn, as for any other check. This will reduce the reserves of the bank by the full amount of the withdrawn government deposit. Let us suppose that the amount involved is $1 million. If the bank had excess reserves, they will then be lowered by four-fifths of that amount (if the required reserve ratio is 20 percent). If the bank had been fully loaned up, it would have, as a result of the government action, a deficit in its reserves of $800,-000.

A shift of government deposits in the other direction would have the opposite effect, increasing the lending power of the banks involved and then indirectly the lending power of the whole banking system. One of the principal defects of the subtreasury system mentioned in Chapter Three was that tax collections, by transferring funds in this fashion from commercial banks to the subtreasuries and later back again, had such effects as we have just outlined, whether or not such results were appropriate to credit conditions at the time. The Treasury now handles its funds in such a manner as to minimize these results. In general, it deposits the proceeds of tax collections or bond sales in accounts at commercial banks. It maintains deposits at the Federal Reserve, however, against which it draws checks for most government expenditures; funds are moved to the Federal Reserve from time to time to maintain the deposits at the Federal Reserve. But by avoiding large swings in the total government deposits at the Federal Reserve, it avoids the erratic results of the subtreasury system. It could, however, use the power to transfer funds to affect bank lending power deliberately if it so chose.

government issuance and sale of new securities

The effect of government sale of bonds or other securities to the public is comparable to the effect of tax collections as described above, except for the fact that the public holds more liquid earning assets as a consequence instead of holding nothing but evidence that they paid their taxes. The effect is to give up deposits for near moneys at the outset. After the government spends the money obtained by selling the securities, the public has the same money supply as before, plus the liquid assets (the government securities).

Another important difference appears, however, if the securities sold by the government are bought directly by banks instead of by depositors of banks. When banks buy newly issued government securities, they create new deposits for the government. There is no initial decrease in the volume of deposits owned by the public, and after the government spends the proceeds of the bond sale, the newly created deposits are received by the public. Thus the money supply is increased when banks "finance" the government by buying its securities directly. To be sure, this operation uses up some of the lending power of the banking system; it is one way of building deposits on top of their reserves.

The money supply might be affected still more if the federal government sold new securities directly to the Federal Reserve. There are statutory limitations to restrict the amount of such government financing. We need not go into the reasons for such limitations at this point; what is relevant here is the effect such sales can have. When the Federal Reserve purchases the government securities, it adds to the deposit account of the federal government the amount of the security purchase. The government then has deposits without either the public or the commercial banks using any of their funds. When the government spends the funds it has obtained, writing checks on its Federal Reserve account, the checks received by the public are deposited in their banks. The increased deposits of the public represent an increase in the money supply by that amount. And as the banks deposit the same checks in their accounts at the Federal Reserve, their reserves are increased by an equal amount. Thus their excess reserves are increased (by four-fifths the amount if the required reserve ratio is 20 percent). With bank lending power thus increased, the banking system may expand the money supply still further.

reducing the public debt

It is apparent that the effect of government bond sales differs according to whether the securities are purchased by the public, the commercial banks, or the Federal Reserve. There would be comparable differences in the monetary consequences of a reduction of the federal government debt. It would be possible, of course, to reduce the public debt by having the government print paper money and pay it to holders of maturing government securities. But this method is not worthy of serious attention as a method of reducing debt. If the real purpose is to expand the money supply, with reduction of the federal interest-bearing debt as incidental, it would at least accomplish this; but it has not been seriously presented as the preferable way of expanding the money supply.

Debt reduction is normally thought of as a matter of increasing taxes and using the proceeds to reduce the government debt. We wish to see how the effects of such debt reduction differ according to the holder of the debt that is paid off. It may be held by the general public, the commercial banks, or the Federal Reserve. The differences in effect will arise with respect to these groups, although the general public includes holders as diverse as private individuals and financial institutions (other than commercial banks). In order to note the effects most easily, we can simplify the mechanics of the payments involved. The taxpayers' checks go to the Treasury. Instead of being deposited and new checks issued by the Treasury to retire debt, we may suppose that they are endorsed by the Treasury and handed to holders of the debt being retired. When people receive such checks, they deposit them in banks, which in effect merely record a transfer of deposits from taxpayers to the former security holders. The money supply is unaffected, as is the lending power of banks. The public holds fewer liquid assets now, however, and this reduction in near money may influence its spending behavior.

When the debt that is paid off is held by commercial banks, the banks receive the taxpayers' checks from the Treasury in return for the government securities being retired. As the checks are drawn against the accounts of the taxpaying depositors, their deposits will be reduced. The money supply in the hands of the public is thus reduced by the amount of the debt retirement. To be sure, since bank deposits are now lower and bank reserves are unchanged by the transactions, the banks have more lending power, which, if they use it, may restore the level of the money supply. But the debt reduction of itself reduced the money supply, whether or not subsequent offsetting credit expansion takes place.

Finally, let us consider the effect of the Treasury paying off debt held by the Federal Reserve. When the Federal Reserve receives taxpayers' checks in return for the retired securities, it collects from the banks on which the checks are drawn, thus reducing their reserves by the amount of the debt reduction. The banks, in turn, reduce the deposits of the taxpayers by that amount. The money supply has been reduced by that amount, and the excess reserves of the banks by the same amount, thus contracting by several times that amount the lending power of the banking system.

These effects of debt increase or debt reduction may be desired in some circumstances and not in others. In general, debt increase would be desirable when an expansionary effect is desired, as in a recession, or, more generally, when unemployment persists due to inadequate spending. Debt decrease would be desirable when a deflationary effect is desired, to a greater or lesser degree, as when one is trying to combat various degrees of inflation. If debt reduction was undertaken at an inopportune time and had an unwanted deflationary impact, it would be necessary for the Federal Reserve to purchase additional government securities in the open market in an attempt to reduce the undesired effects of the debt retirement policy. It is not clear that the public or the banks would prefer the result of debt reduction in all respects, even if undertaken at an appropriate time, for they would then be in need of finding suitable securities in which to invest in order to replace those retired. It might not be possible to make equally satisfactory replacements, although the situation might redound to the benefit of issuers of new securities.

changes in the monetary gold stock

Another type of transaction that should be examined involves changes in the United States monetary gold stock. Again we can grasp the essence of the result by using a simplified example. Let us take the case of domestically mined gold that is sold to the Treasury. A government check, drawn on a Treasury deposit account in the Federal Reserve, pays the mining company for the gold. The company deposits the check in its bank and thus increases the money supply. To be sure, if the Treasury had to replace its reduced deposit by more taxes or by the sale of bonds to the public, the effect on the money supply would be removed as the public would give up an equal volume of deposits. If the gold stock increases at a time when the inflationary effect of increasing the money supply is not desired, the Treasury may sell new securities to replace the funds used to purchase the gold, thus "sterilizing" the gold, as it is said. What has really been done in this case is to offset the effect of the gold purchase on the money supply.

But we must go back to our initial example of the gold purchase. After the mining company deposits the check in the bank, the bank in turn deposits the check in the Federal Reserve, gaining reserves equal in amount to the new deposit. The lending power of the bank is thus increased, and in the system of banks as a whole a multiple-credit expansion is possible.

Let us next consider the Federal Reserve itself. When the bank deposits the Treasury check to its reserve account, the Federal Reserve reduces the Treasury account and gives it back a canceled check. We previously mentioned the Treasury account reduction, but in the sequence of events this would come last, although the Treasury would think in terms of a reduced deposit as soon as it wrote the check for the gold. The new gold may now be the basis for a further operation known as "monetizing" the gold. The Treasury can issue new gold certificates, backed 100 percent by the new gold. These may be deposited in the Treasury's account at the Federal Reserve. The gold can thus be paid for by creating the money to pay for it. There is no need then to tax or to borrow to pay for the gold unless the Treasury wants to "sterilize" the gold, that is, remove the effect on the money supply of the public caused by its purchase. When gold certificates are issued on the basis of the new gold and deposited in the Federal Reserve, this also adds to the reserves of the Federal Reserve. But one should not conclude that the result will be an expansion of Federal Reserve Bank credit and a further expansion of the money supply. The Federal Reserve is not a profit-maximizing institution, and the addition to its reserves will not affect its credit policy. Consequently, no further monetary expansion will be caused by the growth of the Federal Reserve's reserves.

The reverse of the above, namely a reduction in the monetary gold stock of the nation, might result from a foreign bank, which holds a deposit in a New York bank, deciding to reduce its holdings of dollars and to acquire gold with them. For our purpose we can ignore the role of the Federal Reserve and the precise mechanics of the transaction and treat it as a simple purchase of gold from the Treasury by the foreign bank. A check on its deposit in the New York bank is given the Treasury, which deposits the check in its account at the Federal Reserve. The Federal Reserve reduces the reserves of the bank on which the check is drawn, and the bank in turn reduces the deposit of the foreign bank. The Treasury may "earmark" the gold for the foreign bank if there is no demand to ship it abroad. Otherwise it will deliver the gold for shipping. In any case, the Treasury has now to withdraw from its deposit at the Federal

Reserve the gold certificates that were backed by the gold sold. Total deposits in the banks have been reduced by the amount of the gold purchase, but more significantly the reserves of commercial banks have been reduced by an equal amount, and thus the lending power of the banking system has been reduced by several times that amount. Whether this will cause credit contraction or merely reduce potential credit expansion depends upon whether the banking system was fully loaned up previously or how much excess reserves it had. The reduction of reserves of the Federal Reserve (its loss of gold certificates that were withdrawn by the Treasury) normally will have no consequences at all. If the gold transaction takes place at a time when the reduction of bank lending power is undesirable, the Federal Reserve can offset the gold loss by open-market purchases of government securities. This will restore the reserves lost by the banking system and increase the money supply again.

We have observed how a number of monetary and fiscal transactions affect the money supply, the reserves, and lending power of the banking system, and how they affect the Federal Reserve and the Treasury. To avoid an excess or deficiency of the money supply is primarily a matter of controlling credit creation by banks. This is done mainly through open-market operations by the Federal Reserve, sometimes supplemented by its other credit control powers. We have examined how these work. We have also seen that the effect of increasing or decreasing the public debt is greater if the holder of the debt instruments is the Federal Reserve. The monetary effects of changes in the gold stock have also been examined.

sources and uses of reserve funds

We now know that there are numerous factors that influence the reserves of banks, and a number of important transactions that affect reserves. We have also shown how to ascertain the effects of many transactions. One can trace the route followed by the checks used in the transactions, noting effects as the checks pass from initial recipients to their banks, then to the Federal Reserve, on to the banks on which the checks are drawn, and back to the writers of the checks. In some cases the circuits are simpler and in some more complex than this. Some transactions may involve clearing several sets of checks. Approaching a transaction in this manner enables us to find out its effect on bank reserves.

What we would like to have is a way of summarizing all the factors that affect bank reserves. The total number of such factors would be very large, but there would be a clear gain if the problem of finding what factors were most important, in any given case period, could be simplified by identifying in some manner the types of factors that were directly involved in reserve changes. Fortunately, this is possible. There is a table of monetary statistics that is arranged in such fashion that changes in bank reserves can be attributed directly to changes in the small set of variables in the table. One does not know from the table alone the reasons why a given variable changed, but one does know which items to look behind to find the primary reasons for any change in bank reserves. A copy of the table is presented in Table 6.1.

The first column in the table gives the absolute magnitude of the items. These magnitudes and the items themselves are derived by a complicated process involving a consolidation of two other tables, a "Treasury Statement of Circulation of United States Money," and the consolidated balance sheet of the twelve Federal Reserve banks. In the resulting table some items refer to the Federal Reserve, some to the Treasury. There are several informative things to notice about the column giving the totals for items in the table. (1) First, and most significant, it is evident that Federal Reserve credit is extended primarily by buying and holding United States government securities. (2) What is surprising is that the "float" is sometimes as large as it is shown to be on the particular dates given by the table. The float represents dollars credited by the Federal Reserve to reserves of banks (as a result of checks due them) before the Federal Reserve has collected from the banks on which the checks are drawn. The float is a temporary and "accidental" result of the time delay in clearance of checks by the Federal Reserve. (3) The various forms of Reserve Bank credit are similar in that all are a source of reserves for banks, as will be clear if the earlier discussion of rediscounts and open-market operations is reviewed. (4) The acquisition of gold also adds to bank reserves as we have seen earlier in this chapter. It is interesting to note in the table that Reserve Bank credit now provides more reserves to the banking system than does the gold stock. (5) Compare next the amount of Treasury currency outstanding and the total amount of currency in circulation; the latter, substantially larger as it is, includes all the Federal Reserve notes, which is most of our paper money.

What is of more interest to us than the size of the remaining

Table 6.1 Sources and Uses of Reserve Funds
Weekly Averages of Daily Figures
(*millions of dollars*)

	WEEK ENDING 4/6/66	CHANGE FROM WEEK ENDING 3/30/66	CHANGE FROM WEEK ENDING 4/7/65
Federal Reserve Bank credits			
U. S. government securities			
Bought outright—System account	$40,779	$+274	$+3,283
Held under repurchase agreement	145	+145	−84
Acceptances			
Bought outright	76	−1	+19
Held under repurchase agreement	44	−21	−42
Discounts and advances			
Member bank borrowings	623	+115	+53
Other	20		+4
Float	1,637	−104	+228
Total Reserve Bank credit	43,325	+409	+3,462
Gold stock	13,633	+1	−930
Treasury currency outstanding	5,738	+4	+340
	62,696	+414	+2,873
Currency in circulation	41,504	+156	+2,642
Treasury cash holdings	934	−2	+202
Treasury deposits with F.R. banks	309	−251	−419
Foreign deposits with F.R. banks	173	+38	−3
Other deposits with F.R. banks	387	+11	+180
Other F.R. accounts (net)	607	−3	−228
	43,915	−50	+2,375
Member-bank reserves			
With Federal Reserve banks	18,782	+466	+499
Cash allowed as reserves (est.)	3,610	−243	+392
Total reserves held (est.)	22,392	+223	+891
Required reserves (est.)	21,994	+99	+868
Excess reserves (est.)	398	+124	+23

SOURCE: *The New York Times*, April 8, 1966.

items in the totals column is the magnitude and direction of changes in the various items, including those already mentioned. The two right-hand columns in the table show changes in the items, one column the changes in the totals since the preceding week and one the changes by comparison with the nearest weekend a year ago. A positive number or a " + " in one of the right-hand columns indicates that the total given in the left-hand column is bigger by the indicated amount than the comparable figure at the earlier date represented by one of the right-hand columns; a " − " indicates the reverse. It does not mean that the item has been increasing (or decreasing, if there is a minus) over the whole period but that the item is bigger by the indicated amount at the later date by comparison with the earlier date.

Table 6.1 shows the actual change in member bank reserves. Since 1959 when the banks were permitted to hold some of their legal reserve in the form of vault cash, the table has shown the amount of cash held by the bank as legal reserve, as well as the amount of reserve in the form of deposits at the Federal Reserve banks. What we want to find out next from the table is how much each of the items listed there is responsible for the change in bank reserves. We can see at a glance how much each item has changed, but what we must know in addition is in which direction bank reserves will be changed by each of the item changes.

Here an analogy will help us. We may think of a pool of re-serves created by funds from several sources; there are several uses for these reserves. At any given date we may see whether these sources have contributed more or less to the pool than at some other date. And we can see whether the several uses have drained more or less from the pool than at the other date. In each case, the por-tion of the pool that has not been drained off for other uses remains as bank reserves. There are three sources of these reserve funds: Federal Reserve credit, the monetary gold stock, and Treasury cur-rency. An increase in any of these increased bank reserves, other things remaining the same, and a decrease in the funds contributed by these sources decrease bank reserves. The changes in these sources of reserve funds are given in the top portion of the table under discussion, and the net change in the three sources taken together is given as well. The uses to which these reserve funds may be put are listed in the table under six headings, beginning with "currency in circulation" and ending with "other Federal Reserve accounts (net)." Member bank reserves with Federal Reserve banks is the residual item; it reflects the net effect of the changes in all the preceding items. When a larger portion of the pool is drained off for one of the six uses of reserve funds shown in the table (following our pool analogy), less is left for reserves of member banks; while a smaller drain to these six uses leaves more funds in bank reserves.

To analyze the specific set of figures in the table, we begin with the net figures for the changes from March 30, 1966, to April 6, 1966. The change in member bank reserves at the Federal Reserve was + $466 million. Why were these reserves up by that amount at the later date? That is what we must explain. The table shows that sources of reserve funds were $414 million higher and uses of such funds were $50 million lower. An increase in a source of reserve funds tends of itself to increase bank reserves; an increase in a use of reserve funds tends to decrease bank reserves; and a decrease in a use of reserve funds adds to bank reserves. We add the $50 million to the $414 million and find the change in bank reserves to be $464 million instead of the $466 million listed in the table. This error of $2 million arises because the figures we are using are all rounded to the nearest million dollars, whereas the data underlying the table were more accurate. Now we have seen how to tell the effect on bank reserves of a change in a source or a use of reserve funds, and we have seen that in this period the change in bank reserves came primarily from a net change in sources of such funds rather than from a large net change in uses of such funds.

If we look inside these two categories, however, we obtain more information. We notice that bank reserves for those particular dates were increased by $1 million by an increase in the nation's monetary gold stock (although, as we would expect, the gold stock was lower than a year previous, as shown in the column for April 7, 1965). The largest single factor increasing bank reserves was the substantial rise in Federal Reserve credit, amounting to $409 million. And it is interesting here, as it often is, to note why Federal Reserve credit increased—whether by rediscounting, in which the initiative comes from the member banks, or from an increase in the size of the float, which for some dates might be due even to such a factor as winter storms delaying the transmission of checks, or due to open-market operations, which are undertaken as a matter of policy by the Federal Reserve itself. In the period we are now considering, the float went down sharply, which in itself reduced bank reserves. However, this was much more than offset by open-market purchases of government securities by the Federal Reserve—$274 million worth, plus $145 million under repurchase agreement (where dealers agree to buy the securities back, the funds thus being in effect a loan). Banks themselves also borrowed from the Federal Reserve though this made less difference than the open-market operations of the Federal Reserve. The changes in the individual uses of reserve funds will also reveal whether there are any significant movements, even if offsetting ones. In this case currency in circulation increased by $156 million, which is more than offset by decreases in Treasury deposits with Federal Reserve banks.

Looking now at the components of bank reserves, we notice that although bank reserves held at the Federal Reserve increased $466 million, the cash reserves held by the banks themselves decreased $243 million so that total member bank reserves increased only .$223 million. The relationship between the drop in bank holdings of cash and the increase in currency in circulation needs to be explored further. The figures in the table for currency in circulation refer to currency outside the Treasury and the Federal Reserve banks; hence cash held by member banks is included. The figure for currency in circulation may rise because banks need more cash on hand and withdraw some from their deposits at the Federal Reserve. In such circumstances the decline in bank reserves at the Federal Reserve is obviously offset by the rise in cash reserves. Another possibility is that the public increases its cash holdings by drawing on its deposits at the bank. This reduces bank reserves either in cash on hand, or if that is replaced by getting cash from the Federal Reserve, it reduces reserves at the Federal Reserve, as would be shown by a rise in the currency-in-circulation figure in the table. The particular case at hand is more complicated. There is a $156 million rise in currency in circulation, which of itself implies (via our pool analogy) a reduction of that amount in bank reserves with the Federal Reserve. At the same time bank holdings of cash fell $243 million, reducing total reserves still further. The implication of these changes is that the public increased its holdings of currency by the sum of these two amounts, or $399 million.

The reader will do well to analyze the factors causing changes in bank reserves as reflected in the final column of the table, referring back if need be to the above discussion to keep before him the relevant procedure.

Studying this statistical table for a single week enables one to spot the relative importance of various factors immediately responsible for the change in member bank reserves. One then knows which items must be examined further to see what is behind their changes. But one must not draw any conclusions about trends on the basis of the changes recorded in a single one of these "sources and uses" tables. If one wants to observe behavior of these items over time and get some idea of what trends may be present, if any, or what other types of fluctuations in the variables may be present, one must obviously examine successive tables over some period of time. Indeed, it is helpful to look at the past behavior of items in the table, as shown in the *Federal Reserve Chart Book.* Figure 6.1 reproduces such a

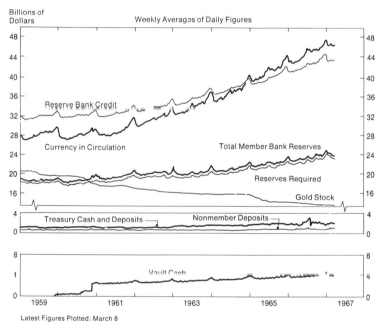

Figure 6.1. Member Bank Reserves and Related Items
Source: Board of Governors of the Federal Reserve System.

chart from a recent *Chart Book;* readers may wish to bring it up to date, which can be done by getting more current data from the latest copy of the *Federal Reserve Bulletin.* (See the first table in the section on Financial and Business Statistics, called "Member Bank Reserves, Reserve Bank Credit, and Related Items.")

money supply

It is now possible to summarize the determinants of the money supply. We have noted that the volume of currency responds to changes in the volume of demand deposits and the public's desires with respect to the proportion of their money balances that they wish to carry in pocketbook money form. We know that the volume of demand deposits depends first upon the volume of reserves in the banking system. Reserves of member banks are changed by amounts that we can calculate when the various sources and uses of reserve funds change by known amounts. Changes in reserves of any banks in the economy, whether members of the Federal Reserve System or not, do not stay confined to the banks where the initial changes occur but spread throughout the banking system. Changes in reserves in the banking system can change the money supply, through changes in bank loans and investments, by amounts that are limited by the legal required-reserve ratios. The legal requirement sets a minimum below which the actual ratio between reserves and deposits may not fall. However, at times the actual ratio may be above this minimum because the banks may be holding excess reserves. How many excess reserves the banks hold is a matter, in the last analysis, of how they view business conditions, the state of security markets, the loan applications they receive, and the degree of liquidity that they feel they need. They can over time adjust their volume of loans and investments to accord with these factors, and hence can choose what volume of excess reserves they want, even though they cannot by their own efforts change the volume of reserves available to the system. This statement need not be seriously qualified by the fact that the banks can borrow from the Federal Reserve, for without denying the loans or rediscounts, the Federal Reserve can offset them if it wishes by open-market operations. The Federal Reserve thus has more to say about the volume of reserves permitted the banks than the individual banks have to say about it. The following outline shows the factors just discussed as determinants of the money supply.

Determinants of the Money Supply

Pocketbook money (Currency)

Total volume of demand deposits (adjusted)

The proportion of their total money balances the public wants to carry in pocketbook money form.

Checkbook money (Demand deposits)

Total volume of bank reserves

Sources and uses of reserve funds (See Table 6.1)

Actual reserve ratio of banks
   Minimum determined by legal required reserve ratio
   Volume of excess reserves
      Bankers' views of business conditions, etc.

The outline does not itself make clear who can affect each of the items it lists. It would be a useful exercise to consider which items in the outline (including within it, as implied, the various sources and uses of reserve funds) can be affected by the general public, which can be affected by the banks themselves, which by the Federal Reserve, and which by the Treasury (or more broadly by government fiscal operations). Consider in what way each may exert some influence on the result, and the relative importance of each of the above at any given point. A rereading of the first part of this chapter may help in identifying the effects of actions by each. From this exercise an appreciation should emerge of the importance of the public's use of banks and its desire for bank credit on the one hand and the bank's responsiveness to changes in business conditions on the other, with recognition of the dependence of the system upon appropriate joint action by the government and the Federal Reserve. We shall consider further in Chapter Fourteen the importance of such joint action to facilitate the needed long-run growth of the money supply, or to check undue rates of expansion at times, or to try to deal with undue contraction. For the present it suffices to have learned how to trace the effects of such actions as may be taken.

questions

1. *Why is there little danger of overissue of currency and coin today?*

2. *When would the Federal Reserve be likely to want to sell government securities? Trace the effects of such a sale on the money supply and on the lending power of the banking system.*

3. *Under what circumstances should the Federal Reserve's rediscount rates be raised? Trace the effects of such an increase.*

4. Compare the monetary effects of paying off portions of the government debt in the hands of the Federal Reserve, or of the commercial banks, or of the general public.

5. Explain how changes in the monetary gold stock of the country may affect monetary conditions. How can we insulate ourselves, in part, from such effects?

the problem of
liquidity

A BANKING SYSTEM IS ABLE TO OPERATE WITH A
fractional reserve because not all depositors want their money back
at once. But a bank that keeps too small a working reserve to meet
occasional drains on reserves, due to an excess of withdrawals over
deposits or to an adverse clearing house balance, may find itself in
serious trouble. Banks that may be solvent, in the sense that they
have enough good assets to cover their liabilities, nonetheless may
fail if those assets cannot be liquidated fast enough to meet claims
upon them. Yet if a bank were to avoid all risk of this sort, it would
have to keep a 100 percent cash reserve behind its deposits, and it
would then probably fail because it could not make enough money to
stay in business. The banker's problem is to make the best compromise possible in various circumstances between the twin requirements of liquidity and earnings.

The compromise between liquidity and earnings is not only a
problem for the individual banker, it is also a problem of a whole

banking system. The consequences for the economy as a whole if the banking system becomes too illiquid for the circumstances are very serious indeed.

required reserves and working reserves

The large number of bank failures in the early history of banking in this country has already been pointed out. Many of these were the result of the banks failing to keep enough cash reserve, though there were, of course, other important causes. If bankers do not keep enough reserves, what seems a more obvious way of correcting the condition and protecting depositors and the public generally than to pass a law requiring them to do so? There have long been laws requiring some minimum ratio of reserves to deposits. The question we must ask is whether this type of legislation solves the liquidity problem, or can it be solved by a fractional reserve requirement. Suppose the requirement is 20 percent, which is higher than was customary under state laws for state banks and is slightly higher than the average requirement now. A net adverse claim on the bank, either for currency or as a result of clearings of checks written by depositors, reduces reserves and deposits by an equal amount. If the bank was fully loaned up, such a drain would put the bank in the position of having a deficit of 80 percent of the total. The reserve required behind a deposit furnishes only 20 percent of the cash needed if it is withdrawn, but the other reserves held by the bank behind other deposits cannot be used for the purpose except on a very temporary basis. Reserve requirements as presently stated for member banks of the Federal Reserve System apply to the average reserve maintained over a period that varies from three days to two weeks for different classes of banks. If for part of the period the bank falls below the requirement, even though it makes it up by carrying more than the requirement later to bring up the average, the bank is subject to penalties. These take the form of fines on the deficiencies and prohibition of new loans and of dividend payments during periods of deficiency. If there are persistent deficiencies, the bank would be closed. Clearly, it pays banks to avoid deficiencies, if possible, and in any case to cover them quickly. It is thus evident that the reserve required by deposits not withdrawn is really not available to any significant degree to cover actual deposit withdrawals. The required reserves are indeed required; they do not form a pool from which the bank can draw to any substantial degree to meet the need for extra liquid funds. They are not intended for use to meet temporary needs for liquid funds. One might almost say that they are immobilized and serve more as window dressing than anything else.

Required reserves do indeed have a use, though the reserve requirement does not, as we have just seen, contribute more than the indicated fraction to meeting liquidity needs. The bank that fails has at least the volume of sound assets held in the cash reserve. Depositors would probably lose less in banks required to keep a 20 percent cash reserve behind deposits than if they had deposits in failed banks without any reserve requirement or with a lower one. More important for the economy as a whole, a banking system with a high reserve requirement may be more stable than one with a low reserve requirement. We saw this when we discussed credit expansion, for the credit expansion multiple is lower the higher the required reserve ratio. One might be tempted to conclude from this, however, that if there were no legal required reserve ratio, the credit expansion multiple would be infinite, but this is not so. Some countries do not impose reserve requirements on their banks, and the bankers learn from experience how much reserve to keep for liquidity needs. The ratio that becomes customary in these circumstances determines the credit expansion multiple. The multiple does tend to be higher than when there is a legal reserve requirement. But the reserves that are kept behind deposits are then more readily available for use in times when more than the usual degree of liquidity is called for. When monetary authorities have power to vary the required reserve ratio, the ratios are important for credit control policy. But the liquidity problem is not solved by laws requiring banks to keep more reserves than they otherwise might.

Nor does it solve the liquidity problem to require the bank's capital to bear at least some minimum ratio to its deposits. Again it would be better for depositors to have their funds in a bank that met some such minimum requirement than in one which fell below it. If the bank failed, there would be a bigger cushion of stockholder equity to protect the depositor. That is, more assets could go "sour" in the former before the depositor would lose anything. But there is nothing about a high ratio of capital to deposits that indicates a bank has its assets in liquid form rather than in illiquid form. ("Capital account" per se does not mean the amount of cash held as some "laymen" mistakenly believe.)

A bank's first recourse when it needs liquid funds is its working reserve. What forms does such reserve take? Primarily, the form of excess reserves. This is liquidity *par excellence*. When banks were not allowed to count their cash on hand as part of their legal reserve, such cash provided additional working reserve. And deposits at other banks, such as is kept by many banks at correspondent banks, is working reserve. The volume of working reserves of a bank is the amount by which it can meet demands for liquid funds directly and avoid deficits without borrowing or taking other action.

As we have indicated, a bank cannot afford to carry a working reserve big enough for all the circumstances that may arise. Yet it wants to have something else to fall back on should unusual circumstances arise. This may be called its "secondary" reserve. The most highly liquid of the bank's earning assets are its secondary reserve. Let us examine the way secondary reserve assets provide a bank with liquidity. We want to be in a position to decide how well various assets can serve as secondary reserves for banks.

commercial loans as secondary reserves

It has sometimes been thought that a bank's liquidity could best be protected by the use of its funds largely for commercial loans. A bank should avoid tying up funds in long-term investments. That is, commercial loans were thought to be a better secondary reserve than other types of assets.

There are several reasons why the commercial loan might be thought to protect the liquidity of the bank. It is a self-liquidating loan. That is, the use to which the loan is put gives rise to the income from which the loan can be repaid. Thus the default risk would seem to be less than it might be with other types of loans. But the essence of liquidity is not the same as safety or low risk. The essence of liquidity is nearness to cash. To state it differently, an asset is liquid if it can be converted into cash quickly and easily without much risk of a capital loss being sustained in the process. Cash can be obtained for any asset if one pays no attention to how much cash one gets; therefore, the question of loss in obtaining the cash is quite important in judging the liquidity of an asset. The bank needs a secondary reserve that enables it to obtain cash when needed easily and quickly without risk of capital loss. The term "self-liquidating," applied to a commercial loan, does not refer to that characteristic but to the use to which the loan was originally put by the borrower and the relation of that use to his ability to repay at the end of the loan period. There is nothing about the nature of the self-liquidating loan that implies that it furnishes the bank cash when needed and without loss.

But there is another feature of the loan that may be examined. If a commercial loan should not be paid when due, the collateral, it is sometimes said, is of such nature that the bank has less risk of loss in getting its cash at that time than may be the case with other types of loans. The commercial loan typically has some readily marketable product as collateral. Usually it is the product whose production, storage, or marketing the loan is designed to finance. The product presumably has a relatively steady market, at least over the period of the loan, so that it might be disposed of without risking much capital loss for the bank. A loan secured by real estate, such as a mortgage loan, may constitute a severe loss for the bank should it have to foreclose to recoup its funds, if the real estate market drops in the meantime, as it may. Securities as collateral for a loan may decline in value with a drop in the securities markets, again inflicting a loss on the bank if it has to rely upon the collateral to get its money back. However, banks have long been wise to the risks entailed by lending on collateral that may drop in value, and they have made it a practice to margin such loans quite liberally. That is, they offset the risk that the real estate or security markets may drop by lending a borrower only a fraction of the amount that his security or real estate is worth at current market values. A drop of some size is thus required before the bank risks any capital loss. Then even if the bank must take over the collateral and dispose of it for cash, the commercial loan may not have less risk of capital loss.

It should be apparent that it is not the inherent ability of the commercial loan to provide cash when needed, which it cannot of itself do, nor the risk entailed by the collateral that provides what liquidity an asset has for the bank. Is it then the short-term character of the commercial loan that makes it good secondary reserve? Typically the loan is for a maximum of ninety days. Funds are thus not tied up as long as in term loans or long-term bonds. The more frequently a loan falls due, the more frequently the bank is in a position to reconsider whether to make another loan or to strengthen its liquidity if it needs to do so. Consequently, the length of time the money is tied up is quite pertinent to the solution of the liquidity problem.

However, the commercial loan does not solve the whole problem just by being short term in character. To begin with, a ninety-day

loan just made is not going to put the bank in possession of funds
again as soon as a longer-term loan that falls due next week. Within
the ninety days the bank can do nothing with the loan itself (unless
it can shift it); it cannot get the funds back from the borrower
short of ninety days. Within that period it does not appear to be
so liquid. If what the bank needs for liquidity is a loan falling due
soon that can give it funds again, then what is most important is not
the length of the original loans but how well the bank's loans are
staggered over time. If a bank arranges its loans so that some fall due
every day, it is clearly more liquid, even if all the loans were term
loans, than if it put all its funds into ninety-day loans that all fell due
the beginning of the next quarter. To be sure, staggering many short-
term loans would be better than having all funds invested in long-
term form but staggered.

In actuality the commercial loan is often not as short-term a loan
as it appears to be. The phenomenon of the continuous borrower
makes its appearance here. Sometimes a borrower will need funds for
considerably longer than the banker is willing to lend them. The
bank, knowing the bank examiner will look with disfavor upon its increasing its long-term loans, may be unwilling to make the loan for
more than ninety days. However, the bank may assure the borrower
that the loan can be renewed upon its expiration, assuming of course
that his credit is unimpaired and so forth. Given this normal expectation, the borrower may commit his funds to a project that is self-
liquidating only over a longer period. The loan is now in fact a
longer-term loan than it appears. It may be renewed repeatedly. Many
borrowers do maintain a certain volume of borrowing from their
banks. But what if at some time the bank gets in a tight position and
cannot renew the loan of one of these continuous borrowers? If it has
to force the borrower to repay instead of renewing the loan, it may
find that the loan is not so liquid even at the due date. The borrower
did not count on having to repay then, and he may be quite unable to
do so. He is not liquid enough either. The bank as well as the borrower may lose if the bank tries to take over the loan collateral to
secure payment. There are several alternatives, and these add up to
"shifting the loan."

shiftability of assets

If the borrower can borrow from another bank to pay off the
first bank, the first bank will have met the need for liquidity by non-

renewal of the loan. The loan has in effect been shifted to the second bank. That is what enabled the first bank to become more liquid. To be sure, a bank can hardly count on the customer coming back very soon again if he has been forced to another bank to continue a loan that he had reasonable expectations would be renewed. Thus the bank in the long run would lose business. Therefore, the bank would avoid resorting to this method of shifting the loan. Another way the bank might use the commercial loan to increase its liquidity is to sell it to another bank; that is, it might rediscount the note of its customer at some other bank, getting the needed funds. Indeed, it might try to do this at any time during the life of the loan. The commercial loan is liquid and good secondary reserve, then, only to the extent that it is shiftable, that is, saleable to another lender.

How shiftable is the commercial loan? Put yourself in the position of the bank to which a bank tries to sell one. The chances are that you do not know the person who signed the note, you have not investigated his credit worthiness, and you certainly did not examine his original loan application. Are you going to purchase this note without an independent investigation of the risk entailed? Likely not. The bank that thought its commercial loans were its most liquid earning assets may find that in fact they are not so easy to market. The bank may be reluctant to sell this asset, rather than another type, even if there were no difference in marketability because of customer reaction. The customer may not react favorably when he finds on receipt of his canceled note after it is repaid that the bank with whom he dealt had disposed of the note to another bank for a time. This anticipated reaction may be enough in some cases to make it preferable for the bank to shift some other asset to another lender rather than to shift a commercial loan, even if the bank could more readily do the latter.

We can conclude that there is indeed no earning asset whose characteristics make it inherently highly liquid apart from its saleability. The bank's secondary reserve provides liquidity to a bank by virtue of its shiftability, that is, saleability. The assets that can be sold most quickly and easily and with least risk of capital loss are not in general customer notes, which are highly individualized, but standard securities, the credit-worthiness of the issuers of which are known without further investigation by other bankers. High-grade corporate bonds might be considered better reserve from this point of view than commercial loans. Government securities are still better, for serious declines in the market are quite unlikely. Short-term United States government securities, or those falling due shortly, should be in ample supply in a bank's portfolio to protect its liquidity.

These conclusions require only one significant qualification. When the Federal Reserve System was established, provisions were written into the law that in effect conferred a privileged status upon commercial loans in bank dealings with the Federal Reserve itself. To obtain a loan from the Federal Reserve, it was provided that a member bank could rediscount paper which met certain tests (of maturity and purpose). This made the commercial loan shiftable to the Federal Reserve though not readily shiftable elsewhere. Among the various arguments that might be adduced for giving even preferential status for rediscount to such loans, the only one that is not seriously faulty is that this type of loan is the commercial bank's special forte, and though encouragement to hold such may be unnecessary, banks would normally have such loans available if they needed to borrow from the Federal Reserve. Indeed, even this turned out not to be the case at one time during the Great Depression, and the Federal Reserve was consequently empowered to lend to banks needing funds on any asset the Reserve might find acceptable. Although banks can shift commercial loans to the Reserve, they are now not restricted to this method of supplementing reserves, and they sometimes rely on other secondary reserve due to some reluctance, already explained, to rediscount customer notes extensively.

We have indicated how the bank must solve its liquidity problem by having an adequate secondary reserve consisting of highly liquid (shiftable) earning assets. But the word "adequate" conceals a problem. The bank finds that in making up its portfolio it can indeed provide a bigger or better secondary reserve by investing in more liquid assets, but it does so at the expense of earnings. The most liquid assets generally do provide the bank a lower rate of return on its investment than less liquid assets. Therefore, the bank has to decide how big a secondary reserve to carry, or (in different words) how much it can sacrifice earnings for liquidity, or how much liquidity it can sacrifice for greater earnings.

liquidity crisis

It is, of course, important that each bank mantain sufficient liquidity as a protection to depositors, but the liquidity of the whole banking system may not be adequately protected even if each bank does provide what appears to it to be adequate secondary reserves. This is because, as we have noted, the liquidity of each bank, taken individually, depends heavily upon the shiftability of assets to some other lender, normally some other bank in the system. When one bank gains liquidity by thus shifting assets, what is happening is that working reserves, usually excess reserves, somewhere in the system are being used in a way that relieves the pressure on some other point in the system. But what happens to liquidity if the entire banking system is under pressure at once, more liquidity being needed in the system as a whole than can be found anywhere in the system? The banks cannot then help each other out because they are all in the same predicament—all scrambling to improve their cash position.

Such a situation can indeed arise, and when it does the consequences are quite serious for the economy as a whole. Something of the sort has happened in some of the country's financial crises in the past. The one that has left the greatest impression on us was that of the Great Depression, which followed the 1929 stock market crash. We shall not review the details of that period here; we need recall a few important parts of the story, though. Conditions arose in which the banks sustained severe losses, many banks failed, the public's confidence in the banks weakened, and deposits were withdrawn. The banks were caught in the middle, unable to stem the tide of deflation, and even adding to it. They needed substantially increased liquidity but could get it only by credit contraction. To reduce loans reduces the volume of reserves required. They had to do this since they cannot in the aggregate generate reserves however badly they need them (unless the central bank expands its credit). At the bottom of the depression of the 1930's the total volume of deposits had fallen about 40 percent and the total money supply about 25 percent. No wonder the Great Depression was so severe! A nation cannot expect to halt a downswing, let alone generate a recovery while the money supply is falling to such an extent as that.

The normal functioning of the economy as a whole involves what we may call "circular liquidity," and this is what broke down in the early 1930's. It was common then to hear people say, "I could pay every penny I owe others if I could just collect what is owed me." The continuous circular flow of payments had somehow been interrupted. Everywhere there were "frozen assets," amounts receivable that could not be collected where normally payment could be counted on. What caused this breakdown in circular liquidity? The whole story involves the complex of factors that caused the depression itself, as well as the inherent instability of the speculative bubble in the stock market. And once business turned down sharply, business failures were a large contributing factor. But the most important single factor aggravating the whole situation was the contraction of bank credit. The 25 percent decrease in the money supply made it impossible for the circular liquidity of the system to be maintained at normal levels. Under the circumstances banks, businesses, and the man in the street all felt that they needed to be more liquid than normal. Therefore, they all scrambled for liquidity, making the situation worse. The banks could not choose not to follow suit. As the public, fearful of bank failure, withdrew deposits, it forced the banks to contract by a multiple of the reserves withdrawn. Payments that normally would have been made partly with the aid of bank credit now could not be made. Because they could not be made, other payments could not be made. Circular liquidity disappeared, the victim largely of unavoidable bank credit contraction.

solving the system's liquidity problem

The reader may question the use of the term "unavoidable" in the preceding sentence, and it should be questioned. But the author's purpose, after trying to outline in the last paragraphs the economic significance of maintaining the liquidity of the banking system as a whole, is to raise the question of how the liquidity of the system *can be* protected. It should now be evident that this cannot be done just by having each bank in possession of enough good secondary reserve. Indeed, it should be clear that unless the system carried a very considerable volume of excess reserves normally, far above what it has usually done, it could not have done any differently when the troubles of the 1930's hit than it did. The solution of the problem of protecting the liquidity of the entire system at once must be approached differently. The banks in the 1930's could not protect themselves by normal methods of shifting assets to each other. Nor could they solve the problem satisfactorily by shifting assets to the public. Security prices had fallen sharply, and the public wanted cash, not more securities.

The solution must lie outside the structure of the commercial banking system. And the key to the solution of the system must be found in the same way that it was found for a single bank. There must be a source of liquid funds that can be tapped by shifting some asset to the holder of the funds. What this comes down to is that the liquidity of a banking system, and hence of an economy, can be protected only by a central bank that serves as a "lender of last resort" for the banks. If a central bank will carry the volume of excess reserves that private banks cannot be expected to carry and will enable bank assets to be shifted to it when there is a liquidity crisis in the system as a whole, the multiple-credit contraction that may otherwise be forced upon the system can be avoided. Usually the credit control activities of central banks receive the most attention, but the role of the central bank as ultimate shiftee for the banking system should not be minimized. It can make a big difference in this respect if it plays the role that only a central bank can play to back up the system of banks and hence preserve the circular liquidity of the economy.

All this may lead one to ask why the debacle occurred to the banks in the 1930's. The Federal Reserve was there, but evidently it did not act with sufficient vigor to deal with the liquidity crisis effectively. What explanation is there for that? The answer that must be given is that the Federal Reserve was neither set up nor operated with a full understanding that its role should be that of a central bank, controlling credit and solving the problem when system liquidity is threatened. We have mentioned earlier the limited problems with which the Federal Reserve banks were to deal and the fear that prevailed that they might indeed do too much. It was believed that if banks were properly supervised so that each one kept its funds in good short-term, self-liquidating commercial or agricultural loans and avoided tying up too many funds in longer-term investments, all would be well. The real nature of the problem of circular liquidity was not understood from the beginning. When the Reserve was in the midst of the crises in the 1930's its thinking had not changed enough to lead to vigorous enough action. It could have done much more than it did to provide, through open-market operations and rediscounts and loans to banks, reserves enough to cover at least those lost through public withdrawal of deposits.

The depression produced some changes in attitudes toward the role of the Federal Reserve. In effect the Federal Reserve was charged with responsibility for taking a more active role as a central bank, and it was given some added powers that could help it handle a liquidity problem better than in the past. One power, enabling the Federal Reserve to vary the required reserve ratio for member banks within certain limits, could help in a liquidity crisis if the ratio was not already at the bottom limit. Lowering the ratio would free many reserves for use to bolster the liquidity of the banks as a whole.

Another power given the Federal Reserve was designed not to deal with a crisis but to reduce the likelihood that bank credit would be extensively used to build another speculative bubble in the security markets, the bursting of which was serious enough itself and which had further adverse effects. The Federal Reserve was empowered to fix minimum margin requirements for purchasing securities. This enables it to reduce the amount of bank credit going directly into security markets.

The liquidity problem can be approached from the side of reducing the demand for liquidity as well as from that of increasing the supply of liquidity. This was accomplished by the legislation of the 1930's. The Federal Deposit Insurance Corporation (FDIC) was established, and all member banks of the Federal Reserve were required to become members of the FDIC. Other banks were also encouraged to become members. Most banks did join. In return for an annual premium of one-twelfth of 1 percent of its total deposits, each depositor's account is now insured up to a maximum of $15,000 (originally $5000). The knowledge that one will not lose even if the bank fails makes it much less likely that the public will ever again lose confidence in the banks to the extent it did in the 1930's and draw out its accounts in such volume. Consequently, the banks will not be forced to scramble so hard for liquidity. This, of course, depends upon the public having confidence in the soundness of the FDIC itself. Its record to date should give solid ground for such public confidence. From its premium income the FDIC has repaid the government and the Federal Reserve banks the original capital with which they helped it start and has built a substantial reserve. The FDIC is more than an insurance agency in that its powers of examination and supervision are designed to enable it to prevent failures, if possible, rather than merely pay off after failures. It has indeed corrected a substantial number of weak bank situations by merging a weak bank with a stronger one. It has taken over assets that the stronger bank finds unacceptable and has slowly liquidated them. The loss record of the FDIC is exceptionally good. To be sure, large deposits are not fully insured, and it would be a gain from the point of view of the liquidity problem if the danger of large deposits being withdrawn for protection were also eliminated. This could be done within the FDIC framework if we chose to legislate such a provision. If in any future crisis there were any fear that the FDIC itself might go under, the nation would face the choice between (1) having the government guarantee the solvency of the FDIC or (2) risking having public confidence so shaken that a vast run on the banks might occur. This could produce the worst liquidity crisis of our history. It would be the height of folly not to have the government stand squarely behind the FDIC at the slightest signs of uneasiness about its strength.

central bank liquidity

The final question to be discussed is the liquidity of the Federal Reserve itself. If it is to be a lender of last resort for the banking system, it must be kept highly liquid. Earning assets do not themselves provide liquidity except through being sold. When the Federal Reserve is called upon to add liquidity to the whole banking system and economic system, it cannot do so by selling anyone its earning assets. Consequently the Federal Reserve must have excess reserves in ample amount at all times. What has protected its liquidity then? What has ensured it substantial excess reserves? Two things have been primarily responsible over the years. First, the unwritten rule or tradition against continuous borrowing from the Federal Reserve. If the member banks borrowed heavily from the Federal Reserve to supplement their reserves even in normal times, instead of using it for purely temporary needs, there would be danger that the Federal Reserve too could become fully loaned up in time. It would then be unable, given the reserve ratio it too was required to maintain (in gold certificates behind both notes and deposits until 1965), to meet the needs of the banking system for additional loans and reserves in times of crisis. The key then was to keep the banks from using the Federal Reserve too heavily in normal times, to restrict them to using it for temporary needs. The Federal Reserve has not always been too successful in this, particularly before the depression of the 1930's. However, in later years the banks seemed properly reluctant to appear very dependent upon the Federal Reserve for reserves except temporarily. The Federal Reserve has tried to cultivate such an attitude. But since the banks can often lend at a higher interest rate than the Federal Reserve charges them, it is not clear why borrowing is as low as it has been. It is good that it has worked this way, for it has enabled the Reserve to keep a high degree of liquidity available for times of need.

The second factor responsible for the preservation of the Federal Reserve's liquidity has been the absence of the profit motive. If the Reserve tried to maximize profit, it would, like a private commercial bank, lend or invest to a point where its liquidity would be adequate for all normal circumstances but probably not adequate for the unusual circumstances for which a central bank is most needed. We would be back to the same situation as under the National Banking Act when banks kept many reserves on deposit in New York banks. These banks as profit-seeking institutions did not remain liquid enough for the central banking function they were involved in performing. If ever the Federal Reserve makes decisions on the basis of the need to increase its earnings to cover costs, rather than on the basis of the welfare of the economy, the day will have come when subsidizing the Reserve will be the only way to have the central banking function properly performed. Fortunately, that day is not likely to come.

If the normal operation of the Federal Reserve is such as to protect its cushion of excess reserves, its position can be eroded by abnormal circumstances (or possibly over a long enough time by monetary expansion). A war can result in such an expansion of money that the reserve base of the Federal Reserve can become inadequate. To forestall this in World War II the required reserve ratio for Federal Reserve notes and deposits was reduced from 40 percent and 35 percent, respectively, to 25 percent. In any liquidity crisis similar action, that is a reduction of the reserve requirement on the Federal Reserve—could solve the immediate problem, giving the Federal Reserve all the excess reserves the situation might require.

Not a domestic liquidity crisis but a loss of gold due to an unfavorable balance of payments has raised the question of why there should be a required reserve ratio applied to the liabilities of the central bank at all, especially if, as appears to be the case, any time that the needed monetary policy is hindered by it, the ratio can be lowered. The answer is that historically there was the fear that a central bank might be so mismanaged as to inflate its credit too much without such a restriction. And the same misplaced notion that requiring some amount of reserve would itself solve the problem of protecting the liquidity of the bank carried over from the commercial bank level to people's thinking about a central bank. In fact a reserve requirement performs no function whatsoever at the central bank level. It is irrelevant except when it hampers some desirable central bank policy. Central banks do not expand their credit to the limit permitted by the requirement, so it is normally irrelevant. Its removal would make no difference except where it removed an obstacle to a needed policy.

In time this may be sufficiently understood that central banks will be operated without minimum reserve requirements. But although this would eliminate any possibility that the Federal Reserve might itself be insufficiently liquid to meet some conceivable liquidity crisis in the the nation's banking system, it would not render irrelevant or useless the two factors mentioned above as having protected the liquidity of the Reserve, namely the tradition against continuous borrowing at the Reserve and the absence of the profit motive in the Federal Reserve. For under a no-reserve-requirement arrangement, these two features of the present system would be needed to help ensure that the Reserve did not expand its credit except in accordance with the needs of the system. The same restraints as now would be needed to check unwarranted credit expansion, but the danger of insufficient liquidity at the top would be removed completely.

In 1965, as a result of the reduction of the nation's monetary gold stock by continuous balance-of-payments deficits and the need to make more of our gold available to maintain the international value of the dollar, Congress did remove the requirement that a gold reserve be held behind the deposit liabilities of the Reserve. This is a significant movement in the direction that we have just discussed. Even if the loss of gold does not continue, as it may, to the point where the reserve requirement behind Federal Reserve notes is likely to be dropped, Federal Reserve liquidity for domestic needs has already been greatly strengthened. This will be apparent if one realizes that the Federal Reserve can now supply additional reserves to the domestic banking system in any domestic liquidity crisis without being blocked by inadequacy of the gold stock. The Reserve can simply lend to banks or buy in the open market, by merely increasing the size of member bank deposits at the Federal Reserve. Only if the liquidity crisis should proceed to the point where the public's demand for Federal Reserve notes exceeded the number that could be issued on the basis of the gold stock would the question of how to provide the required liquidity reappear. Even a severe crisis is not likely to go so far if the Federal Reserve acts vigorously to maintain the liquidity of the banking system (as it now unquestionably can) and if the government stands firmly behind the FDIC to maintain confidence in it. In the final analysis, however, it would be absurd to maintain a reserve requirement behind Federal Reserve notes if this were to prevent the public from having whatever portion of its money supply it chose in note form rather than deposit form. This is particularly true if such refusal came at a time when the public was indeed scrambling to convert to notes, for then the scramble and its consequences could only become worse. This is not the same as saying that the money supply should not be limited; it is saying that the present limitation on its form is not useful and could conceivably be harmful. Reserve requirements on a central bank like the Federal Reserve can detract from, but cannot contribute to, the solution of the liquidity problem, a problem that has plagued us in the past and one that we should never allow to cause serious trouble again.

These considerations have involved reference to the nation's balance-of-payments situation and to one aspect of the gold reserve requirement. Both of these matters will receive fuller treatment in subsequent chapters. Suffice it here to add a comment about the gold reserve requirement and the total money supply. Our study of the Federal Reserve's liquidity should dispose of the idea that the gold reserve requirement is the factor that most of the time has actually been the effective brake on the overexpansion of the money supply. The fact is, as we have seen, the Federal Reserve has normally kept substantial excess reserves. That is to say, the Federal Reserve has kept the money supply from expanding as far as the gold reserve requirements would have permitted. Monetary policy, not gold reserve requirements, has been the effective brake on credit expansion in the past, and will continue to be so in the future. Therefore, the removal of any or all of the gold reserve requirements does not signify lack of the normal restraints on the money supply. Removal does make more certain that we can have our money when we need it, and in the form we may want it, without our effort to get it causing a banking crisis and general economic decline.

questions

1. *What are good working reserves for a commercial bank? What is not? Why?*

2. *What are the relevant factors in evaluating the commercial loan as a form of secondary reserve for a bank?*

3. *Explain the importance of the liquidity of the banking system for the circular liquidity of the economy.*

4. *How are we prepared to prevent future liquidity crises by*

action on both the side of demand for liquidity and the side of supply of liquidity?

5. Discuss the role of the required reserve ratio applied to a central bank.

·EIGHT·

financial intermediaries and their role

THE COMMERCIAL BANK IS INDEED ONE OF OUR most important lending institutions, but it is by no means the only source of loans. Nor is new money creation the only source of loanable funds. In actuality, the larger portion of the total supply of loanable funds is "current savings." Therefore, we must extend our discussion to fit commercial bank operations into the broader picture of the total flow of loanable funds and the total pattern of financial institutions.

In tracing the flow of loanable funds, we can identify different sectors of the total market. Each sector is characterized by a group of financial institutions that attract a portion of the savings of the economy and make loans of certain types. Since these institutions are performing essentially a middleman function, transferring funds from lending sources to borrowers, they are termed "financial intermediaries." A good starting point for our examination of the loanable funds markets is a consideration of the borrowers in these markets and the purposes to which they put their loans.

borrowers

In general it may be said that any economic unit may seek to borrow when its own resources are not sufficient to finance some expenditure that it plans to undertake. When "internal financing" is possible, there is no need for financial institutions except perhaps as temporary means of handling accumulating funds.

The borrowers are those who seek "external financing." Any classification of borrowers is somewhat arbitrary, and the following classification is open to the objection that the classes are overlapping. Nonetheless, it is a useful classification when related to the structure of the loanable-funds market. (1) *Business firms* of all sorts borrow for short terms for what is called "working capital"; for example, they may borrow to purchase something for which they will be reimbursed when they sell it, with or without further processing. Firms also seek funds to invest in "fixed capital"; for example, they may undertake construction of a factory, store, or warehouse. (2) *Households* may borrow to meet emergency or temporary expenses or to finance the purchase of consumer durables, such as cars, refrigerators, and the like. (3) *Housing builders or purchasers* borrow to help finance the construction or the purchase of housing. (4) *Farmers* as producers may borrow to purchase a farm, to add to their farm equipment, or to tide them over until a crop is marketed; as consumers they borrow for the same purposes as other households. (5) *Government* bodies at all levels borrow for capital projects, such as building public schools or roads and later repay out of tax proceeds. In addition, the federal government sometimes borrows rather than tax to finance a budget deficit that may be either undesired or deliberately undertaken to have certain economic effects. (6) *Financial institutions* sometimes borrow from one another to meet loan demands from their customers.

savings

The primary source of funds to satisfy these borrowers is savings. Some of the saving is done directly by business firms. When they save enough to finance their own investments, we speak of "internal financing." But often business firms have to borrow the savings of others, that is, from households who are the ultimate source of savings as they divide their income between consumption and saving. In addition to savings, loans can be financed by an expansion of bank credit, that is, new money can be created and lent to borrowers. Since only commercial banks can create demand deposits directly, they are unique among financial institutions in this regard. As loans mature and are repaid, the funds can be lent again. The largest annual addition to the pool of loanable funds comes from current savings rather than from new money creation. There are times when the stream of loanable funds can be augmented slightly by tapping funds which had been lying idle; this is referred to as "dishoarding." It is sometimes argued that an increase in credit granted by any seller to any buyer constitutes an additional source of loanable funds. This is incorrect, however; when a business extends credit to buyers of its products, it must either borrow enough from banks to enable it to finance its customers, or it must draw down its cash balances (a form of dishoarding), or it must tap the savings stream to avoid either of the other alternatives. When government lends, it may tap the sources of funds or it may use tax proceeds. The incidence of taxes is uncertain; they may reduce idle balances, or current savings, or current spending in varying degrees.

If savings are the principal source of the funds that financial institutions can draw upon to make loans to the various types of borrowers, how can they obtain control of the savings? Savers typically do not want their savings to lie idle, earning nothing. They want to lend their funds, but they do not want to have to seek out borrowers, evaluate their credit-worthiness, or go to the bother of negotiating the loans in a form that protects them, involving as this may a choice of legal forms, of collateral, and so forth. Thus it is advantageous for the saver to have a middleman—a financial institution—specialize in lending his savings. Financial institutions, in turn, are advantageous to the borrower, who does not then have to find for himself a saver who is willing to lend on terms that are suitable.

To attract savers, the financial institutions have to provide certain inducements so that the saver will entrust his savings to their care. First, the saver must be offered safekeeping of his savings. Second, the saver must be paid something for the surrender of the use of the funds; he must share in the gain from lending them to the final borrower. Various savers will also require various degrees of liquidity, upon surrender of their savings. Some will want to be able to get the funds back quite readily, while others will be satisfied to tie them up for specified periods of time. In general, the saver finds that financial institutions can offer him higher rates of return on his savings only by providing him a lower degree of liquidity. There may also be an inverse relationship between earnings and safety, or we could say a direct relation between earnings and risk. The saver, of course, reduces his risk appreciably by having his funds lent by a financial institution instead of lending them directly himself because he obtains greater diversification among final borrowers of his funds. At least the small saver thus avoids the risks entailed in "putting all his eggs in one basket."

The operation of financial institutions, then, involves attracting savings (and idle funds) and lending them to various borrowers. There are two sets of loans involved, and both can be spoken of as "investing" money. The saver lends to the financial institution, instead of always lending directly to final borrowers, and the financial institution lends to the borrowers classified above. These financial investments must be distinguished from the actual production of capital goods (reported as investment in national income statistics) although the two may be to some extent interrelated. It is obvious that not all borrowers use the funds to produce or buy capital goods.

financial instruments

There is generally some evidence of a financial investment or loan. It may be nothing more than an entry in a savings bank book held by the household saver. Or it may be any of a wide variety of securities that the investor speaks of having purchased in making his financial investment or loan. The security or other evidence of the loan specifies the terms of the loan. Securities growing out of loans frequently are in effect "promissory notes." They involve a promise by the maker to pay a specified sum at a specified time. These notes may be unsecured, or secured, by collateral that the lender can sell in order to recover his funds in case of default. In many cases the rate of interest payable is stated.

Credit transactions sometimes involve the use of a different type of credit instrument called a "bill of exchange." This is essentially a draft or order requiring another party to pay a specified sum at a determined time. The drawer must, of course, be entitled to require such payment by the payee. A "bank check" is a form of bill of exchange.

There is a market for those credit instruments that are negotiable, that is, for the instruments that are legally transferable from one party to another. The participants in the securities markets are the lenders, the borrowers, and the middlemen they sometimes use (the various financial institutions). The negotiability of credit instruments is a very important characteristic since it greatly increases the holder's liquidity, that is, his ability to reconvert to money should he need to do so. Lenders would often be much more reluctant to part with their funds if there were not a ready market for the securities they hold. Consequently, the market facilitates borrowing and minimizes hoarding. Funds that might otherwise lie idle are put to work.

Equities or shares of stock of corporations constitute another type of security actively traded in the market and involving the same three parties they bring together, namely, those seeking funds to use and those with funds to invest in financial instruments. The ultimate issuer is not obtaining funds by signing a promissory note and paying interest on the funds; the issuer obtains the needed funds in return for sale of a partial interest in the corporation, a share of ownership going to the purchaser of the stock. The purchaser hopes to gain dividends (rather than interest) paid out of corporate profits and perhaps hopes to sell the security later for more than he paid for it, making a capital gain on the transaction.

Financial institutions then deal in various forms of promissory notes, bills of exchange, and equities. External financing takes place through any of these forms, and a financial investment may take any of these forms. The rate of return on investible funds, and in general the cost of obtaining them, are determined by the forces of demand and supply in the money and capital markets. The term "money market" is usually applied to the markets for short-term loans, while the term "capital market" covers markets for longer-term funds. The specific terms on which funds flow through these markets vary widely since investors have different preferences as to the nature of the financial investments that they are willing to make and since those seeking funds similarly have different needs and requirements and differ as to what they will commit themselves to. The resale of securities by original investors provides alternatives for new investors so that the general condition of securities markets determines the terms on which new funds can be drawn from those markets. The price of an old issue is determined in part by the returns obtainable by owning it.

Some securities, notably United States Treasury bills (short-term obligations, typically ninety days, on which the Treasury frequently borrows) are sold at auction to the highest bidders on a discount basis. That is, the buyer pays less than the face value of the bill and upon maturity receives the face value. The yield on the investment is the interest thus earned divided by the initial investment. The less the buyer has to pay to obtain the fixed sum at a given later date, the higher the rate of return on his investment. Most dollar claims, that is loans, involve either a specified discount rate or a specified rate of interest to be paid on the principal. A bond, for example, specifies the "coupon rate" or rate paid per $100 of the face amount of the bond. This means that periodically the bond issuer will pay the holder of the bond a fixed and known sum. If the bond can be bought for less than that principal sum (the par value), the rate of return or yield on the actual amount invested in buying the bond is higher than if bought at par. Similarly, if the market price of the bond rises above par, a buyer getting the same fixed interest payments will be earning less on his actual investment in the bond.

savings institutions

The classification of lenders, like that of borrowers, is somewhat arbitrary. We shall examine primarily institutions specializing in serving the several classes of borrowers. There are, however, some financial institutions that tend to be identified primarily in terms of their service to household savers instead of in terms of the type of borrower they serve. These may be called "savings institutions," although the term could be applied much more broadly. The principal institution of this type is the savings bank, which holds savings deposits rather than demand deposits. The savings departments of commercial banks also fall in this category. A strong competitor in recent years for household savings is the savings and loan association. Savings held in these associations are usually withdrawable at any time in practice, although associations are not legally required to pay out savings invested in them except as they are able since the investor is in fact purchasing a share in a mutual company. One of the largest outlets for household savings is life insurance. It is true that the purchaser of insurance is buying protection, but except for some term insurance policies he is also building up a reserve for some future time against which he may draw, as against other forms of savings, if need be. The United States Postal Savings System, established in 1910, provided a savings outlet for people who were wary of savings banks, but it never held a very sizeable volume of savings. A type of savings institution that is based on groups of people associated together in some fashion, as a common place of employment or a club, is the credit union. This not only provides a place for the saver to put his funds, it is at the same time a sort of mutual-help institution, making small personal loans to its saver-members.

long-term capital market

Business borrowers and seekers of capital funds are served by financial institutions in the long-term and in the short-term capital markets. In the former are found investment banks, investment trusts, and stock exchanges. Investment banks serve as middlemen in the process of raising long-term capital for business. Corporations obtain more capital by issuing more stock or bonds. Frequently such issues are planned in conjunction with an investment bank, which then underwrites the issue, perhaps forming a syndicate with other investment banks for the purpose if the issue is large. That is, the investment bank undertakes to sell the new issue to others, selling of course at a higher price than it pays the issuing corporation. Some new issues are placed directly by the corporation with buyers, but the middleman provides enough advantages that his services are widely used in floating new securities. Often the investment bank must temporarily supplement its own capital by borrowing from the commercial banks to help it carry a new issue until marketed.

An investment trust is a very different kind of a financial institution, although it also serves to improve the market for long-term securities. It offers the saver its own securities, called "trust certificates," and uses his funds to invest in a variety of marketable securities of others. This provides the saver diversification even with a relatively small investment. In the past the record of this type of institution has been rather spotty, but in recent years there has been a rapid growth of mutual funds, which are a form of investment trust. They are free to alter their holdings of securities at will in order to increase earnings for the participants. The latter can generally sell their interest in the fund whenever they choose, but what they get for it will depend upon the current value of the assets it represents.

Stock exchanges and security brokers and dealers serve to provide a ready market in which securities may be traded. The exchanges are regulated by their members through whom all transactions on the exchange floor must be made. The New York Stock Exchange is the best known. Not all securities are listed on security exchanges. Some are confined to trading "over the counter," in an unorganized market. The security exchanges do not provide the initial market for raising new capital, but they make it much easier for such capital to be raised by providing a ready market for resale or purchase of outstanding issues of securities. A buyer or seller can get a broker to execute his order for a commission, or he may be able to do business with a dealer who uses his own capital to carry an inventory of securities for resale.

The whole process of issuing and trading in corporate securities, important as it is to the financing of the long-term capital needs of business, has at times exhibited results that were so widely regarded as unsatisfactory as to lead to a substantial amount of government regulation, supplementing the self-regulation within the "industry." State legislation in the field proved ineffectual, and federal regulation entered the field in 1933 with the passage of the Securities Act, which has since been amended. The main objective of the regulation is to improve the market so that investors purchasing securities have an opportunity to know what they are buying. That is, the purpose is to prevent fraud and misrepresentation and to provide disclosure of sufficient information for an intelligent decision to be made by prospective buyers. The law does not regulate the quality of securities issued or traded. It seeks to ensure disclosure of relevant facts. The Securities and Exchange Commission is empowered to exercise broad supervisory powers over the exchanges themselves and over the activities of their members. Corporations whose securities are traded on the exchanges must file financial reports in accordance with regulations prescribed by the commission.

Commercial banking and investment banking have been separated by law so that the same firm cannot do both types of business. The Board of Governors of the Federal Reserve System has been empowered to fix the minimum margin requirements for the purchasing or carrying of securities so as to enable the amount of bank credit flowing into securities markets to be limited.

short-term capital market

For the short-term credit needs of business the commercial bank is the most important institution, but it does not have a monopoly of this type of business. There are several other types of lenders who share the business, although they sometimes supplement their own capital by borrowing temporarily from commercial banks. What are called "commercial-paper houses" serve as middlemen in the purchase and resale of open-market commercial paper. This is a type of promissory note issued in standard denominations of $5000 or more by well-known firms wishing to borrow for a shorter period than a single bank is likely to provide. The commercial-paper house charges a commission for "retailing" an issue of open-market commercial paper. The issue and the loan may thus be divided among a substantial number of banks, perhaps including small ones whose funds could not otherwise have been effectively tapped for the purpose. The interest paid on these notes tends to be rather low, and is set by the issuing firm, always with an eye on current market conditions.

There is also a market for bankers' acceptances, especially since the Federal Reserve has stood ready to back up the market by buying such acceptances when necessary to provide them greater liquidity. These are used chiefly in financing foreign trade. Being drafts drawn upon and accepted by a bank, they are a negotiable kind of credit instrument. Acceptance dealers (or bill brokers, as they are called in England) buy such drafts from exporters who want dollars for their claims on foreign banks and sell the drafts to commercial banks that want short-term liquid assets.

Another source of short-term credit for business is called the "factor." In general, a factor provides the business credit on a short-term basis against the security of its "accounts receivable." The money owed the business by its own cutomers, but not yet paid, is the basis (the collateral) for the funds loaned. Sometimes the factor actually takes over the accounts and collects to secure repayment. At times factors have operated in other ways to help provide funds in certain industries.

Finally, the sales finance company may be mentioned as providing finance not only directly to the consumer, but also, especially in the automobile field, to the retailing business itself. Some of its funds are obtained by sale of its own finance paper (like open-market commercial paper) that it places directly with commercial banks, without the commercial-paper house middleman.

consumer finance and personal loan market

The most widespread use of credit by consumers today is for purchase of consumer durable goods on the installment plan. The type of financial institution that provides the credit for such purchases is known as a sales finance company. The largest bloc of such business is in the automobile field, where the finance company pays cash to the car dealer and collects the installments from the buyer. For other consumer durables the seller often holds the installment contract himself. Interest rates on installment purchases vary widely, and it is often very difficult to tell exactly what rate is involved. The stated rate may be misleading. The buyer may not know the actual cash price at which the purchase could have been made. Other charges have sometimes been lumped with interest charges. And interest can be made to appear low by padding service charges instead.

Commercial banks have become important lenders of consumer credit in the last thirty years. In addition to installment loans, they make loans to consumers repayable in a lump sum. By keeping their loan standards relatively high, they have been able to hold interest rates for this type of lending down to relatively low figures (for example, 6 percent discount on a one-year installment loan, which amounts to close to 12 percent per annum). A recent innovation is the revolving-credit account for the depositor. This enables the depositor to overdraw his bank account, as it were, by design, when he needs additional funds, repaying by installments with interest on the unpaid balance. (Interest is usually about 1 percent a month.)

Another type of institution in this field is the personal loan company (or consumer finance company). It specializes in making small personal loans. A few large companies share the field with numerous small local firms. As a result of abuses in the past, state laws now partially regulate this type of business, usually under the Uniform Small Loan Law. The maximum size loan permitted is still $300, but the companies seek to have this raised to accord with the increase in price level since that ceiling was fixed. Maximum interest rate is usually 3.5 percent per month on unpaid balances. The costs of handling such small loans, which are usually amortized monthly, is high, even though the loss record is not bad (even on unsecured notes), and these costs keep up the interest rate.

Credit unions have already been mentioned, but it should be noted here that their members treat them not only as a place to save but also as a place to borrow small sums.

The pawnbroker provides what is in effect a loan, although in form there is a sale of some item to the pawnbroker with an option to repurchase at a specified higher price within a certain period of time.

The most notorious of all lenders, the so-called "loan shark," still operates, taking advantage of needy and ignorant people whom he often manages to keep in debt to him continuously. Threats enable him to collect exhorbitant interest despite the illegality of his operation.

Consumers are often able to buy "on credit," paying later (as at the next billing period for a store) and with no apparent interest charge. The seller in this case either borrows what is in effect lent the customer, or foregoes interest he could have earned by lending the same amount elsewhere if he had made a cash sale. This cost is covered in the sale price even though there is no distinction made between cash and credit purchaser. Alternatively, the sale on credit without interest charge could be looked at as providing the credit customer a discount in order to make the sale. A recent innovation is the revolving-credit account by which stores can convert more sales into installment loans with interest charged at a rate (usually 1.5 percent per month) that more than covers their costs.

mortgage market

The construction or purchase of housing normally involves long-term credit on a mortgage with the property as collateral. Such loans are heavily margined; that is, the loan is limited to perhaps 60 percent or 80 percent of the current value of the property. The principal lenders in this field are life insurance companies, savings and loan associations, and banks (both commercial banks and savings banks). The mortgage market has been revolutionized since the depth of the depression of the 1930's when very large numbers of mortgage loans became almost uncollectible and many people lost their property. The difference in the mortgage market today from that of the 1930's has come about through the development of a number of new financial institutions established by the federal government. The key innovations in the field were brought about by the Federal Housing Administration (FHA), which is not itself a lender but insures mortgage loans when the underlying transaction meets certain conditions that it lays down. Regular monthly payments to amortize the mortgages are central. The degree of standardization introduced by the FHA into the mortgage field has been supplemented by the Federal National Mortgage Association (popularly called Fannie Mae), which by its readiness to purchase FHA insured mortgages (or resell them) has created a secondary market for mortgages and has thus given them more liquidity. In addition, a Federal Home Loan Bank System was created in 1932, composed of eleven regional Home Loan banks, membership in which is open to institutions making mortgage loans. Federal savings and loan associations are required to join, and are supervised by, the Federal Home Loan Bank Board. The main function of the Home Loan banks is to provide loans, short-term or long-term, to their members. The capital for the purpose, temporarily provided by the Treasury, now consists of subscriptions to stock by the member institutions; it may be supplemented by issuing bonds for sale to the public.

Other federal agencies make grants as well as loans for certain types of construction, primarily public housing, public works, urban redevelopment, and some college construction programs. Insurance is also provided through the Federal Savings and Loan Insurance Corporation for accounts in savings and loan associations; some associations insure privately, though the experience of such insurers has not always been good. The Veterans Administration operates somewhat like the FHA for mortgages for veterans, though terms are more liberal.

agricultural credit institutions

Farmers have often felt that they were not treated fairly when it came to the availability of loans. Commercial banks have sometimes been reluctant to lend farmers the amounts that they need for the lengths of time that they need the funds. And the farmer typically cannot resort to some of the methods of financing his operations that other businesses can. Consequently, special financial institutions have been developed under the auspices of the federal government to mobilize credit for farmers. In 1916 a system of twelve Federal Land banks was established to make loans on mortgages of farm property. The funds are raised by sale of bonds and are disbursed through what are called national farm loan associations, formed by groups of borrowers. Three other systems of regional agricultural credit institutions were established within the federal Farm Credit Administration—banks for cooperatives, production credit corporations, and Federal Intermediate Credit banks. The last two of these have now merged. Like the Federal Land banks, all of these help to mobilize private capital for loans through local organizations of farmers. Thus long-term, short-term, and intermediate-term credit for farmers is now available. Other agencies provide funds for special purposes: the Farmers Home Administration, the Rural Electrification Administration, and the Commodity Credit Corporation. The last of these is the agency through which the government price-support program for basic farm crops is carried out.

allocation of loanable funds

Although there are many lending institutions, the total supply of loanable funds is limited. The limitation could be overcome by giving banks power to create credit without limit; but this would be undesirable. The resources over which borrowers obtain command are limited; therefore, there must be a comparable limitation on loanable funds. Without such limitation on loanable funds the resources that a dollar could command would necessarily decline. Since there are only so many resources to go around, the question is who gets them. We can assume at this point in our discussion that the economy generates income and hence claims on products and services equal to the volume of products and services it produces. When someone saves part of his income and lends the savings to someone else, he in effect transfers command over some resources to the borrower. When some resources are unemployed, credit creation may put additional purchasing power in the hands of borrowers, thus giving these borrowers command over additional resources. But an overall limitation remains, and borrowers as a group get command over resources not employed by others. Borrowers, however, are numerous; potential borrowing sometimes quite exceeds the indicated limitation on loanable funds. What determines which borrowers will get command of resources and which will not? The answer is important since loan allocation affects the allocation of the nation's resources, for not all borrowers use the funds the same way.

Two factors may be said to determine the allocation of loanable funds: a price and an "institutional" factor. The price in question is the rate of interest. Interest is the price of a loan; like any price, this one eliminates from the market those for whom the price is not worth it or who for any reason cannot pay the price. As we have indicated earlier, there is more than one price for a loan. The prices of loans differ with a variety of things, including the term of the loan, its purpose, and the amount of risk involved for the lender. The amounts lenders are willing to make available on these various terms as well as the amounts people want to borrow on various terms determines these interest rates. This is to say that the rates are determined by the demand for and supply of loans and securities of various kinds.[1] The demand for any kind of loan, the amount people will want to borrow for any purpose, will be lower the higher the cost of the loan, other things being equal. And the higher the return to the lender, the more he may be willing to lend. Who gets loans (and hence resources) and who doesn't is then changed by changes in the aggregate supply of or demand for funds, as well as by changes in the composition of either. Any increase in interest rate differentials among markets for different types of securities gives an inducement for some borrowers and lenders to shift their supply or demand to the relatively more favorable markets, limiting the effects of changes in the composition of the markets for loanable funds.

The other factor that explains the allocation of loanable funds at any time is the pattern of financial institutions. This chapter has surveyed the types of financial intermediaries and has thus shown the extent to which various middlemen have specialized in serving the needs of various classes of borrowers.[2] Where a type of borrower does not have his needs served very adequately, his command over resources is substantially less than after some financial institutions develop in the direction of serving him. Thus the development of installment credit for consumers by banks and sales finance companies alters the allocation of loanable funds and hence of the nation's resources. Similarly, the development of a whole battery of agricultural credit institutions has made possible a rate of mechanization of agriculture that would otherwise have been impossible or, at least, unlikely.

One can, of course, contend that this "institutional" factor is merely the price factor operating over a longer period of time. Something can be said for this view. If the price of some type of loan exceeds the cost at which it can be provided, the profit prospect will lure lenders, and the structure of financial intermediaries will be altered to provide the services needed by borrowers. This is all right

[1] The significance of interest rates is discussed in another connection at the end of Chapter 10.

[2] A more extended treatment of financial institutions and their economic significance, with supporting statistical data, is given in one of the supplementary volumes of this set: Raymond Goldsmith, *Financial Institutions* (New York: Random House, to be published in 1968).

as far as it goes and explains in part the historical development of our financial intermediaries, but it is apparent that in some areas, for example, agricultural credit, there was the possibility of profitable lending. However, specialization of financial institutions to meet the need did not occur. It required government action to find the formula under which private capital could more adequately serve the farmer. The institutional pattern has to be explained in terms that are not exclusively "economic," and this affects the prices of different types of loans. Thus price factors and institutional factors between them may be said to determine the allocation of loanable funds, with its implications for allocation of resources in the economy.

We have not thus far dealt with governments as borrowers, though borrowing is done by governments at every level. The federal government at times deficit spends and borrows to cover the deficit. But other units borrow similarly. For example, school districts float bond issues to erect new schools; that is, they borrow the money from whoever buys their bonds. As borrowers, governments have no financial intermediary as specialized to their service as those developed for other types of borrowers. State and local governments do find, however, that they can secure help floating their bond issues through the regular machinery of investment banking. The federal government has been able to enlist widespread help, especially from commercial banks, in selling savings bonds to the general public, and marketable federal government securities are traded by a dozen firms that act as dealers in such securities. This group of dealers constitute the sole highly specialized financial intermediary in the field of government borrowing. The borrowing of governments, like that of private borrowers, gives command over resources to the borrowing units. The federal government is unique among borrowing units in that its borrowing may not be only for the sake of the "product" of those resources, but also may be for the purpose of providing employment of otherwise idle resources. When the latter is the purpose, the government is properly concerned with obtaining loanable funds without depriving others of such funds. This implies that such borrowing should come from idle bank funds or the Federal Reserve.

power of the creditor

The relationship of lender and borrower is, barring force or fraud of obvious kinds, a mutually beneficial relationship, else it would not be freely entered into. Nonetheless, there is asymmetry in the relationship. Shakespeare advised us if we wanted friends, neither a borrower nor a lender be. But the lender has often made out quite well, well enough that many institutional lenders have found profit in the business. Indeed, Shakespeare aside, the economy needs lenders, and that is why their operation is so well rewarded. Yet the lender, to whom one might suppose all would then be grateful, is often not well loved, as Shakespeare knew. The reason is, essentially, that the creditor, the one to whom the borrower owes the money, has a certain amount of power over the debtor, which the latter can hardly welcome.

How much power the creditor has over the debtor is in large measure a matter of the law. For civilized relationships to be maintained when, for example, the debtor refuses to pay back his loan, society requires the establishment of regularized procedures. Protection of the creditor is provided by the creation of legal "rights" against his debtors and by legal processes that enable the creditor to recover what is due him, insofar as possible (as by attachment of wages, foreclosure of mortgages, and the like). Such law has contributed greatly to economic development through the progressive accumulation of physical capital goods. The requisite lending was facilitated by providing legal recourse for those who lend the funds for investment.

However, the debtors' jail has been evidence that the results were sometimes rather onesided. Harsh laws could be invoked to throw a man in prison for nonpayment of even rather small sums and to keep him there until both debt and prison charges were paid. It is said that as late as 1829 in the United States there were as many as 75,000 persons annually imprisoned for debt.[3] How much protection the debtor should have is a very old question. The moral code of the early Christian church forbade taking interest on a loan. In those days loans were more frequently a matter of helping someone over a period of extraordinary need than of employing funds as productive capital, and the moral issue of profiting by others' misfortunes was the foremost social consideration. However, that moral censure was insufficient to prevent the practice of charging interest. The moralists gave up trying to prevent interest and inveighed against usurious rates of interest as exploitation of the needy. This led to legislation limiting the rates of interest that could

[3] E. L. Bogart, *Economic History of the United States*, 2nd ed. (New York: Longmans, Green & Company, 1935), p. 426.

legally be charged. To this day there are some unfortunate people who become victimized by loan sharks operating illegally.

The problem with respect to business loans is somewhat different. In general, the independence of a business from those from whom it borrows is highly prized. It is thought to be bad for a business to pass into the hands of the bankers from whom it borrowed or to be controlled by other important lenders. Today there are large accumulations of liquid funds in the hands of managers of pension funds, mutuals, and the like. The management of these funds could give them potentially considerable power over businesses in which they invest heavily.[4] Although financial power has sometimes been used deliberately as a way to obtain control of corporate enterprise, as through vast holding company operations, banks' and other financial institutions generally do not want to control the businesses to which they lend. They do not want to be so powerless in the relationship either that they cannot protect their interest, and usually they are not. The lender, by his power to lend or withhold funds, inevitably exercises some influence over the firms dependent on him for credit.

questions

1. *Compare broadly the economic roles of commercial banks and the whole group of financial intermediaries discussed in this chapter.*

2. *What determines the total volume of loanable funds in the economy?*

3. *What determines the allocation of these loanable funds and what economic significance has this allocation of funds?*

4. *Classify loanable-funds markets. In which of these markets is the commercial bank most active?*

5. *Is it ever possible for savers to shift their lending from one loanable-funds market to another or for borrowers to make*

---

[4] Peter Drucker, *America's Next Twenty Years* (New York: Harper & Row, 1957), Chapter III, "The New Tycoons."

a comparable shift in the market from which they obtain funds for a given purpose? What might be the reason for either trying to make such a shift, and what would the effect be on the total loanable-funds market?

the changing value
of money

WE HAVE SPOKEN EARLIER OF THE SLOW PROCESS of developing a satisfactory money. To be satisfactory, money must be reasonably stable in value. But what is meant by the value of money? Money is unlike other things of economic value in that when it is put to its primary use, the nation's money supply is not used up. Money is that which is used as a medium of exchange. By the "value of money" we mean the amount of other things that one can get in exchange for a unit of the money. The value of money is said to fall if there is a decline in the volume of goods and services which the unit of money will purchase. The "value of money" and the "purchasing power of money" are, therefore, synonomous terms.

measuring changes in the value of money

To measure changes in the value of money is then a matter of measuring the changes in the volume of other things obtainable with a unit of the money or, what is the same thing, the changes in the number of units of money required to purchase other things. If the dollar prices of things in general rise, the extent of the rise is a measure of the extent to which the purchasing power of money fell. The price level and the value of money move in opposite directions. Here we encounter an argument that must be avoided because it is based upon a simple confusion. It may be contended that the value of money fell because the price level rose; others may say that it is the reverse procedure—the price level rose because the value of money fell. The problem here is not to find which way a causal relation goes between two different things. There is only one thing to consider—the exchange ratio between money and other things in general. An alteration of this ratio can be referred to either as a change in the price level or as a change in the value of money. All that is meant by a fall in the value of the dollar is that there is a rise in the price level. We must seek elsewhere for the causes of the phenomenon that can be referred to equally well by the use of either term.

Price indexes have been developed to measure the changes in price levels. These indexes show the change in the average of a set of prices. The best known of the price indexes is the consumers price index, computed regularly by the United States Bureau of Labor Statistics (BLS). This index measures the average change in price of the goods and services bought by the typical household consumer in urban environments in the United States. Figure 9.1, based on Table 9.1, shows the movement in recent years of the consumer price index and the Gross National Product (GNP) deflator. The GNP deflator indicates the change in the average of prices of currently produced goods and services. It is evident that the two indexes give a similar picture of the rate at which the value of the dollar has been changing lately.

If our economy matched the economist's picture of perfect competition, the task of computing an index number would be much easier than it is. For each commodity a single price quotation, obtained from any seller, would suffice, for the price of the commodity would be uniform throughout the market for it. As it is, competition is far from perfect, and a sampling problem arises at the very start. The problem is to obtain a "representative sample" of price quotations for each commodity to be included in the index. The same sort of sampling problem presents itself in the choice of what specific goods and services to include. The number of such bought by con-

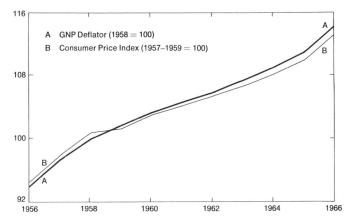

Figure 9 1   Two Price Indexes, 1956-1966
Source: Table 9.1.

sumers is so large in the aggregate that not every slightly differentiated product can be included.

The averaging process itself is not as simple as might be thought. Simple arithmetic averages of numerous prices would yield quite different answers when different sized units were used for the price quotations. Should the price of eggs be quoted in units of one egg, a dozen eggs, or a crate of eggs? You can readily think of other examples that would affect the results. There is no right or wrong about the different units that might be used. If, however, the units used include one Ford car, one ton of coal, one pound of butter, one dozen eggs, one man's suit, one quart of milk, and one haircut, among other things, it will be apparent that a "small" change in the expensive units may quite outweigh in the average what might appear to be "large" changes in the less expensive units. One way to overcome this is to average not the absolute prices in some "base period" and those in some other period but to average the relative changes in prices. Call the price of each commodity in the base year 100, and compute the prices in other years as percentages of the base year price. Then average the resulting "price relatives."

Both the simple arithmetic average and the simple average of relatives involve an implicit weighting of the items included in the index. In neither case is there any certainty that the weighting of the different items is preferable to, or as defensible as, some alternative weighting. It would indeed be quite obvious that an indefensible

Table 9.1 Two Price Indexes, 1956–1966

YEAR	GNP DEFLATOR 1958=100	CONSUMER PRICE INDEX 1957–1959=100
1956	94.0	94.7
1957	97.5	98.0
1958	100.0	100.7
1959	101.6	101.5
1960	103.3	103.1
1961	104.6	104.2
1962	105.8	105.4
1963	107.2	106.7
1964	108.9	108.1
1965	110.9	109.9
1966	114.2	113.1

SOURCES: GNP Deflator—Table, "The National Income and Product Accounts of the United States, 1929–1965," Statistical Tables; *A Supplement to the Survey of Current Business*" (Washington, D. C.: Department of Commerce, Office of Business Economics, 1966); *Survey of Current Business.*

Consumer Price Index—*Federal Reserve Bulletin* (January, 1966), p. 102 and (July, 1967), p. 1230.

weighting was involved in the example given above. One would not obtain with such an index (in which one car and one pound of butter and the like were included) anything but a misleading measure of the change in the value of the consumer's dollar if, say, the prices of various items moved in different directions or to substantially different degrees. Weighting of different prices in an index requires, then, something better than the accidental weighting that results from either of the two averaging methods mentioned. It has become customary to weight prices or price relatives in an index according to the relative expenditures on the items in question in some selected period. This gives a defensible measure of the change in value of the dollar to the typical consumer because the changes of different prices will be treated as affecting the value of his dollar in proportion to his expenditures on the items in question.

index number problem

Unfortunately "the index number problem" is not quite so easily disposed of as the above suggests. Further difficulties will become apparent if we think of using a price index to find the change in the value of the dollar since grandfather's day. Suppose we take prices fifty years ago of the things that the average consumer buys today. Some of the items could not be bought fifty years ago. We cannot enter into our computations any meaningful comparison with some current prices. So, we are not able to say how much it would have cost grandfather to buy what we buy today or how much more his dollar was worth than ours. We may have the feeling that many things have gone up in price since his day, but we run into a difficulty in trying to quantify the decline in value of our dollar. To be sure, we might approach the problem the other way around. We might start with what grandfather bought fifty years ago and see how much the same things would cost us today. We would weight the prices in the index by the relative expenditures on them in grandfather's day. We would then have less difficulty, for we could doubtless get everything today that he bought (though we might have to have "custom made" for us some things that grandfather bought but which have disappeared from use). We might thus get an index number figure, taking the weighted average price of goods bought fifty years ago and expressing today's average price of the same combination of goods as a percentage of the earlier average price. But would this be a good measure of the change in the value of the dollar? Would it be significant to us, or for that matter to grandfather if he were still alive? Not really because the present prices of many things used fifty years ago would be of very little interest to anyone today. We simply use a different bundle of goods. The index figure we might compute would conceivably be an accurate measure of the change in average price of a certain bundle of goods, but it would be quite irrelevant because nobody consumes such a bundle of goods today.

If weighting prices in the index by expenditures in a much earlier period gives an irrelevant result and these prices cannot be weighed by current expenditures (because the latter set of weights includes items which could not be had at any price in the earlier period), the obvious thing to do, some might contend, is to use current weights for current prices and the weights of fifty years ago for prices of fifty years ago. But if one thinks for a moment about this enticing solution, he will realize that he is in effect comparing the prices of two quite different bundles of goods, not measuring the change in the average price of some particular bundle of goods. One cannot measure the change in the value of the dollar by saying that commodity X used to cost X dollars, and today commodity Y costs Y dollars. One can get two figures, but they are not comparable because they do not relate to the same commodity. Is there any way out of this dilemma? The answer is that there is no completely satisfactory way out of it. Various index number formulas have been developed over the years which are more complicated than those implied by the discussion in this chapter, and some of them have distinct merits, but there is no truly "ideal" way out of the index number problem that we have just examined.

If one caution is observed, however, one can avoid being impaled too sharply on the horns of the dilemma. The dilemma is serious when comparisons are made over long periods of time, during which the relevant weighting has changed a great deal or during which completely new products have achieved real importance in expenditure patterns. As long as the index numbers are used to make "short-run" comparisons, the changes in expenditure patterns may not be great. When comparisons are attempted over quite long periods, any index numbers obtained should be taken "with a grain of salt." This, alas, takes much of the fun out of the sport, for the comparisons over long periods are those that we would most like to make if we could.

what index?

It is not too difficult to see how there can be disagreement over the amount by which the value of the dollar has changed over the past. There are different ways to compute the index numbers that measure such change, and the weights used may refer to expenditure patterns of one period or of another. One may quarrel with the representativeness of the sample of prices averaged even if one agrees on how broad the index should be. But there is a question of how broad it should be, and so people using different indexes may legitimately disagree on the amount of change in the value of money.

Thus far we have referred primarily to one common index, the BLS consumer price index. This index does not measure the change in the prices of everything for which money is spent. Nor does the other index quite commonly used—the wholesale price index. Narrower in coverage than the consumer price index, the wholesale price index is more sensitive to forces beginning to change prices. Any individual or group of persons may be quite right in contending that none of the published price indexes gives a true picture of the change in the value of the dollar for them. The fact is that any single index can measure only the change in the value of the dollar in purchasing some particular bundle of goods. If that is not much like the bundle of goods one actually purchases, the index does not measure the change in the value of the dollar to the person in question. To get the change in the value of one's dollar over the things one purchases, one would need to make his own index number, weighting items appropriately for his own expenditure pattern. But such an index number might be inapplicable to anyone else. Whose purchases of what should economists and others consider when they talk about measuring changes in the value of *the* dollar?

We might consider the implicit deflator used to correct national income figures to ascertain the amount of change in output represented and the extent to which national income statistics merely reflect price changes. This would enable us to measure the change in value of the dollar in purchasing current output of goods and services in general. However, it still excludes a vast number of transactions in previously produced goods, in real estate, and in claims (or securities). If we really wished to construct an index that would measure the value of money over all its uses, we would have to sample all transactions in which money purchases something at a price. This has been referred to as a "transactions price index." Unfortunately, we do not have any index that is as ambitious an undertaking as this. Conceptually, it is the only index that would measure changes in *the* value of money in general. But it would not be worth the work to compute it because changes in some of its main components would likely hold more direct interest than this most general index. We shall understand better why this may be so after we consider the reasons for our interest in the changes in the value of money.

significance of changes in the value of money

If people are concerned over changes in the value of money, it must be because it makes some difference to them. Certain economic effects flow from the changes in the value of money. But before we consider these, it will be worthwhile to see why there are any effects. It is sometimes asserted that if the value of money changed to the same degree in all uses, there would be no economic effects. Imagine, a situation in which the dollar, as a unit of account, were suddenly to be cut in half. Every place where there had been a dollar sign before, now put the dollar sign again but multiply by two. All prices would then be doubled; all incomes would also be doubled; all debts would be doubled, as would the value of all assets. It would be as though we had suddenly shifted to another unit of account with a fixed rate of exchange with the dollar. Nothing would be changed except the language used since the new unit of account would have a different name, and everywhere we spoke of one dollar before we would now speak of two of whatever we called the new unit. This example enables us to understand that the economic effects that flow from changes in the value of the dollar really arise because the dollar does not change to the same degree in all its uses at the same time. In other words, when the price level changes, price dispersion occurs; not all prices change by the same proportion. A rise in any price index will not be accompanied by a rise of the same amount in every other price index or by a rise of the same proportion in every price included in the index. Changes in relative prices occur when the average of prices changes, and we use a price index that measures only the change in the average as a simple way of getting an idea of how great has been the change in relative prices. The more the index changes, the greater the short-run changes in relative prices, and the greater the economic effects of these relative price changes is likely to be.

But what are the economic effects of price-level changes? They are of three general types: effects on the distribution of wealth, effects on the distribution of income, and effects on the level of production. Some generalizations can be made with respect to these types of changes. Inflation, a rise in the price level, benefits debtors and hurts creditors. The debtor pays back dollars that have less purchasing power than the dollars he borrowed if the general price level has risen in the meantime. As we turn to examine the effect of deflation, we immediately note that there is an asymmetry between inflation and deflation, which we shall have occasion to note several times. The term "deflation" is not normally defined as the exact opposite of "inflation." When we say that the economy is undergoing "inflation," we mean that the price level is rising. But when the economy is undergoing deflation, though there will be downward pressure on prices, the prices may be "sticky" or somewhat rigid going downward with the consequence that the decline may occur in income rather than price level. "Deflationary" is synonymous with "contractionary" and the opposite of "expansionary" rather than of "inflationary." Looking now at the effect of deflation, we cannot reverse the earlier proposition and say that deflation benefits creditors while it hurts debtors. It does hurt debtors, for the dollars they repay have greater purchasing power than the dollars they borrowed. If creditors could always collect under such circumstances, it could be said that deflation benefited creditors. But deflation often depresses the economy and the level of production. If it results, as it may, in a depression, the debtors may indeed be ruined, but with their ruin goes the creditor's chance of collecting what is owed him. Deflation may harm creditors also then.

We recognize also that inflation and deflation alter the distribution of wealth because different forms of wealth are affected to different degrees, and people distribute their wealth differently among the various forms. For example, if one person has most of his wealth in real estate and another has most of it in bank accounts and bonds, it is quite conceivable that price inflation will raise the value of the real estate in proportion to the rise in the general price level (if the person made wise investments), while the person whose wealth took the form of dollars and claims upon dollars had no increment in wealth brought about by the inflation, but stood to get back dollars whose value had fallen. Inflation is like a tax upon those forms of wealth that do not appreciate in value in proportion to the rise in the price level or more than that.

Everyone would like a foolproof way of keeping his wealth so that it would not be adversely affected by either inflation or deflation, and possibly would even benefit by whichever came about. In the nature of the case there is no such ideal to be found. The only way that everyone can avoid adverse consequence on his wealth from either inflation or deflation is by preventing either from seizing the economy. To be sure, some people make a living by advising others as to what to do with their savings; and some of the advice may be very good since people can be quite foolish in such matters. But basically what people seeking such advice are doing, at least when it comes to beating inflation or deflation, is trying to outguess the public. Even where this is done successfully for them, the solution for them, in the nature of the case, cannot be generalized for the public at large. No allocation of savings among different assets would safeguard them for all people if all people simultaneously chose the same distribution of their wealth in an effort to save them from the ravages of inflation.

Changes in the price level may have effects on the distribution of current income as well as upon the distribution of accumulated wealth. Those with relatively fixed incomes lose when there is inflation, for the purchasing power of their income falls. They gain from any decline in the price level if the deflation that occasions it does not also destroy their jobs. Some people's incomes manage to outpace inflation while others lag. Some people manage to hold onto jobs without pay cuts in deflation, while the incomes of others fall— some to zero as jobs disappear. The most volatile functional share in national income is the profit share; this varies the most with inflation and deflation.

The level of production may also be affected by inflation and deflation. Deflationary pressure on the economy is apt to involve a decline in production and employment. This is not an unexpected result of the squeeze on profit margins and decline of profits. The effect of inflation on production is not so simply stated. Very rapid inflation has generally had an adverse effect on the level of production. Hyperinflation has been quite disruptive. On the other hand, very low rates of inflation may stimulate the economy if the inflation is due to strong demand for goods and services, for this tends to widen profit margins and increase profits. A rise in the finished-goods price level brought about by an increase in costs of production may have the opposite consequence, however, as profit margins are squeezed and profits decline.

should the price level be changed?

It is apparent that price-level changes affect different groups within the economy differently. Is it possible to say what is in the general interest and what is against the general interest? We started this chapter with the proposition that reasonable price stability was desirable. But price levels have changed from time to time. Depressions have often produced substantial declines in the general price level. Booms, and more notably wars, have generated price inflation, the wars producing some of the inflationary effects in periods after the wars were over. Since World War II popular journals have from time to time printed alarming articles claiming that we now have only a 50-cent dollar or a dollar depreciated to some other extent. Is there some value of the dollar that provides us a suitable norm to which we should return if we can? This question is equivalent to one asking if there is one price level at which the economy will work better than at some other. It is easy to draw erroneous inferences from the discussion of the changing value of the dollar. Once the economy has worked for a while at one price level and has become adjusted to that price level, it works just as well as at any other price level. To say that the dollar today is worth only 50 cents really says no more than that the price level today is twice as high as at some other day. This of itself is neither bad nor good. Compared to a still different day, the dollar would be worth something quite different still. What is the right day to compare with the present? Obviously, there is no such day. The only thing about which judgments of good or bad can be made are the economic effects of moving from one price level to another, in either direction.

Thus, one may judge, if he chooses, the effects of postwar inflation to have been bad because they in effect taxed away much of the lifetime savings of people who had retired before this period and who therefore found their savings had less purchasing power than when they deposited them. It does not follow, of course, that everyone is worse off when prices rise, for some incomes rose as much or more than prices. Indeed, the per-capita real income of the nation rose in the period of the postwar inflation.

The real question is whether it would be good to try to reverse a change in the value of money. If the value of money falls, as it did during the postwar period, should we try to restore it to its previous level? That is to say, should we try to reduce the price level to its previous level? If so, how far back should we go; how low a price level should we seek? It is immediately apparent that there is no merit in trying to make the value of the dollar rise as high as possible. It is per-capita real income that we want to make as high as possible for the nation—not the value of the dollar. Since raising the value of the dollar means lowering the price level, we must consider all the ramifications before embarking upon a policy of that sort. The economic effects of such an effort will not be simply to put everything back where it was before, undoing the adverse effects that inflation may have had upon some. Deflation, to get prices down to, say, prewar levels, would certainly bring on a depression of sizeable proportions as profit margins were squeezed and profits fell. The unemployed would increase without restoring the losses that inflation had inflicted upon quite different people. In short, the attempt to reverse inflation does not remedy its evil effects; instead it adds a new set of evil effects of its own. Bewailing the 50-cent dollar should not be taken as warranting an attempt to return to the price level of the year used for the comparison. A second wrong will not make the first one right.

Is the same sort of thing to be said about reversing a decline in the price level? Let us look at the situation in 1933. Prices had fallen sharply from the 1929 levels, and the country was in a serious depression. President Roosevelt did many different things to try to raise the price level again. Was his objective a mistaken one? Here the asymmetry between inflation and deflation arises again. In a private enterprise economy the prospects of a revival of production in the 1930's was not good until profit margins could be restored and profits increased. This was the logic of the move to "reflate" the price level, or get it back nearer to previous levels. The deflation had also made the burden of private debt excessively heavy, and a reasonably quick return to the 1929 price level would have relieved this excessive burden. To be sure, it makes a difference how the price level was raised. Raising wage rates directly, whatever merit it may have had from other points of view, was not the sort of price-inflating effort that would have the effects sought on production. Nor would it do simply to widen profit margins by marking up prices, for that did not represent any improvement in the market and would not of itself ensure an increase in total profits. What was needed was enough of an increase in demand to increase sales enough to produce a rise in competitive prices.

The way to judge, then, whether to try to reverse a change in the price level is in terms of the most likely economic effects of the proposed effort. Resisting sharp changes in the price level is widely conceded to be desirable. But after changes have, nonetheless, taken place, a better case can be made for reversing short-run declines in the price level (via increased demand), if the declines have been associated with recession, than can be made for trying to get prices back down to earlier levels after an inflation.

The room for different judgments about slow long-run changes in the price level is wider. If the price level declines very slowly over a long period of years, say at a rate representing the rate of growth in labor productivity per hour, no adverse effects on production would be expected. And if in these circumstances full employment can be maintained without the stimulus of rising prices, there would be little objection. Some people, however, will judge the general interest to be better served by either a steady price level or by one that sees the price level rise very slowly over the years. The case for a slowly rising price level is, of course, the view that this added stimulus to business assures a fuller level of employment. Others will point out that even a slow rate of inflation over a man's earning years can take quite a bite out of the purchasing power of his savings. The appropriate degree of long-run stability is thus arguable.

questions

1. *What is "the index number problem" and what can be done about it?*
2. *Why do we not develop a more scientific price index and use it for all purposes?*
3. *Explain the usages of the terms "inflation" and "deflation" in which they are not exact opposites.*
4. *What generalizations do you think you could support with respect to the economic effects of price-level changes?*
5. *Formulate a price-level policy that you think would be optimal and defend it.*

the circular flow of

money and real

income

THE CHANGES IN THE VALUE OF MONEY AND THEIR economic effects lead naturally to the inquiry as to what causes these changes. That branch of our subject dealing with this inquiry is called monetary theory. Several theories of money have evolved setting forth different determinants of the value of money and also different explanations of the relationship of money to and effects upon other important economic variables such as interest rates and the level of production or real income. These relationships are of as much interest and of as much or more economic significance than the changes in the value of money. In reality, it is not possible to give a satisfactory explanation of the value of money except as part of a more general explanation of the role of money.

When one explores the factors that lie behind any economic phenomenon, such as a change in the value of money, one embarks upon what can be literally an endless quest. The economy is very complex, and each of its parts is tied to some other parts. So everything in the economy is related, at least indirectly, to everything else. Because all parts of the economy are tied together, each part can affect the rest. And a complete account of everything that affects the phenomenon in question could indeed never be given. Any attempt at an exhaustive account would be exhausting. To be useful, a theory must abstract from the multitudinous factors that have some connection with the outcome being explained, and must concentrate attention on a relatively small number of explanatory factors. This accounts in substantial measure for the admitted unrealism of theory; it is a deliberate oversimplification. It is, of course, dangerous to oversimplify thus, even though it is necessary. A good theory, as distinct from a poor one, is one that selects those causal factors that are the most important, and neglects those that are less important. And there is the further problem of managing to identify correctly the relationship that exists between these important factors and the thing being explained. One can get in much trouble by relying on a theory that selects the wrong factors as basic, or that makes serious errors in depicting the way the basic factors are related to the variable being explained. The ultimate in simplification is of course to reduce the explanation to one involving a single causal factor. But even if this does correctly identify the most important single causal relationship, such a theory may not yield a sufficiently good approximation to the reality it seeks to explain. How many factors need to be taken into account varies both with the portion of reality being explained and with the degree of approximation required in applications to be made of the theory.

circular-flow diagram

It will be helpful for our discussion of monetary theory to provide at the outset a simplified picture of the role of money in the economic system that can serve as a framework for subsequent discussion. Such a picture, usually referred to as a circular-flow diagram, is a useful tool in visualizing the main features of the economy as a whole. The particular manner in which it is drawn may vary, depending upon the interpretation of the person presenting it. (After the student understands Figure 10.1, he may wish to draw it in his own way.)

In Figure 10.1 the economic system is divided into two types of economic units—firms, the units in which production is organized,

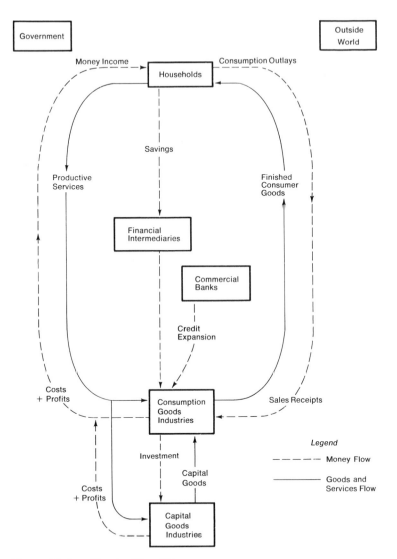

Figure 10.1. Circular-Flow Diagram

and households, the consuming units. Households are also the source of productive services, and firms are the users of such services. So the diagram shows a flow of the services of land, labor, and capital (all owned ultimately by households) to business firms. The firms transform these productive services into finished goods and services that are then sold to households. This inner stream may be called the "real-income" stream, to distinguish it from the "money-income" stream, which is shown on the diagram flowing in the opposite direction. Business firms pay out wages, rent, interest, and profits to the households for the productive services that they have used. Households receive this income and spend much of it on the goods and services that they purchase. This stream of outlays by households constitutes the sales receipts of the business firms selling the goods and services, and it is, in turn, the source of funds from which they pay their costs of production and profits. But some of the income received by households "leaks out" of the circular flow in the form of savings. If these savings were a permanent leakage from the income stream, the size of that stream would, of course, shrink as a result. But much or all of the savings may be injected back into the income stream in the manner shown on the diagram. At various times business firms have need of additional funds to invest in new equipment to improve their productive process or to expand their productive capacity. We have represented the capital goods industries that make the necessary capital goods as a separate block of firms in the diagram. These firms hire productive services from households also so that there is a portion of the flow of such services diverted to them. These services are transformed into capital goods and sold to the other firms. The other firms borrow from the savings stream to cover the cost of the capital goods, and the money paid for the capital goods is used in turn by the capital goods industries to pay for their productive services. Thus the savings are injected back into the income stream. If all savings are returned in this manner, the size of the income stream is unchanged.

leakages and injections

The above discussion leads to the first set of simple generalizations that flow from a consideration of the diagram. If investment is equal to saving, income is constant. This is, in effect, an equilibrium condition, namely that investment equals saving. If saving exceeds investment, income declines. And if investment can somehow be brought to exceed saving, the income stream would be increased. This brings us to a consideration of how the financial institutions are represented on the diagram and what their role is. In the circular-flow diagram commercial banks and other financial institutions have been separated. Commercial banks are related to the income stream in two distinct and unique ways. They provide the mechanism through which most of the money payments represented by the money-flow stream are made, namely the checking facilities. Since demand deposits are the major portion of the money supply, most of what is flowing in the money stream takes the form of checks on such deposits. The changes in the money supply are brought about by the commercial banks, and the money supply is increased when the banks expand credit. This is represented on the diagram by a dotted line from the banks to business firms when they are borrowing increasing amounts from the banks. Such an expansion of bank loans to business can make possible the excess of investment over saving, which was mentioned above. The function of the other financial institutions is to serve as middlemen between savers and those who want to borrow savings. This has been discussed in greater detail in Chapter Eight and need not be repeated here.

The center portion of the diagram represents only the private sector of the domestic economy. To present a more complete picture of the economy it would be necessary to show the relationships existing between the economic units in the center diagram to government on the one hand and to the outside world economy on the other. To draw these connections would clutter up the diagram so that it would be very difficult to read, but the student should realize that additional goods and services flows and money flows do tie all these units together.

The introduction of government and the outside world into the diagram makes it incumbent upon us to recognize that there are other leakages from the income stream besides saving, and leads us to look for other offsets to those leakages. When government (federal, state, or local) collects taxes, this draws funds out of the income stream. Taxes, therefore, are a leakage just like saving. Similarly, when we spend some of our income on imports instead of on domestic goods, that money leaks out of the domestic income stream. But the corresponding injections are not hard to find. When government, at any level, spends money, it injects funds back into the income stream. When we export goods to the outside world economy, this adds to the domestic income stream. It should at once be apparent that what stabilizes income or increases or reduces it is not simply the balance between saving and investment, but that between total leakages and total injections. The equilibrium condition is that total injections equal total leakages from the income stream in any period. An excess of leakages over injections reduces income, and an excess of injections over leakages increases income. The balance between each pair of leakages and injections is not important to the level of income if an imbalance in one pair is exactly offset by an opposite imbalance on the part of one or both of the other pairs together. This is the simple insight that led to the controversial policy of offsetting the depressing effect when investment falls short of saving by having the government spend more than it collects in taxes. A government deficit can make up for deficient investment, or if one wishes to express the discrepancy that way, for surplus saving.

These simple statements of the relationship between saving and investment, leakages and injections, will serve our purpose well. In the diagram all saving has been treated as though it was made by households and all loans are made to business firms. Neither is literally true. The diagram was so drawn to keep it as simple as possible without omitting what was essential for our purpose. The reader should keep in mind that business firms frequently save directly and later use the savings to help finance their own investment, instead of turning over all profits to their ultimate household owners and then trying to borrow to obtain investible funds again. Similarly, borrowing is done by other than business firms, as indicated in the chapter on financial intermediaries. The diagram treats households as net lenders in the aggregate, and that is quite correct. There is no need to represent the gross saving flow from households as this would not alter materially the monetary theory analysis. Government borrowing and foreign capital flows need to be considered for some purposes.

Not all leakages and injections are the result of decisions by the same people; different people are involved in different decisions leading to leakages or injections as the case may be. The motivations behind these decisions is not the same either. The household deciding how much to save out of current income is considering different factors from those weighed by the executive of a business firm deciding how much to invest in new capital equipment in the coming year. It would thus appear to be quite accidental if at any one time the amount people decided to save equaled the amount people decided to invest in real capital goods. Similarly, with respect to other leakages and injections, import and export decisions are not necessarily equal at any given time, and governmental units in the aggregate do not always try to cover all outlays with taxes. Sometimes they deliberately run a deficit or surplus, as well as doing so unexpectedly at times. When decisions that lead to leakages and injections to the income stream do not match, as they do not automatically, the consequences we have described follow until an equilibrium is established or until the trend is altered by new discrepancies impinging on the situation.

price, interest, and income

The price level, or value of money, does not appear anywhere in the diagram. It might be visualized as a sort of gauge attached to the money-income and real-income streams and measuring the changes in the relative rates of flow of the two streams. A rise in the money flow relative to the flow of goods and services would be reflected in a rise on the price-level gauge—conversely, by a fall.

The general level of interest rates, a matter in which we are also interested, might be thought of as a sort of average of the prices of the loans that are represented by the flow of savings to financial intermediaries and the loans from them to the borrowers.

Our discussion has given us a general picture of the circular flow and an understanding of how the principal sectors of the economy and the money- and real-income flows are represented there. The remainder of this chapter will be devoted to an elementary inquiry as to how various factors may be important in determining the value of money, the cost of a loan, the level of real income, and some interrelations among these. This exposition will be a simple one and thus will not show all possible relationships among the variables considered, nor will it probe deeply behind their behavior.[1]

money equation

Our inquiry begins with the money supply. If the money supply is increased, it will increase the size of the money-income stream,

[1] These matters are considered further in the author's supplementary volume in this set: Harlan M. Smith, *Elementary Monetary Theory* (New York: Random House, to be published in 1968).

other things being assumed unchanged. The opposite result would, of course, follow from a decrease in the money supply. Though nothing could be simpler, this is not at all unimportant.

When we refer to the money supply we refer to a stock of a particular type of asset that serves as the medium of exchange and that people find it convenient to have a stock of. Money income, on the other hand, refers not to a stock of anything, but to a flow over time. The relation between the money stock in a period and the income flow in a period is found in the rate of use—in other words, the number of times the money turns over in making income payments in the period. If we call this the income velocity of money (V), and represent the money stock by M and money income by Y, we have the following simple relationship: $MV = Y$. Money income would then change in proportion to a change in the money supply, other things remaining the same—more specifically, if the velocity of money remained unchanged. If there were a change in the rate at which the money flowed around the economy, the amount of the change in income could not be stated so simply.

The speed with which money flows through the economy, the number of times it turns over as income during any given period, is affected by many factors. The degree of development of the payments mechanism is itself one of those factors, and has led historically to a change in the amount of money needed to "finance" any given level of income, that is, to make possible any given level of income payments per period. Psychological factors also play a part, however, in determining the velocity of the circulation of money. For example, if people begin "hoarding" more money, the average velocity of circulation of money will fall. Or if people expect that the price level may soon rise, they may try to buy before the prices rise some things that they know they will want later, and this will increase the rate at which money circulates in the economy. We can refer to these last two examples as cases of increased and of reduced demand for money. In the first case people try to hold on to larger stocks of money than usual. In the second case they are willing to spend more quickly, at the possible cost of a reduction in the size of their cash balances (cash in this context meaning the same as money, and not referring just to currency).

There are broadly speaking three motives for holding money— (1) the transactions demand, (2) the precautionary motive, and (3) the speculative motive. As the medium of exchange function of money implies, we hold money to be ready to make the payments involved in planned transactions. There is, usually, no close coincidence between the magnitudes of our money receipts day by day and the magnitudes of our expected expenditures day by day. So we hold receipts ready for the expenditures. We call this the transactions demand for money. The higher our income, the higher the expected expenditure level, and so the more money we tend to hold for the purpose. In addition, we may hold money to be prepared to meet unexpected expenditures. Both the magnitude of these and the ability to hold money for these tends to increase with our income. We refer to this as the precautionary motive for holding money. There is of course the possibility of holding other assets, especially income-earning assets, in place of money for these purposes, and then selling them for money just when we need to make a money payment. The cost, trouble, and risk of loss entailed in trying to do so underlie our liquidity preference, that is, our preference for holding some amount of money. At the same time, the interest we could earn by holding a money substitute can be viewed as the cost of remaining liquid. And, other things being equal, the higher that cost, that is, the higher the interest rates, the more people tend to be willing to part with liquidity, to cut down on the size of their cash balances, and to lend, investing in some security. Changes in security yields, however, introduce another motive for varying the amount of money people desire to hold. If they expect yields to rise (that is, security prices to fall), they may do better to hold money for later investment. Thus they may avoid a capital loss that would be incurred if they had to resell to get back money after the security prices fell, and by waiting they buy at more favorable prices and hence earn a higher rate of return on their investment. This reasoning is referred to as the speculative motive for holding money. Consideration of these reasons for holding money opens up numerous possibilities for variation in the demand for money.

It is now possible to conclude that there may be circumstances in which changes in the demand for money or in the velocity of circulation of money (whichever term we use being a matter of indifference) may have effects upon money income. A decline in the demand for money (that is, a willingness to try to get by with smaller balances in our pocket and checking account), which is an increase in the velocity of money, tends, other things being equal, to increase money income. The opposite change in V would of course have the opposite effect on Y.

Next we encounter the most troublesome question for monetary theory. When something changes the money-income stream, what portion of the effect will be reflected in the price level or value of money and what portion in the size of the real-income stream? To aid in answering this question, we may rewrite our income equation in a form that enables us to distinguish between changes in price level P and changes in output X: $MV = PX$. Output multiplied by its average price gives the value of output; this is the same as the money income of the nation. Changes in X stand for changes in the size of the real-income stream in our circular-flow diagram as Y stood for the size of the money-income stream.

If for any reason the real-income stream does not change, a change in money income will be a proportionate change in the price level. Since there are circumstances in which real income cannot change very much, if at all, this can have practical importance. For example, when the economy is already at full employment, aggregate output cannot be increased in the very short run, and even over a longer period of time it may be able to be increased only very slowly. In these circumstances price inflation can be expected if the money supply is increased substantially. The asymmetry between expansion and contraction, or between inflation and deflation as it is usually put, is also seen here. There is no reason why real income must remain constant if money income falls. What the actual outcome depends upon is a more complex story that will not be explored here.

In our circular-flow diagram we saw that money income would change unless a certain equilibrium condition was met, namely, that the injections into the income stream exactly offset the leakages from the stream. From the previous discussion it is apparent that it does not matter whether the income changes involve changes in the stock of money or in its rate of turnover. It would be of some interest to know why changes occur, however. There are a number of distinct possibilities wherever the stream changes. The factors studied earlier as determinants of the money supply may have changed. For example, the monetary authorities may have altered the money supply directly through open-market operations. Or the "psychology" of the public, or of important segments of it, may have altered so far as their desire for liquidity is concerned (this is considered a change in the total demand for money or in total liquidity preference). At this point it is advisable to examine directly the leakages from or the injections into the income stream. We need to look at the motives for spending on capital goods or on consumer goods and services and at the motives for not spending, as well as into changes, if any, in taxes and government spending.

An analysis of the historical record of economic fluctuations does seem to shed some light upon which of the several possibilities has been of most importance. It tells us that the most important single driving force in changing peacetime income levels has been the change in the rate of private business investment. To make it clear that this refers to a component of the real-income stream, rather than, simply, to money or financial investment, we can state that the change in the rate of production of capital goods is the most important in generating income changes.

investment multiplier

The explanation of these changes in real investment is not simple and will not be detailed here, but we can explore some of the consequences of such changes. When real investment changes, this produces a discrepancy between total leakages and injections, assuming an equilibrium situation initially. To examine the manner in which income may continue to change until the equilibrium condition is met again, we shall consider a case in which real investment increases, initiating a rise in income. This income rise is not blocked on the real-income side by full employment. In other words, we are considering a situation of substantial unemployment, and so real income can be increased in the short run. What, if anything, will restore equilibrium if investment continues at the new higher rate period after period? What will happen in the absence of a deliberate effort by government to offset the change? Such an effort would be very unlikely in our example, and even more unwise if people desire full employment. Let us also abstract from conceivable changes in the foreign trade component of income because, for our economy, this is not likely to be the source of most of the adjustment. This leaves saving as the adjusting factor. But what will cause saving to rise to match the new higher rate of real investment? Clearly the main factor causing changes in the rate of saving in the economy is a change in the level of national income. However, this must be a change in the level of real income, for people will generally not change the fraction of their income that they save if the price level rises as much as their money income. They do save a higher fraction of income when their real income rises. Thus equilibrium can be restored, with saving rising to match investment, if real income rises sufficiently. We must ask what are the components of real income. Real income, or total output, consists of total production of consumer goods and services, capital (or investment) goods, and government goods and services. This can be expressed in short-hand form by writing

$$X = C + I + G$$

X stands for real income and the other symbols for the obvious components just mentioned. Now we know that when people's incomes rise, they increase not only their saving but also their consumption. Normally this results in a rise in production, replacing the inventory disinvestment that would otherwise take place. Thus real income will rise, in the case we are considering, both because the rate of production of capital goods has increased and because this rise in income for someone generates a further increase in real income as a result of consumer spending. Nor is this the end, for the rise in production of consumer goods, in turn, raises income. This, in turn, raises consumption again. The rise in income is not without a limit. The limit is due to the fact that saving does rise, too, as income rises. The new equilibrium will be reached when saving is leaking out of the income stream at the same rate that investment is injecting funds into the stream. The relationship between the increase in the equilibrium level of real income and the initial increase in the rate of investment is called the multiplier (k).

$$k = \frac{\triangle X}{\triangle I}$$

Changes in the rate of production of capital goods (real investment) then produce changes in the level of real income that can be estimated.

Let us suppose, for a very simple example, that as income rises we save one-third of the increase and spend the other two-thirds and that other leakages from the income stream do not increase. (It would be just as well to assume that they increased too, so that the sum of the added leakages was one-third of the added income, leaving consumption two-thirds of it.) Under these circumstances income of the nation would continue to rise, as a result of a $100 million per period rise in the rate of real investment, until income was high enough to raise saving (or leakages) by $100 million per period. Obviously if one-third of any increase in income goes into savings (or leakages), income will have to increase by $300 million per period before leakages and injections will again be equal and an equilibrium income level reached. The multiplier magnitude in this instance is three. And, as is now apparent, its size is in this case the reciprocal of the marginal propensity to save $\triangle S/\triangle Y$ (that is, the fraction of additional income that is saved or not spent on consumption).

Although the example has been oversimplified, this analysis is sufficient to show the general sort of relationship involved.

output and price level again

It is not clear from anything said about the multiplier, however, whether the change in the rate of production of capital goods will also result in a change in the price level or not. We posited a case in which the new rate of production of capital goods remained constant, and we shall consider that case a little further. We supposed also that there was enough unemployment to start with so that the full multiplier effect on real income could be achieved. But there are various types of factors that may cause the price level to rise as the economy pushes closer to full employment. For one thing, the closer the economy moves to full employment, the more the principle of diminishing returns may become applicable. Not every sector of the economy is likely to have the same amount of idle resources to put to work; consequently, "bottlenecks" develop in some lines earlier than in others. Labor unions may also push up wage rates before full employment is reached, or some business firms may try to increase their profit margins, and either or both of these things may begin to raise certain components of the price index. The closer to full employment production goes, the more these price-raising forces may come into play.

Had our example been a decrease in the rate of real investment, we would have had to analyze the relative strength of factors leading business firms to maintain their prices and of factors leading them to reduce prices. The empirical evidence shows that in recent years the price level has become quite resistant to deflationary forces, though it is not so inflexible when it comes to expansionary forces operating on the economy. This suggests that the economy may have an inflationary bias. This may indeed be the case, but the record since 1958 suggests that it would be a mistake to take alarm, for the extent of the inflationary bias in this period, apart from war escalation, is not as great as might be concluded from the above comments. The various forces operating on the price level seem to vary from time to time so that the task of prediction is very difficult indeed, and in the nature of the case it becomes more of a matter of informed guesswork than a science.

The change in real investment discussed was a change originating in the real-income stream for reasons that we did not explore. Can we say anything about the likelihood of the real-income stream being affected by changes originating in the money-income stream? Fortunately, something can be said, although it is not as strong as one might wish. In an economy in which the profit motive plays an important role in production decisions, we can expect production to rise in response to a rise in business sales and vice versa. However, sales rise and fall as the money-income stream rises and falls unless prices have simultaneously changed proportionately. This qualification is not a very serious one, for in most situations the price level is apt to change in response to changes in the income streams and to change proportionately to the money-income stream only when that increases at full employment. For other cases, then, a change in the money-income stream leads normally to a change in spending, which changes business sales, and thus may motivate a change in production or real income.

interest rate

As the rate of interest is the price of a loan, it is not surprising that we may start a brief treatment of its determination by reference to the forces of demand and supply. The circular-flow diagram showed the supply of loanable funds coming chiefly from savings, but supplemented by new money creation by commercial banks. The diagram could not show how the quantity of funds available for loans varied with the rate of interest itself or with the level of income, and the demand for loanable funds was reflected only in the fact that firms borrowed. The demand for loanable funds might be thought of as reflected in the supply of securities of all types offered to potential lenders, for some sort of security must be given in order to obtain the funds desired. Obviously, the quantity of loanable funds sought will not be independent of their price. We should expect that like most demand curves this one too would show a greater quantity demanded at lower prices than at high prices. And we should expect that various factors would from time to time shift the whole demand curve. To speak of *the* rate of interest as determined by the demand and supply of loanable funds is an oversimplification.

There are many different types of loans. Some funds are available for some types of loans and not for others. Demand and supply of each type of loan may then be said to determine the whole complex of interest rates covering such loans. When we speak of a change in *the* rate of interest, we may have reference to a change in the general level of interest rates. Or we may be abstracting from various institutional factors in loanable funds markets, from market imperfections, and from the risk element involved in loan operations to postulate a "pure rate of interest." In any more extended analysis of interest determination it is necessary to go behind demand and supply and uncover various monetary and nonmonetary factors and to distinguish their operation in the short and long run. Other theories of interest thus find their place in a more complete analysis. The demand and supply of loanable funds will in any case be equal in conditions of full equilibrium.

significance of the level of interest rates

Our final concern in this chapter will be to discuss briefly the importance of the level of interest rates (or "the" interest rate, for short) on certain asset values and thence on rates of real investment (the production of capital goods). We have already noted the importance of changes in the latter for changes in real income and the general price level (or value of money).

What rate of interest people are willing to pay to borrow money depends upon the advantage they expect to receive from the use to which they put the money—whether it be obtaining certain satisfactions sooner than otherwise or increasing their income through the employment of additional productive capital equipment. The demand for loanable funds, and hence their cost, is changed significantly by changes in the aggregate rate of investment in capital goods. But for the individual investor in such goods, the interest rate is a factor that he cannot change and that he must take into account in making investment decisions.

If a firm is to invest in productive capital equipment, the return on the investment would have to be better than that obtainable simply by buying a security. The interest rate on the loan alternative thus sets a lower limit to the prospective rate of return that the capital goods must yield if indeed it is going to pay to produce the latter. If 5 percent a year could be earned by lending money (that is, earned on some security purchase), the capital good whose expected rate of return is lower will not be produced. Changes in interest rates thus can alter the rate of production of real capital goods. A rise in the interest rate tends to cut out marginal investments that would otherwise have been profitable, and a fall in interest to open up some added opportunities at the margin.

The problem is complicated by the fact that productive capital goods typically cannot be expected to yield the same net returns each year of their life. On the contrary, their costs of operation and gross returns from use are both likely to vary from year to year, and the net return will reach zero in some year. It is then not so easy to determine the rate of return to be compared to the relevant rate of interest. To comprehend the solution, it is advisable to find out first how to discount a stream of varying returns to get its present value. Let us suppose that the interest rate is 5 percent. Lending $1000 now would return $50 interest a year hence, plus return of the principal. Therefore, to get $1050 a year hence, one must invest $1000 now. To get one dollar a year from now one would have to invest $1000/1050, which is $1/1.05 or $.952. In the more general case, with i standing for the rate of interest, the amount invested now to get a dollar a year later is $1/(1 + i)$. Suppose next that one invested $1000 now and a year hence reinvested the $1000 plus the $50 interest for a second year, also at 5 percent. One would then obtain at the end of the second year $1102.50. This is the sum of $1000 plus interest on it at 5 percent for two years, or 2 times 5 percent times $1000, plus 5 percent earned on reinvestment of the $50 interest (which is then $1000 times 5 percent times 5 percent again). This can be written more simply as

$$\$1000 + 2 \times .05 \times \$1000 + \$1000 \times (.05)^2$$

or for the general case for each dollar invested $\$1(1 + i)^2$. Or for each dollar received two years hence, one needs to lend or invest currently $\$1/(1 + i)^2$. If the number of dollars receivable varies from year to year, the amount to be invested now to yield the variable future income stream is given by the following formula:

$$P = \frac{A_1}{1 + i} + \frac{A_2}{(1 + i)^2} + \frac{A_3}{(1 + i)^3} + \cdots + \frac{A_n}{(1 + i)^n}$$

In this formula the A's are the expected net returns at the end of each year hence (from 1 to n), and i is the rate of interest at which we "discount" the future returns. Each quotient is the amount to be invested now for the number of years indicated to get the relevant dollars at the end of that time. The P, or sum of these amounts, is called the "present value" of the future income stream, or the present value of the asset that will yield that income stream. If a productive capital good yielded a variable future income stream, one can apply the above formula to find out how much one would have to lend now in the indicated way to get the same future returns. If one can buy the capital good for a lesser sum, then one would expect to earn more than the current rate of interest on it. If it costs more than that sum, it would clearly be a poor investment and would likely not be bought. An alternative way of approaching the same decision problem would be to find what rate of discount would make the present value of the future income stream equal to the cost of the productive capital good that would generate that income stream. If such discount rate (called the marginal efficiency of capital) exceeds the current rate of interest, this would be an indication that one expects the capital good to yield a higher rate of return than a loan at the current interest rate. The solution of the problem can be viewed from either angle.

From the above it should be evident that the rate of investment in real capital goods will vary with changes in interest rates or in the expected net dollar returns on the capital goods. Policies that affect interest rates may thus affect the rate of real investment. The magnitude of such an effect may differ from time to time, and it certainly differs with the length of time into the future over which returns must be expected by the investor if his investment is to pay. Small changes in interest rates will have much greater effect on long-term investments, such as housing, than on short-term investments, such as those in inventories. If we look at changes in total investment in capital goods over the business cycle, it is apparent that changes in expected dollar returns on such investments and changes in the confidence people have in such expectations are more influential than are interest rate changes generally in altering real investment.

questions

1. *What minimum set of factors should be taken into account in any monetary theory that hopes to give a satisfactory explanation of changes in the value of money?*

2. *In considering the decisions that lead to leakages from and injections into the income stream, do you see adequate ground for expecting that they would generally produce an equilibrium level of income without change?*

3. *Under what circumstances could changes in the money supply, up or down, be expected to change the price level proportionately?*

4. *What are the major possible sources of changes in the stream of money expenditures?*

5. *Explain the multiplier effect and its relation to price-level changes.*

6. *Discuss reasons why the demand for money might change.*

7. *How are interest rates, values of earning assets, and rates of real investment related to one another.*

the domestic role
of gold

IN PRIMITIVE MONETARY SYSTEMS MONEY WAS
some commodity that had value as a commodity before it came to
be used as money. In a modern monetary system, such as our own,
the money may retain some tie to a commodity base. What is the
significance of that tie? Our coins are made of metals with value as
commodities, but they are only "token coins" not "full-bodied," that
is, the metal in the coin is not worth as much as the coin is as a
medium of exchange. This is quite deliberate; otherwise there is a
danger that the market value of the metal might rise a little and give
people an incentive to melt down the coins and sell the metal for
more than the face value of the coin. Indeed the recent rise in the
value of silver has led to modifications in our coins to reduce the use
of silver and help forestall just such a problem. Our paper money
in the past has merely represented silver or gold. It has been exchangeable for coins but circulates in their place because of the
greater convenience of the paper bills by comparison with the quan-

tity of coins they represent. Today bank deposits, transferred by check and created by the extension of bank credit, are the main forms of money. Yet, until quite recently the whole money supply rested ultimately, like an inverted pyramid, upon gold. Bank deposits were backed by reserves held at the Federal Reserve, and the Federal Reserve, in turn, was required to hold gold certificate reserves behind its note and deposit liabilities. Recently the deposits at the Federal Reserve have been exempted from this requirement in order to free more of the nation's gold stock for international payments. For some time the Congress seemed reluctant to take such a step, despite the international pressure on the dollar. The tie to gold has been the commodity backing that some people have regarded as the backbone of our monetary system, and they feared that any change in this would be unwise. Let us examine this in more detail.

why a commodity backing for money?

People benefit from having money with reasonably stable purchasing power—in other words from "sound money." It was discovered long ago that if money is issued to excess, relative to the amount of goods and services to be purchased with it, the value of the monetary unit will decline. Thus the problem of sound money is essentially the problem of placing appropriate limitations on the volume of money issued. A gold reserve, with minimum reserve ratios fixed by law, has been one device for limiting the money supply. At times this has been reinforced by the convertibility of other money into gold or gold money. When such convertibility is possible, those issuing other money take on added risks if they allow their issue of money to get too far out of line with the likely demand for redemption of the money in gold. Quite apart from the problem of excess money issue, originally the acceptability by the public of the issue of a new money sometimes depended entirely upon their faith in the convertibility of the money. They had to believe it was "as good as gold" and could indeed be exchanged anytime for gold; otherwise they would not accept it.

This takes us back to the question of why gold was thought to be so good, indeed so superior, to serve as money. The answer, of course, is that gold was thought to have a stable value, that is, a stable purchasing power over goods and services in general. The way to have sound money, then, was thought to be to tie the money firmly to gold. In the days when there were many private issuers of money (the private banks), this would protect the public against the issuers' greed, which otherwise would lead them to overissue money. But if unregulated money issue were the initial problem to be overcome, "managed money," which is government control of the issuance of money, also came in for some brickbats. Some argued that managed money and unsound money were virtually synonymous in practice. When government is free to issue money itself, it was charged, the door is open to the politicians. And since bread and circuses are the old route to political success, they can be trusted to abuse the money-creating powers for their own political benefit. In short, governments must be restrained in the exercise of money-creating powers, just as the private bankers must be restrained, else the public suffers from unsound money.

In the gold standard it was thought that a monetary institution had been found that would restrain monetary issue and give the public a solid basis for confidence in the money. There are those even today who say that any money that is not tied to and exchangeable for gold is a fraud, is dishonest money. The only honest and stable money is said to be gold money. Is all this sound economics, or are these people still worshipping a golden calf?

Gold still plays an important role in the international economy, but its domestic role has shrunk progressively in modern monetary systems. Is this a big and potentially dangerous mistake, or is it a clear gain? What experiences support one view or the other? What lay behind the charge of the "silver-tongued" orator, William Jennings Bryan, that the nation was being crucified upon a cross of gold? Is the issuance of "fiat" money (money issued by government without gold or other commodity backing), likely to lead to run-a-way inflation or hyperinflation? The answers to questions such as these will become clearer as we proceed.

If it is the lack of restraint in managing money on the part of the politicians or government officials that worries us most today, then a gold standard will indeed prevent their depreciating the money, but only if two conditions hold. First, they must be prevented from altering the relationship between money and gold. Second, the value of the gold must be determined by its nonmonetary uses. If not, government monetary operations could still alter or manipulate the value of the money. Whether a domestic gold standard can thus insulate the value of money and protect it against government mismanagement needs to be explored. In the preceding chapters we have discussed the value of money, but there is one approach to its explanation that we did not examine—the commodity theory of money.

gold and the domestic value of the dollar

Like the quantity theory, the commodity theory is not reducible to a single proposition or line of argument. It is, if anything, even older than the quantity theory approach. Over the years proponents of this theory have differed somewhat in exactly what they were asserting. Indeed, one of the main difficulties for the student analyzing the reasoning involved in the commodity theory is that adherents to this approach often regarded their conclusions as so obvious that they saw no need to develop a complete and systematic exposition of the reasoning upon which they rested. Hence, our treatment of the theory must piece together various strands to see how strong a position can be constructed by this approach.

The general argument is that the value of money is determined by the value of the commodity (such as gold) that it represents. This is obviously the sort of theory used to explain a primitive commodity money system. If applied to the United States today, it would say that the value of the dollar is determined by the value of the gold represented by the dollar. This is at present one-thirty-fifth of an ounce of gold, for the Treasury buys gold by giving $35 in exchange for one ounce of gold. When the deficit in our balance of payments leads to partial payment to foreign countries in gold, they receive one ounce of gold for $35 that we owe them.

The value of money would then change, if the exchange ratio between gold and the monetary unit remained fixed, only with changes in the value of gold (that is, its purchasing power over goods and services). It was held that this value remained relatively stable. But what was supposed to determine the value of gold? The answer: the value of gold is determined like the value of any other commodity— according to economic laws. As our understanding of economic laws has changed over time, so have the ideas as to just how the value of gold is determined. At one time it was thought that the values of commodities were determined simply by their real costs of production. That is, for example, if the amounts of land, labor, and capital required to produce one commodity were twice as great as those required to produce a second commodity, the former would have twice the value (cost twice as much) as the second. However, market prices of commodities can be determined by cost alone only if produced under conditions of constant cost. And any extractive industry, such as gold mining, operates under conditions of increasing cost at any given time. Value in a market must, therefore, take into account not only the costs of production, which operate on the supply side, but also the factors that operate on the demand side. Demand and supply may then be said to determine the value of commodities including gold.

The supply of gold does not change very rapidly. Annual production adds only slowly to the world's gold stock, and the nonmonetary demand for gold grows slowly too, it is alleged. With the demand and supply of gold stable, any changes in the general purchasing power of gold must originate not on the side of gold but on the side of other goods. The price of goods in terms of gold will change only as a result of a general change in the demand for goods or in the supply curves for goods in general. To ensure the economy, then, against government influence on the value of money or other disturbances originating on the side of money, it should suffice to fix the exchange ratio between the monetary unit and gold. But if this is to suffice, it must be correct that the value of the gold is not itself in any way determined or influenced by its use as the monetary metal. It must be the supply and nonmonetary demand for gold that must be the determinants of its value in relation to demand and supply of other goods in general.

Can we accept the view that the monetary use of gold merely enables governments to rest their monetary unit upon a "rock of Gibraltar" without influencing it? Do they merely tie their money to something with a value so stable that it is independent of this subsequent tie? Let us examine the monetary demand for gold when governments decide to employ a domestic gold standard. What does a government do when it goes on such a standard? It undertakes to buy at a fixed price whatever gold is offered to it or to sell at that price any gold that others wish to buy. (To be sure, in practice the buying and selling price are not quite identical, the small spread being a small charge levied for the transaction. We can ignore this as of no great importance for the question at hand.) The buying price sets a floor below which the market price of gold can then not fall, but at the same time it cannnot rise above the selling price either as long as the government has gold to sell and is willing to continue selling it at that price. It appears that the monetary demand for gold is indefinitely large at a certain fixed price and that changes in the nonmonetary demand can be simply offset by selling more gold to or buying more gold from the monetary authorities. This is hardly a situation where nonmonetary demand and supply determine value and money merely rests on this stable and independent value. A variable, but sometimes large, part of the annual gold production is devoted to monetary rather than nonmonetary uses. Annual production is only about 3 percent of the monetary gold stocks. (See Table 11.1) In the unusual situation where hoarding and nonmonetary uses exceed production, as in 1965–1966, the supply of gold for such uses is augmented by drawing down monetary gold stocks.

Does anyone really suppose that if governments cease to use gold as a monetary metal today its value would be unchanged? Let them propose such a change and see what gold-mining interests say If the United States alone were today to cease buying gold for monetary use, its market value would fall. But the fact that we have kept the dollar exchangeable for one-thirty-fifth of an ounce of gold since 1934 has not prevented the value of the dollar from falling continuously since then, and the purchasing power of gold has fallen just the same amount as the purchasing power of the dollar. Is it not more realistic to assert that the value of the dollar determines the purchasing power of gold than it is to contend that the purchasing power of gold determines the purchasing power of the dollar?

devaluation of the dollar

The answer to the above question can perhaps be found in an experiment that, though not the sort of "controlled experiment" used in the natural sciences to test a theory, comes as close as we are likely to get in economics to yielding us a clear answer. The devaluation of the dollar in 1933 should contribute to our understanding. If the commodity theory reasoning, as set forth above, is correct, devaluation of the dollar should immediately produce a proportional rise in the price level. Thus, if the value of the dollar is determined by the value of the gold "in" the dollar and if the value of the gold is determined by economic laws of supply and demand (but independent of monetary use of gold), then reducing the gold in the dollar reduces the value of the dollar proportionately. We might look at three ratios involved in this: (1) the exchange ratio between goods in general and the dollar is the one we presumably explain on the basis of the other two ratios; (2) the exchange ratio between goods in general and gold is the one presumably fixed and unalterable by government; and (3) the exchange ratio between gold and dollars is the one altered by devaluation. If the purchasing power of gold is the basis of the purchasing power of the dollar, then reducing the number of dollars obtained with an ounce of gold reduces the volume of goods obtainable with a dollar, and the reduction in the goods obtained should be in the same proportion as the reduction in the number of dollars obtained with an ounce of gold. Let us consider this proposition from another angle. When the number of dollars that have to be given for an ounce of gold is increased, the number of dollars that have to be given for goods in general should be increased to the same degree. The general price level should be increased by the same proportion as the dollar price of gold is raised. Did it work this way in 1933? Was the dollar price of goods changed in proportion, or was it the gold price of goods that changed and the dollar price that was the controlling factor?

The dollar price of gold was raised during 1933 from $20.67 an ounce to $35 an ounce. Figure 11.1 and supporting Table 11.2

Table 11.1   Gold Production and Monetary Gold Stocks
(*millions of dollars*)

	1 ESTIMATED WORLD TOTAL GOLD RESERVES OF CENTRAL BANKS AND GOVERNMENTS*	2 INCREASE IN WORLD GOLD RESERVES	3 WORLD GOLD PRODUCTION*
1958	39,445	—	1,050
1959	40,195	750	1,125
1960	40,540	345	1,275
1961	41,140	600	1,215
1962	41,470	330	1,295
1963	42,310	840	1,350
1964	43,060	750	1,395
1965	43,350	290	1,440
1966	43,180	−170	not available

* Estimated; excludes U.S.S.R., other Eastern European countries, China mainland, and North Korea. Column 2 is computed from Column 1.

SOURCE: *Federal Reserve Bulletin* (March, 1966), pp. 426–427 and (July, 1967), pp. 1258–1259.

show the behavior of the price level over the same period. It is clear that the price level did not rise to the extent it would have if the commodity theory of money had been correct. In April, 1933, the United States government gold price was $20.67 an ounce. In September of the same year this price was increased to $30.77, an increase of nearly 50 percent. To be sure, the United States Treasury was inactive in the gold market in much of the interim, but the increase just quoted is close to the change in the London price of gold in dollars. The price index from August to September rose only about one point, and from April to September it rose only from 71.7 to 78.2, a rise of about 9 percent. Subsequently the United States gold

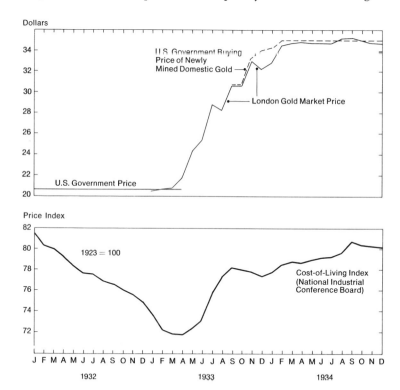

Figure 11.1.   Gold Price and Cost-of-Living Index, 1932–1934

Source: Gold Price—George F. Warren and Frank A. Pearson, Gold and Prices (New York: Wiley, 1935), pp. 168–169. Cost-of-Living Index—Survey of Current Business Supplement, 1936, p. 11.

Table 11.2   Cost-of-Living Index and the Dollar Price of Gold, 1932–1934

		COST-OF-LIVING INDEX* 1923=100	GOLD PRICE LONDON†	U. S. GOVERNMENT‡
1932	Jan.	81.6		$20.67
	Feb.	80.3		.
	Mar.	80.0		.
	Apr.	79.3		.
	May	78.3		.
	June	77.6		.
	July	77.5		.
	Aug.	76.9		.
	Sept.	76.6		.
	Oct.	76.0		
	Nov.	75.6		.
	Dec.	74.9		.
1933	Jan.	73.7	$20.58	.
	Feb.	72.2	20.65	.
	Mar.	71.8	20.71	.
	Apr.	71.7	21.71	$20.67
	May	72.3	24.29	
	June	73.1	25.36	
	July	75.7	28.85	
	Aug.	77.3	28.34	
	Sept.	78.2	30.68	$30.77
	Oct.	78.0	30.71	30.82
	Nov.	77.8	33.10	33.34
	Dec.	77.4	32.32	34.03
1934	Jan.	77.7	32.87	34.27
	Feb.	78.5	34.48	35.00
	Mar.	78.8	34.77	.
	Apr.	78.7	34.85	.
	May	79.0	34.78	.
	June	79.2	34.79	.
	July	79.3	34.77	.
	Aug.	79.7	35.13	.
	Sept.	80.8	35.18	.
	Oct.	80.5	35.01	.
	Nov.	80.4	34.80	.
	Dec.	80.3	34.79	.

price was increased until it was stabilized at $35 an ounce beginning in February, 1934. This was an increase over September, 1933, of nearly 14 percent. The price index increased from 78.2 to 78.5 over the same period. Is it plausible that the domestic purchasing power of the dollar is the direct consequence of the dollar being representative of so much gold, with the purchasing power of the gold being immutably determined in its nonmonetary uses? There is a possible explanation for the failure of the price level to behave as the commodity theory suggests that we must examine to see if it will enable us to say that the theory is still correct. If other forces had arisen independently during the period to offset the effect of the devaluation and hold the price level down, then the theory and the devaluation experience would still be compatible. Unfortunately for the theory, however, one will look in vain for such factors during this period. It appears rather that the Great Depression had already hit its bottom at about the time of the devaluation and that the forces of recovery, though they operated very slowly and feebly, were at work. Further, the depression of the price level was not in the picture. Devaluation did not just offset factors pushing the price level down by almost the amount that devaluation was pushing it up. Indeed, one of the major government policies initiated shortly after Franklin Delano Roosevelt took office, the National Recovery Act (NRA), had the effect of raising prices under government proclaimed codes.

It cannot be said that devaluation does not affect the price level. Such effect as it has comes about in a different manner than just indicated, and the degree of price change is in general much less than the degree of devaluation. When the dollar was devalued in terms of gold, it made other country's currencies more expensive than before, and it made the dollar cheaper to foreigners in terms of their currencies. Consequently, the dollar prices of imports rose, and since imports enter either directly into consumption or enter into further processing for later consumption, the price index is affected.

---

† Monthly averages of pound-price of gold at the London gold market, evaluated at the month-end exchange rate. George F. Warren and Frank A. Pearson, *Gold and Prices* (New York: Wiley, 1935), pp. 168–69.

‡ The U. S. government discontinued sale and purchase of gold on April 19, 1933, began to purchase newly mined domestic gold at $29.62 on September 8, 1933, and again fixed the price on February 1, 1934, at $35.00. The prices from September, 1933, until February, 1934, are monthly averages of the daily prices. Warren and Pearson, *op. cit.*, pp. 161, 168.

* SOURCE: National Industrial Conference Board, *Survey of Current Business Supplement* (1936), p. 11.

As demand shifts in favor of import-competing products because imports or import-using products cost more, their prices may rise some. And the increased demand for exports may increase their prices as well. So a number of components of the domestic price index may be affected to some degree by devaluation. All these factors taken together are quite sufficient to explain the amount of price inflation actually experienced by the United States following the devaluation, and none of it by the alleged constancy of the value of gold. Gold did not retain its value but rather had its value determined by what happened to the value of the dollar due to other forces and by the change in the amount of gold obtainable with a dollar. This discussion demonstrates more than adequately that the value of the dollar is *not* determined by the immutable value of the gold on which it rests. It was the value of gold that had to adjust when the exchange ratio of dollars and gold was changed, not the other way around.

gold stock and the money supply

If gold, used as a reserve behind the money, has an affect on the value of the money, it is in some other way that is not explained by the commodity theory reasoning. In particular, changes in the gold stock of a country may alter the money supply. We have seen in Chapter Six that this is so. But changes in gold stock are not the sole determinants of the money supply, and hence, even to the degree that that is important, not sole determinants of the value of money. Indeed it has become increasingly common since World War I for nations using gold in their monetary systems to offset at least in part the effects on the money supply of changes in their gold stock. Thus under modern circumstances gold does not govern even the money supply, let alone determine its value alone. To be sure, this is what the advocates of the gold standard complain about, namely, that governments have interfered with the normal effects of changes in gold stocks, and they argue that if a nation's money supply were to move in proportion to its gold stock, all would be well. There would never be danger of too much money causing inflation, which is a decline in the value of money, nor danger of too little money in the economy. Let us, therefore, consider the experience with the gold standard to find if the interference with its working by government has been an irresponsible attempt of politicians to escape the safeguards that the gold standard provides the country or to note if governments have acted responsibly in the public interest in managing money instead of being managed by it.

It is a misconception of the gold standard to suppose that it assures stability of the economy for the individual nation. If more than one country is on a gold standard, and permits gold to move freely into or beyond its borders as it then does, any change in wants, resources, technology, international capital flows, or government policy with respect to trade or capital movements may change the total flows of money among countries, adding to or subtracting from the individual country's gold stock. But every redistribution of world gold stocks due to economic or policy changes anywhere can cause changes in money supplies, national income, and price levels in each country whose gold stock is thereby changed. Would it be irresponsible for our Federal Reserve to decline to expand the money supply in proportion to the increase in gold stock in a period such as the 1920's when we already had a boom and did not want price inflation, or would it have been irresponsible on their part to have permitted an increase in the gold stock to have expanded the money supply proportionately? The British government faced the opposite situation for a time; British industries were depressed but gold was flowing out of the country. Would it have been in the public interest to have allowed the money supply to be contracted in proportion to the nation's gold stock, thus further depressing the economy, or was it a responsible government policy to try to promote economic growth despite the decline in the gold stock? It should be apparent from examination of experience that the reason that the gold standard has not been allowed to rule the roost is that it did not give the world stability. Governments have been able to follow wiser monetary policies than would have resulted from a doctrinaire adherence to the gold standard. It is good gold standard dogma that strict adherence to the standard stabilizes a nation's economy, but it betrays a lack of understanding of what is really implied by such adherence in a world of economic change where gold stocks can be expected to change from time to time. And it involves a distrust of government authorities that does not do justice to the actual record of monetary management since World War I.

To be sure, the dogma is not entirely without evidence to lend it credibility. After both world wars a number of countries experienced very serious inflations. In some cases governments so expanded the money supply that the money depreciated to worthlessness. The slate had to be wiped clean and a fresh start made with new money.

It is implied by gold standard adherents that these governments could have solved their problems and adhered to fixed gold reserve requirements. However that may have been, the conclusion is drawn that any time a government does not adhere to fixed gold reserves it is courting the same disaster. Moreover, governments are presumed to be without any other brakes upon monetary expansion and likely in the absence of such brakes to resort to unrestrained deficit financing, made possible by monetary creation. The fear of hyperinflation is rationally based when a nation finds itself in the circumstances that led to such postwar inflations in a number of countries, but it is not rational to fear such inflation as the consequence of all deficit spending in depression in countries as stable and with economies as healthy as that of the United States. The economic circumstances differ tremendously in the two cases, but they are treated by some as though they were the same.

domestic convertibility into gold

The unwarranted fear of hyperinflation in this country in circumstances where this is not the danger has led gold standard exponents to support policies that unwittingly court serious deflation. The favorite device of gold standard advocates to prevent inflation and enable the individual citizen to protect himself against monetary mismanagement by government is convertibility of all forms of money into gold coin at any time. Accordingly, if government undertakes policies such as deficit spending that citizens believe will cause inflation, reducing the value of their dollars, they can simply demand gold coins in place of other money. This will reduce the nation's monetary gold reserves, forcing a contraction of the total money supply and forcing the government to halt any program that depended upon its increasing the money supply. Experience shows that the public does not tend to become fearful of their nongold dollars during periods of prosperity, even if booms are accompanied by rising prices. The time when they become fearful is in times of recession, especially after some banks have failed. That is when the public has been much more apt to seek special safety for its money, pulling it from banks (and thereby causing other bank failures) and converting it into gold. If the government is obliged in these circumstances to reduce the total money supply as its gold stock falls and is thereby prevented from offsetting the decline in private spending by creating a government deficit, the depression is certain to be worsened. Hoarding of cash nearly wrecked the banking system in the 1930's as it was, and if all deficit spending had had to be eliminated, an intolerable situation would have been created.

True, economists do not know all that it would be helpful to know to manage money wisely, and government officials cannot be counted upon to pay attention to all that is known about the subject. But the record is not as bad, especially in this country, as is painted by those who focus only on the experiences with hyperinflation in some countries. And their remedy could itself be quite disastrous. If we forced government to be guided not by the processes that now govern the monetary policies of the country, but by the impact on monetary gold stocks of the panicky reactions of a public threatened in recession with loss of bank deposits, we would indeed have rendered our domestic economy quite unstable, even apart from possible foreign repercussions such as were discussed earlier in this chapter. A fear of inflation where inflation is not a danger leads gold standard advocates to create a situation where aggravation of deflation is a grave danger and can do great damage. When democracy is functioning at its best in respect to monetary policy, it operates through the various bodies that impinge on monetary policy and involves the opportunity for judgment and deliberation on the economics involved, requiring as it does the defense of policies in terms of the public interest. If this is not certain to avoid all mistakes—and it is not—who could say that we would be better off to be at the mercy of democracy at its unreasoning worst when the public is gripped by panic and a wave of gold hoarding depletes the gold reserves of the nation? Clearly, the gold standard does not provide the salvation that it has been alleged to provide.

gold and monetary management

At its worst, the gold standard can unstabilize a country's economy through the reactions of its own citizens or through the impacts of change on its international position. But at its best, to tie a nation's money stock rigidly to gold is to trust to luck rather than to try to develop good management of our monetary affairs. It is not possible to state with precision just how much the nation's money stock ought to grow year by year. However, if we take as our objective a money of reasonably stable value (sound money, as that was defined above), it should be obvious from the analysis of the preceding chapters that the money supply needs to grow roughly in proportion to real national income, that is, to total production. If there is a tendency for velocity to rise slowly over the years or to fall slowly over the years, this would affect the rate of growth of the money supply that would be consistent with stability of the price index. With this qualification in mind, let us ask what the likelihood is that the gold stock will grow at the rate that money then needs to grow, namely at about the same rate as total output grows. Gold production depends upon the price of gold and its cost of production. The former must be fixed for relatively long periods by the government if it is to use gold as a monetary reserve at all. The costs of production of gold depend upon such factors as the returns available to the factors of production in alternative uses (and these tend to rise), the rate of depletion of existing sources of gold, the rate of discovery of new sources of gold and the "quality" of those new sources, and the degree of improvement in the technology of gold mining or gold recovery. It should be plain that there is no reason to expect all these factors to behave in such fashion as to give us the rate of growth in gold stock for the world as would be needed for sound money, that is, for the needed rate of growth in money supplies. In any case, no individual nation would have reason to expect that it would get the desired increment in gold each year or even on the average. We certainly should not need to trust to luck; if men prefer to do so, they ought to be able to learn how to manage their monetary affairs so as to come out better than if they trust to luck. Regardless, they should be able to avoid the worst consequences that a rigid gold circulation standard would be apt to impose upon them.

To dispose thus of the arguments for the old gold standard is not to say that gold is necessarily useless. It is to say that gold should be our servant, not our master. In the present state of the international economy gold is useful in settling international balances and helping provide some stability in foreign exchange rates. More will be said about this elsewhere. Suffice it to say that having gold available in the nation's Treasury and central bank is useful and need not entail any of the rigid controls over the domestic economy just discussed, though any international stabilizing arrangements do reduce to some degree the amount of domestic economic flexibility. What needs to be said further, however, is that the usefulness of the gold is confined to its international role. Domestically it is not needed. It need not be allowed to influence the domestic money supply when its influence is in the wrong direction, and it does not have to be relied upon to change the money supply in the right direction or by the right amount. There is no other way in which it can have any influence upon the value of the dollar except through permitting some influence on the money supply. We now effectively prevent its hurting us domestically, but it does not really help us domestically. It is pure window-dressing, and even that does not matter to those who understand the economics of it and are not still under the illusion that their money is better by virtue of the gold behind it.

questions

1. *Why do some people think that gold backing for the dollar is very important? What monetary experience can they cite to support their case? Does it really establish their case? Explain.*

2. *What can we learn from the devaluation of 1933 about the domestic role of gold?*

3. *Is our money supply now at the mercy of changes in our gold stock? Are changes in our gold stock completely without effect?*

4. *Evaluate the arguments for and against making the dollar convertible into gold domestically.*

5. *What reasons are there for thinking that a gold standard could not be depended upon to provide automatically a stable economy?*

the international payments mechanism

ECONOMIC TRANSACTIONS DO NOT STOP AT A NA-
tion's borders because political boundaries have little bearing on the
economic advantages of transactions between regions. The policies of
governments with respect to international transactions vary, however.
Governments frequently place restrictions on such transactions or promote only those deemed to be "in the national interest." In any case,
transactions crossing national boundaries are complicated by the fact
that different nations use different currencies and have different national monetary systems. Generally, the money of one nation is not
used in another nation. Thus payments from a person or firm in one
nation to some party in another involves a complication not present if
both are in the same country.

money, credit, and banks in international payments

The ways that have evolved for making international payments are
numerous and differ in detail, but an overall understanding of the

essentials is possible if we use an example, illustrated in Figure 12.1 on page 180, of one way in which such payments may be made. An exporter, Mr. Brown, in New York (1) makes a sale of cotton to Mr. Windsor of London. Mr. Windsor agrees to pay £1000 (English pounds) ninety days from the date of shipment of the goods. The payment will normally involve the use of a credit instrument. Mr. Brown might draw a draft upon Mr. Windsor, ordering him to pay the sum at a specified date. This "trade bill," as it would be called, might be sold by Mr. Brown so he could get the dollars in which he really wants payment in the end, provided someone could be found who was willing to accept payment in English pounds. The saleability, or negotiability, of the credit instrument can be increased if Mr. Windsor writes "accepted" on the note and signs to indicate that he has indeed accepted the legal obligation to pay the indicated sum at the specified date. Mr. Brown may, however, prefer a banker's acceptance to a "trade acceptance" because Mr. Windsor's bank may be better known, and its creditworthiness less subject to question in New York than Mr. Windsor's. Accordingly, if Mr. Brown attempts to sell the credit instrument in the New York bill market, he will probably find that he can discount it at a lower rate if the draft is drawn upon a London bank than if drawn upon Mr. Windsor directly. Mr. Windsor, therefore, may be required, as part of the terms of sale, to arrange with his bank for a draft to be drawn upon it by Mr. Brown for the sum of £1000. Mr. Windsor would then go to his bank, explain (2) to them the transaction with Mr. Brown, and (3) get them to issue a "letter of credit" to Mr. Brown that will authorize him (4) to draw the draft directly on the bank. Upon acceptance of this draft (5) by the London bank, it becomes a highly negotiable credit instrument. It should be noted that Mr. Windsor will enter into an agreement with his bank to pay it the £1000 on (or before) the date that the draft is payable, and he may, and likely will, have to give the bank a legal right to attach certain assets (perhaps the cotton involved in the underlying transaction) if he should fail to pay the bank on the due date. The bank, therefore, takes very little risk; it performs a service in allowing the draft to be drawn on it and obtains a commmission for the service, but it does not itself advance any funds to either party.

We return to Mr. Brown, who, upon acceptance of the draft by the London bank on which it is drawn, can sell the bill any time and get his money in the form of dollars. Bill dealers and brokers in New York act as middlemen in purchasing bills originating in foreign transactions and otherwise and finding buyers for them. The buyer may very well be a New York bank. By selling the draft to a middleman Mr. Brown does not have to take time from his business to find a bank willing to buy his draft when he wants to sell it. We can follow the essentials of the operation, however, if we simplify the process by supposing that Mr. Brown does make the sale (6) directly to his own bank. His bank may be happy to buy this banker's bill because it is a highly liquid credit instrument. It will earn interest on the face amount of the bill from the time the bank buys it until it falls due and is paid. In buying the bill the bank deducts this interest in advance, paying Mr. Brown less than the face amount; this is called "discounting" the bill. The New York bank holds the bill until due and then collects the full amount from the London bank.

When Mr. Brown sells the bill to his bank, he is paid in dollars, and the dollars are added to his checking account at the bank. The bank could not invest in this credit instrument if it did not have excess reserves, for it needs reserves to back up the demand deposit it gives Mr. Brown. When it does give him the added deposit, the bank has increased the money supply by that amount. What determines the number of dollars paid Mr. Brown, in addition to the discount or interest rate on that type of credit instrument, is the rate of exchange between dollars and pounds, or, in other words, the dollar price of pounds.

Let us consider next the transactions when the bill falls due in London. The New York bank will present the bill to the London bank (7) and the London bank will pay the New York bank by creating a deposit of £1000. On that same day (8) Mr. Windsor will pay the London bank £1000. He will probably do this by writing a check for that amount on his deposit in the bank; he will have built up his account in advance in anticipation of his need to meet the obligation on a certain date. In effect, the London bank will transfer a deposit of £1000 from the bank account of Mr. Windsor to that of the New York bank. There will be no change in the total volume of bank deposits in England. Instead of Mr. Windsor or some other Englishman having that £1000 to pay to someone in the normal course of business, the deposit has for the time being leaked out of the circular flow within England and come to rest in the ownership of the New York bank. The money supply of the importing country has not changed, but a deposit has become temporarily idle.

These effects may be quite temporary. Let us ask what use the New York bank has for the deposit of pounds of English money that it acquired. It does not want to maintain an idle supply of "foreign exchange," as these pounds are called from the viewpoint of America. It was willing to buy a draft on a foreign bank instead of confining its loans and investments to domestic claims (that is, securities) so that it can sell the pounds subsequently and earn a commission on the sale. Let us see who might wish to buy the pounds. This will enable us to illustrate another way in which an international payment might be made.

Suppose that a New York importer, Mr. Jones, (9) imports some cutlery from a London exporter, Mr. Beadle. The terms require immediate cash payment of £1000 by Mr. Jones. To simplify our exposition we shall imagine that Mr. Jones does not use the middlemen in the New York bill market. Instead (10) he approaches his bank, which is the same bank that bought pounds from Mr. Brown. He tells the bank that he would like to make a payment in England of £1000 and asks if the bank can sell him £1000. The bank is happy to oblige. It draws a draft on its account in the London bank and sells this draft to Mr. Jones. The price again depends upon the current rate of exchange between dollars and pounds. Mr. Jones writes a check on his deposit in the bank to pay for the pounds. The drop in demand deposits in the New York bank reflects the effect of paying for imports; this is a reduction in the money supply.

Mr. Jones next (11) sends the draft to Mr. Beadle, who promptly presents the draft to the London bank for payment. The London bank (12) reduces the deposit account of the New York bank by £1000 and increases Mr. Beadle's account by the same amount. In this case the exporting country experiences no change in the money supply, but pounds previously idle will now return to circulation, since Mr. Beadle will spend them in the normal course of business.

These examples of the flow of international payments have been presented diagramatically in Figure 12.1.

In our two examples of international payments the banks were involved in three ways: (1) they lent their good name to a credit instrument in the first case, making it more readily negotiable; (2) they purchased a time draft, thus in effect financing a credit transaction in which the seller decided he wanted his money sooner than the ninety days provided by the terms of the sale; and (3) banks sold foreign exchange. In each case the businessman was able to pay in his own currency or receive his own currency. Currency itself did not move from country to country, but credit instruments did. It is possible to generalize from the examples. We may say that anything that involves payments coming to us from other countries, as in the case of exports,

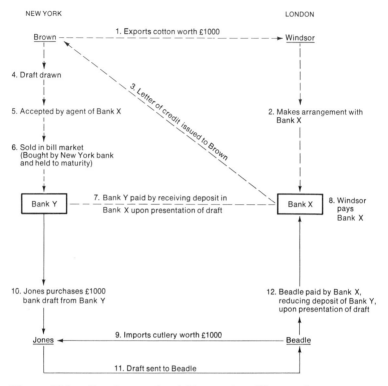

Figure 18.1. Two International Transactions Illustrated

would raise the domestic money supply and provide a supply of foreign exchange to us, or it would return dollars from foreign ownership. Similarly, anything that involves our making payments to foreign countries, as in the case of imports, reduces the domestic money supply and uses up foreign exchange (or it provides foreigners with a supply of dollar exchange).

When the total in-payments and out-payments are equal, these two tend to neutralize each other as far as effects on money supply and foreign exchange are concerned. The volume of deposits in each other's banks might grow equally, or might remain constant, depending upon whether banks felt that the volume of international transactions made it desirable for them to carry larger "inventories" of foreign exchange or not. We shall return to the concept of a balance between in-payments and out-payments.

external value of a currency

In our example we referred several times to the rate of exchange between the two currencies as that which determined the number of dollars exchangeable for a given number of English pounds. But what determines the rate of exchange between the currencies of two nations? This is a matter in which governments often play a role, but in the absence of such intervention economic forces govern. International payments involve purchases and sales of foreign currencies; there is then a market in which the currencies (or bills stated in terms of the currencies) are bought and sold. And the forces of demand and supply determine the price prevailing in any such market. Our demand for a foreign currency is generated by any transaction involving payment to someone in that currency; the supply of any foreign exchange is generated by any transaction involving payment from that country to us.

The rates of exchange for a nation will tend to rise, other things being the same, if its demand for foreign currencies rises and to fall if various factors cause the supply of foreign currencies to increase. Thus a rise in the nation's demand for imports tends to raise the nation's exchange rates, while a rise in its export tends to lower exchange rates. It will be noticed that the term "rate of exchange" of a nation is used to refer here to the price a nation pays in its own currency to obtain foreign currencies. Unfortunately, usage of the term is not entirely consistent. Consequently, one must tell from the context whether the term is being defined as here or in exactly the reverse sense—to refer to the price foreigners pay for a nation's currency.

In an earlier chapter the value of money was defined as its purchasing power over goods and services in general. At this point it is necessary to distinguish between the internal and the external value of a country's currency. The internal value of the currency is that which was explained earlier, and we measured changes in the internal value by changes in some price index. The meaning of the external value of a currency is quite obvious if the currency is used to purchase foreign currencies as the intermediate step in purchasing foreign goods and services. The more of a foreign currency that can be purchased with a unit of some national currency, the more foreign goods and services it can purchase, other things being unchanged, and so the higher the value of the national currency being considered. In other words, given the domestic prices of goods and services in each country, the more of various foreign currencies a dollar will purchase, the higher the external value (that is, purchasing power) of the dollar. One might measure changes in the external value of the dollar by the changes in some index of foreign exchange rates vis-à-vis the dollar. Thus, if at some point the United States finds itself facing rising rates of foreign exchange (that is, if the dollar prices of foreign currencies is rising), this is a matter of a decline in the external value of the dollar. Exchange rates and the external value of a currency move in opposite directions, just as do domestic prices and the internal value of the currency. Or we may say the price the foreigner pays for a currency and its external value move together.

As with the components of a domestic price index, there may be and normally are changes in relative prices, as well as changes in the price level. In the foreign exchange market the exchange rates on some currencies then may move relative to others. But, as in any well-organized market, the exchange ratios will tend to be uniform throughout the market; that is, the exchange ratios among dollars, pounds, and francs will be the same in New York, London, and Paris.

A question with which there is understandable concern is that of the relation between the internal and the external value of a country's currency. One very simple notion is that the two must be equal, or will be made so by international trade since people will buy domestically or abroad depending upon where they receive the most for their money. Price levels will then adjust. Not only do transportation costs alter this, but also many other factors negate doctrines of this sort, which are called "Purchasing power parity" doctrines. For one thing, many of the goods and services that enter into the determination of the domestic purchasing power of a currency are not and sometimes cannot be traded between countries, and so they do not enter into the determination of the exchange rates. The latter are also affected by international capital movements, which alter the demand and supply of foreign currencies but do not directly change domestic price indexes. For such reasons, and because a change in the domestic price index does not normally involve all domestic prices changing in the same proportion or affecting international transactions to the same degree, it is not even true that the internal and external values of a currency must change in the same proportion.

It is true, however, that a change in either one will normally change the other to some degree in the same direction, other things being equal. Suppose, for example, that foreign exchange rates rise.

This is a fall in the external value of the currency. The country will now find that imports are more expensive. This will have both a direct and indirect effect on internal prices. It will directly raise the prices of those domestic commodities that require imported ingredients. And indirectly, it will tend to shift demand from other imported goods to import competing goods and thereby raise the prices of import competing goods. As all these domestic goods enter into the domestic price index, a decline of some magnitude, though in general not a proportionate decline, will be registered in the internal value of the currency. Or suppose, for an example of the causal relationship running in the opposite direction, that the country experiences an internal inflation. The effect will be to make it more difficult for the nation to compete in foreign markets, and so its exports will decline. Imports, however, will now compete more favorably in local markets; so imports will rise. The former lowers the supply of foreign exchange, and the latter increases the demand for foreign exchange. The result will be a rise in the foreign exchange rates, which is a lowering of the external value of the currency.

exchange rate stability and gold

When foreign exchange rates are governed simply by the forces of demand and supply, they are subject to almost continuous and substantial fluctuations. Even if over a year a nation's demand and supply of foreign exchange would be equal at some fixed exchange rate, the month-to-month and day-to-day quantities of foreign exchange demanded and supplied at that rate probably would not be equal, thus causing exchange rates to vary rather unpredictably in the short run. These fluctuations introduce an additional uncertainty and hazard into international economic transactions. If a businessman does not know from one day to the next what he will have to pay to obtain a foreign currency when he needs it to pay for goods that he buys or what he can get when he sells the foreign currencies obtained from exporting operations, he is taking a big risk that transactions that looked quite profitable when initiated may turn out to be very unprofitable by the time the payments are concluded. International investment is similarly hampered by the added risk of alterations in exchange rates over time. It is not sufficient to try to work out arrangements in which the exchange rate risk is always put on the other fellow. Not only may the effort not always succeed, but even when it does, a sufficiently adverse move in exchange rates may bankrupt the party at the other end so that he cannot pay. To be sure, the risk of future change in a price can be dealt with in part by the development of a market in "futures," and "forward foreign exchange" may be bought and sold. That is, one may buy or sell now, at prices determined now, foreign exchange for delivery at some specified future date. Thus one may hedge against unfavorable price changes but at a price which will vary with market factors.

For such reasons national policies to introduce some greater measure of stability into foreign exchange markets is very common. Countries that are members of the International Monetary Fund have agreed to peg their exchange rates within narrow limits. This is done simply by having each country peg its currency to the American dollar. Each government stands ready to buy or sell dollars at something close to the official rate of exchange between its currency and the dollar. This introduces a very high degree of stability into exchange rates. As we shall see later, however, when it becomes difficult to maintain the pegs, the official rates may be changed. Another way of stabilizing exchange rates among countries was for nations to peg their currencies directly to gold, as under the international gold standard, and buy and sell gold at fixed prices in terms of their own currencies. When they do this, the rate of exchange between two currencies is determined by their rates of exchange with gold at the mints of the respective countries. This is called the "mint par of exchange." If the demand of Country A for the currency of Country B were to increase, there would be a limit to how high the price of B's currency could go. As it rose, it would become cheaper at some point for citizens of Country A to use their currency to purchase gold at their treasury, ship it to Country B, and make their foreign payments in that currency. The cost to the payer could then not exceed the official exchange rate (the mint par of exchange) by more than the cost of shipping (and insuring the gold in transit, and so forth). Similarly, the exchange rate on B could not fall by more than the small cost of shipping gold. This keeps exchange rates stable. They can vary only within the rather narrow limits referred to as the gold points.

When changes in demand and supply are not permitted to determine exchange rates, their effects manifest themselves in other ways. These will be examined briefly in connection with the discussion of disequilibrium. It will be apparent that if a country chooses to peg its exchange rates at a level too far from the equilibrium rates that would be determined by the forces of demand and supply, it will have difficulty maintaining the official rates.

The gold standard, which dominated international economic relations in the last quarter of the nineteenth century and until World War I, broke down in the interwar period. The effort to maintain fixed exchange rates by a gold standard in the face of substantial or rapid economic changes that affect the international payments of nations tends to induce gold flows between countries to help settle disequilibrium in their balances of payments. These gold movements alter the reserves of their banking systems and may thus tend to have expansionary or contractionary effects. Sometimes these effects are unstabilizing for a country or otherwise undesirable domestically, which explains why monetary authorities sometimes tried to offset the impact of international gold flows. After we explore these matters briefly we shall examine how international monetary cooperation has been organized through the International Monetary Fund. This cooperation also provides for stabilization of exchange rates. Gold, however, still serves an important role internationally. It is still the most generally acceptable means of settling net imbalances between countries. Therefore, it is useful for countries to keep gold reserves for that purpose.

balance-of-payments statement

If we wish to have a picture of the international economic transactions of a country, we look at its balance-of-payments statement. This statement summarizes the in-payments and the out-payments and the transactions that gave rise to them. Table 12.1 shows the United States balance of payments for 1965.

It is informative to see the magnitude of different types of transactions, and for this purpose they are classified under several headings. Imports and exports of goods and services are shown in what is called the "current account," while foreign investment and various flows of capital are reported under the heading "capital account." Unilateral transfers may be shown as a separate category of international payment. Finally, the statement shows any net flows of gold into or out of the country. Not all transactions are officially recorded, of course, but they will have their impact, nonetheless, on the country's foreign exchange reserves or gold stock or on foreign holdings of monetary assets (including bank deposits) in the country. This check provides the basis for the "errors and unrecorded transactions" entry in the balance-of-payments statement.

The credit and debit entries in the statement may be explained initially by reference to the examples of international transactions

Table 12.1   United States Balance of Payments, 1965
(*millions of dollars*)

	DEBITS	CREDITS
I. Current account		
Goods and services transferred under military grants		1,624
Merchandise	21,492	26,285
Income on investments	1,130	6,054
Other services	9,358	6,721
Total	31,980	40,684
Balance		8,704
II. Capital account		
Transactions in U. S. assets abroad (net)		
Long-term	4,254	
Short-term		728
Transactions in foreign assets in U. S. (net)		
Long-term	169	
Short-term		197
Total	4,423	925
Balance	3,498	
III. Unilateral transfer account		
Private remittances	612	
Government	5,157	
Total	5,769	
Balance	5,769	
IV. Changes in U. S. official reserve assets		1,222
Total of all accounts	42,172	42,831
Errors and unrecorded transactions	659	
Corrected total of all accounts	42,831	42,831

SOURCE: *Survey of Current Business* (March, 1966), p. 22.

used earlier in this chapter. The export of cotton from the United States would be a credit item in our balance-of-payments statement, as would any other transaction that increased the amount owed us by foreigners (or, we might say, that created additional claims on foreigners). The import of cutlery into the United States would be entered as a debit, as would any transaction that made us owe more to foreign sources (that is, gave them more claims on us). There was no net change in balances held abroad by American banks as a result of the two transactions together, but it will help us to consider each payment separately. When the American bank bought the draft payable in pounds and subsequently accepted a deposit in a London bank, it was in effect buying an I.O.U. of the London bank; this investment in a London bank account, or foreign exchange, is an outflow of short-term capital. As such, it is entered as a debit in our balance-of-payments statement. Similarly when the pounds were sold to Mr. Jones, who subsequently paid them to Mr. Beadle, the United States disinvested short-term funds abroad. This would be considered a credit entry in the balance-of-payments statement, as would any capital inflow.

When all items are entered, the debit and credit totals in the balance-of-payments statement are always equal. This is seen if we realize that the statement includes as above both the underlying transactions and the payments for them, and these must balance or offset. The underlying transaction creates a claim, and this claim is met by the debtor relinquishing a claim on the currency of the other country or by the other country accepting a claim on the debtor country. Or, finally, payment may involve the movement of gold, though this is normally a very small portion of total payments, and in equilibrium no gold would move at all.

disequilibrium in the balance of payments

Although the statement of international transactions is drawn up in such a manner that total debits and total credits are necessarily equal, this does not indicate that a country's international economic position is necessarily an equilibrium position. Evidence of disequilibrium is the necessity of "balancing items" in the form of gold movements or movements of short-term capital. A country is said to have a deficit in its balance of payments, or to have an adverse or unfavorable balance of payments, if the net effect of the transactions of a period is net claims against it that are settled either by an outflow of gold or by a net inflow of short-term capital, or by both. The inflow of capital may take the form of foreigners building up the volume of deposits that they own in the banks of the deficit country. The country or countries that build up such balances or receive gold are called "surplus countries," or countries with a favorable balance of payments.

If a country has a deficit in its balance of payments for successive years, it will eventually find that those in other countries who have been accepting increasing amounts of bank deposits in the deficit country will eventually decide that it is not profitable for them to continue to build up such deposits. They may then decide to withdraw some of the deposits by using them to buy gold from the deficit country and that country's gold stock will begin to flow out. Since there is a limit to the amount of gold a country has to lose, there is a final limit to how long it can remain in a deficit position and still continue to peg its exchange rate at the official level. The deficit country is thus under some pressure to correct any deficit before it has lost all its gold. The surplus countries are under less pressure to correct disequilibrium, although it is hardly profitable for them to continue indefinitely to build up foreign deposits or to accumulate gold. One of the main concerns in the area of international monetary relationships concerns the correction of disequilibrium in a nation's balance of payments, and more particularly the elimination of a country's deficit position internationally.

This often leads to national policies that in themselves may be undesirable. For example, a country with an adverse balance of payments may resort to protectionism to reduce imports and thus the claims against it. The reduction in imports reduces the country's demand for foreign exchange and the number of debit entries (in the statement of balance of payments) that it has to offset. Or a country may try to reduce its general price level so as to be able to export more and earn more foreign exchange, thus eliminating its deficit. This, however, is easier said than done, and in modern conditions national policies that put downward pressure on the price level are apt to run aground costs of production that do not fall fast enough, with a resulting squeeze on profit margins. The net result may be a depression or chronic large volumes of unemployment. Another method by which a deficit may be tackled is through an exchange control scheme. The government may set up an agency through which all foreign exchange purchases and sales must be made at official rates. The usual result is that some foreign currencies become surplus and others in short supply. To even things out the government puts pressure on its citizens to keep them from using scarce currencies and to get them to earn such currencies even if business considerations would lead to better transactions with other countries. In the end trade tends to become bilateral with some balance being struck with each other country, one at a time, instead of multilateral with a general balancing involving as it does freely convertible currencies. The result is something less than optimal patterns of international trade and investment.

An alternative, to which countries sometimes resort, is "devaluation" of their currency, that is, an alteration in the level at which the currency is pegged relative to other currencies. It is in general easier to alter official exchange rates than to alter the whole price and income level of a nation with an adverse balance of payments. Devaluation may work by making it easier for foreign countries to buy the currency and hence the goods of the devaluing country and harder for citizens of that country to buy foreign currencies and goods. Thus it increases the supply and reduces the demand for foreign exchange, and if a happy choice of rate has been made, a new equilibrium may be restored with in-payments and out-payments equalized without special balancing capital flows or gold movements. This is not always an ideal answer, however, for if the cause of the deficit is, for example, a continuous inflation in the country with the adverse balance of payments, the devaluation will have only a short-lived effect and the deficit will then reappear. The more frequently devaluation is resorted to by various countries, the less stability there is in exchange rates. Enough has already been said about the desirability of stability in rates.

If one country takes unilateral action to improve its international position by using measures which disadvantage other nations, it may encounter retaliatory measures by other countries. In such a setting it is clear that some measure of understanding of each other's problems is called for, and cooperation may be needed from time to time if the mutual interest in maintaining a stable international monetary system is to be well served. In particular, countries that develop an adverse balance of payments need to have a way of covering their international payments deficits temporarily without losing too much gold or resorting to devaluation or other measures even more restrictive of normal international economic transactions.

International Monetary Fund

In 1944 the International Monetary Fund (IMF) was established expressly to avoid retaliatory measures or breakdown of the international monetary mechanism under the pressures of disequilibrium, and, on the positive side, to help by making available additional foreign exchange on a temporary loan basis for countries that develop an adverse balance of payments. Perhaps the most important contribution of the IMF is to provide for member countries a regular meeting ground out of which mutual understanding and actual international monetary cooperation can grow. The member nations pledge themselves to stable exchange rates, as indicated earlier, but within this framework exchange rates may be altered if necessary to correct "fundamental disequilibrium" without the same danger of provoking retaliation as otherwise.

The IMF does involve an actual fund consisting of gold and currencies of member countries, each country contributing a quota based on a number of factors (such as its national income, volume of foreign trade, and the like). The original resources of the IMF totaled $0.0 billion (valuing all currencies in terms of dollars at official exchange rates), and the United States quota was $2.75 billion. The IMF has since been enlarged twice, first by 50 percent in 1959 and most recently by about 25 percent in 1965. A member nation may borrow as much as 25 percent of its quota from the fund, in any one year, and it may continue to do so for five years at the most. It is obligated to repay its indebtedness to the fund as its balance of payments improves to make this possible. Thus, the fund helps a country tide over temporary disturbances in its balance of payments or gives it time to correct the situation if longer-run changes have impinged on it.

The IMF was established as a result of international discussions that terminated at Bretton Woods, New Hampshire, in July, 1944, but for a decade after World War II ended the Fund was hardly operative. The postwar period proved to be one in which reconstruction needs and international disequilibrium were so overwhelming that most countries maintained varying degrees of exchange control. The fund began to come into its own with the resumption of general convertibility of currencies about 1958.

international economic position of the United States

In its early history the United States was a large importer of capital. Europeans invested heavily in the growing industries of the country. The large sums invested provided the foreign exchange to finance a large surplus of imports. In due course the United States had to increase its exports to earn the foreign exchange to pay interest and profit on the foreign capital invested. World War I marked the change-over from a debtor to a creditor nation in its international position. And the United States has since then continued to lend and invest more abroad, either privately or through government programs. It remains today the largest supplier of capital internationally. The bulk of the funds thus provided to others are employed to buy goods and services from the United States. So even though a creditor nation the United States continues to have an export surplus rather than an import surplus.

However, various sorts of changes have gone on continuously in the international position of the United States, changing the composition of foreign trade and other international receipts and payments. Since 1958 the country has for the first time become keenly conscious that the net result of recent changes has placed it in the position that other countries have often experienced—that of being in need of correcting an adverse balance of payments.

An examination of the balance-of-payments statement has led different people to select different categories of transactions as responsible for the deficit. While some factors, such as the sharp rise in United States purchase of foreign securities beginning in 1958, may be considered more significant than others, it would be a larger truth to say that the aggregate of inflows did not adjust to the increase in aggregate outflows. At first this did not bother the authorities even when some of the gold stock was lost, because the country possessed a disproportionate portion of the world's monetary gold stock at the time. More concern was expressed as foreign deposits in the United States, subject to withdrawal in gold, became much larger relative to the gold available to meet such withdrawal.

Various measures have been undertaken to help correct the disequilibrium, with some success but not enough. For example, most foreign aid is now tied directly to United States exports; that is, the funds must be spent on United States exports. Other efforts are being made to reduce foreign restriction on American exports and to promote exports otherwise. Given time, these measures may suffice to correct the disequilibrium; if not, more drastic measures may be needed, such as restriction of the outflow of funds to purchase foreign securities until such time as exports can be expanded to provide the foreign exchange needed to balance such capital flows.

The problem is whether in the meantime those who hold such large short-term balances in this country will decide to pull them out, which would mean converting them to gold and taking the gold. This sort of short-term capital flight wrecked the gold standard in the inter-war period, and it is a real danger against which various international measures have been devised recently by cooperation between central banks and the like. Since the United States dollar is a widely held foreign exchange reserve for other countries and their currencies are pegged to the dollar, the whole international monetary mechanism is dependent upon the international stability of the dollar. But the alternative ways of approaching the current problem and the longer-run strengthening of the international monetary mechanism are beyond the purview of this chapter.[1]

questions

1. *Discuss the merits of fixed versus fluctuating exchange rates.*
2. *Show how imports and exports may affect a nation's money supply and alter its holdings of foreign exchange.*
3. *Could it ever operate to the disadvantage of a country if foreign nationals held a large volume of deposits in its banks?*
4. *What role does the International Monetary Fund play?*
5. *Compare the merits of various ways a country might try to eliminate a balance-of-payments deficit.*

---

[1] A fuller treatment of international monetary relations, with further attention to the position of the United States, is provided in a supplementary volume in the set: Delbert A. Snider, *International Monetary Relations* (New York: Random House, 1966).

THIRTEEN

the development of central bank policy

IN A BROAD SENSE MONETARY POLICY MAY REFER to action of or public policy toward the whole range of financial institutions and the volume, cost, and rate of expenditure of financial assets. The term is more frequently used in a narrower sense to refer to the policies of a nation's central bank. We use it here in the latter sense.

There is a great deal of interest in monetary policy today and much reliance upon it, but this has not always been true. It has sometimes been thought that if a country's monetary and financial system were properly structured, there would be no need for a *central bank*. Or if a central bank existed, perhaps to supervise commercial banks or perform other mechanical functions, it should have no "monetary policy." It was feared that if the central bank pursued a monetary policy, it could involve misuse of the bank's powers in such manner as to worsen economic conditions. Good intentions are not sufficient to ensure that monetary policy will improve things rather than make matters worse. Consequently, there is great appeal in the idea that the monetary and financial system will work automatically to yield the desired results if it is just structured properly and then allowed to operate according to its own inherent logic. The theory of the gold standard is the outstanding example of such an idea. It held that the money supply would be properly and automatically regulated by variation in the country's monetary gold stock. There was no room for a central bank to have a policy at all, unless it be said to be a policy of keeping its gold reserve ratio constant.

The commercial loan theory of banking, a comparable theory, did much to determine the structure and behavior of the Federal Reserve System for many years. Before we examine the influence of this theory in depth and in order to have a basis for evaluating monetary policies, it is advisable to determine the commonly accepted purposes for which monetary policy may be used.

objectives of monetary policy

Generally the prosperity, stability, and growth of the domestic economy and the maintenance or restoration of equilibrium in the nation's balance of payments have been the objectives of monetary policy. The promotion of a high and stable level of employment has become a universal objective of monetary policy. We might assert that the objective is the promotion of "full employment." That term, however, must not be understood to mean that nobody is ever out of work but that there is no deficiency of aggregate demand. It refers to a situation in which there are jobs enough to go around, even though at any given time there may be some people unemployed for other reasons. Full employment is thus consistent with some seasonal and frictional or structural unemployment of a temporary nature.

In recent years increasing attention has been paid to the promotion of economic growth and progress through monetary policy and other measures. Usually this objective is stated in vague and general terms rather than by specifying any particular rate of growth in Gross National Product (GNP) or in some other variable. Insofar as the objective is taken seriously, rather than being merely a reassuring sound, it may be taken to indicate a desire to prevent the rate of growth of GNP (or for the more sophisticated the rate of growth of productivity per man-hour) from falling behind the nation's own long-run average, or even a desire to improve a little on that rate.

Stabilization of the domestic price level, as well as of the level of employment and economic activity, is generally a goal of monetary policy also. The prevention of deflationary price-level movements is an inherent part of the promotion of high employment and growth, but the prevention of inflation may be made more difficult by the latter objectives. When conflicts between objectives arise, monetary policy inevitably weights some objectives higher than others; some of one must then be sacrificed to achieve more of another. To say that the objective of monetary policy includes price-level stability merely excludes substantial or rapid price-level movements; the term "stability" is usually taken to leave room for several alternative price-level patterns. The objective may be to have the general price level fall slowly to reflect increasing productivity. Such price-level behavior would distribute the gains of technological progress directly to final consumers. If those gains were divided instead among the factors of production, the general price level might remain constant. Some would favor a policy that permitted a slowly rising price level, on the grounds that this stimulates business more than the alternatives and, hence, is more compatible with objectives of high employment and growth.

Any nation not economically cut off from the rest of the world may have to concern itself at times with its balance of payments vis-à-vis the rest of the world. The problems that arise in this area were examined briefly in Chapter Twelve. Here we need to indicate that one concern of monetary policy is to maintain or restore equilibrium in the nation's balance of payments. For small countries whose foreign trade or investment is an important part of their national income, this objective of monetary policy may be of foremost practical importance. The United States has generally been in the fortunate position that balance-of-payments problems did not exert much pressure on monetary policy. That situation has changed in recent years, however, and especially since 1958 monetary policy has had to be formulated with balance-of-payments objectives clearly in mind. Just as domestic objectives of monetary policy sometimes conflict with each other to some degree, so domestic and balance-of-payments objectives sometimes conflict to some degree. When they do, monetary policy must seek an acceptable compromise, pushing a little harder in one direction at the expense of some loss in another.

The question that we must ask of any monetary policy, therefore, or of any substitute for a monetary policy, is how well it achieves each of the objectives in various circumstances. And when conflicts arise among objectives, how it weights the various objectives, or what sacrifices are entailed for the gains obtained.

federal reserve system and the commercial loan theory

The Federal Reserve is our central bank, and it operates as such to try to achieve the objectives just discussed. But the Federal Reserve was not established for the purpose of operating in such fashion, with the powers it has, to achieve such objectives. We learned in Chapter Four how the establishment of the Federal Reserve System was expected to remedy certain defects in our monetary system. We shall next consider how this restructuring of the banking system was expected to take care of other matters more or less automatically.

The division of the Federal Reserve System into twelve regional banks was done to resolve the fear that a central bank might wield too much power. Obviously, this did not constitute a formula for more effective pursuit of the objectives of modern monetary policy. Insofar as any of these objectives were considered at all, there was strong opposition to giving the Federal Reserve powers to use or misuse to achieve such objectives. The problem as it was seen then was not to design a monetary institution that could stabilize the economy, but so to design it that it would not unstabilize the economy while correcting the inelasticity of the currency, and so forth. In particular, it was thought necessary to safeguard the economy against the danger that the new monetary institution might produce inflation. Stability was to result not from giving a central authority certain powers, but from restricting its powers so that it would not itself cause trouble. With the System properly designed, economic stability would be maintained automatically—so it was thought.

How was the Federal Reserve to be restricted so that it could not exert an inflationary influence while it was providing the needed elasticity in currency and credit? In regard to Federal Reserve notes, overissue was to be prevented by requirements of reserve, collateral, and convertibility. The reserve requirement was fixed at 40 percent in gold or gold certificates, and the notes could be exchanged on demand for any lawful United States money, including, when gold coins and gold certificates were in circulation, for gold. Thus the nation's monetary gold stock, or more exactly the portion of it available to back the note issue, placed an upper limit on the volume of Federal Reserve notes. It was characteristic of adherents to the gold standard to contend that this limit would never be inappropriately high, or inappropriately low. In any case there was another limit, and the relation between the two was not considered. The other limit was the deliberately elastic limit implied by the collateral requirement. The notes were to have as collateral the commercial loan paper rediscounted by the Federal Reserve banks for commercial banks. Initially set at 100 percent, the collateral requirement was subsequently reduced so that reserve and collateral together were 100 percent.

The purpose of the collateral requirement was to permit the volume of notes issued to increase along with, but no more than, the increased need for notes. Needs of the economy were thought to vary chiefly with the volume of commerce and business, which involved a variation in the volume of commercial loans by banks. When more notes were needed, banks could then rediscount commercial loans to get them, and this would provide the Federal Reserve with the needed collateral, but only the amount required to satisfy the need. Note issue could thus not become excessive and lead to inflation and depreciation of the value of the notes. This was the logic applied.

Demand deposit expansion has become more important than currency issue as a potential cause of inflation. Although this was not widely recognized at the time, the Federal Reserve Act did incorporate restrictions designed to deal with the problem indirectly. There was thought to be no problem if bank credit expanded only when needed to finance an expansion of production. The solution lay, therefore, in preventing the Federal Reserve from extending its credit to member banks except to the degree that the member banks were forced to borrow from it in order to accommodate the needs of commerce and business. To make it work this way, member banks were permitted to rediscount at the Federal Reserve only the type of loan used to help finance the production and marketing of goods. We discussed in Chapter Seven the relation of this "commercial loan," as it is called, to the liquidity of banks; now we are considering its relation to the money supply and the inflation problem. The Federal Reserve could not cause inflation, it was thought, nor indeed would the banking system, if only commercial loans were eligible for rediscount at the Federal Reserve Bank credit and, in turn, Federal Reserve credit would expand only as needed to finance increased output. In the $MV = PX$ equation, M would change to accommodate changes in X, and P would remain stable.

This idea that the commercial loan could play a role which

would automatically ensure the right money supply, neither too much nor too little, is called the commercial loan theory of banking. Clearly it lies behind the restrictions on note issue and rediscounting by the Federal Reserve. It is not incorrect to claim that the structure of our central bank was originally based in part on this theory.

from qualitative to quantitative guides

The commercial loan theory also had a great influence on the policies of the Federal Reserve until the depression of the 1930's. It is said to have provided a "qualitative guide" to credit policy. That is, the Federal Reserve concerned itself only with the quality of the paper offered it for rediscount; if the paper met the tests of eligibility for rediscount, there was no concern with the total volume of rediscounts granted the banking system. But various economic circumstances began slowly to force the Federal Reserve to pay some attention to quantitative considerations. As time went on, Federal Reserve practice involved more and more instances of what might be considered "cheating" by adherents of the commercial loan theory. If the result were regarded as bad from that point of view, it constituted a vast improvement from the viewpoint of the economics of the situation.

In the early years of the Federal Reserve its discount rate policy was purely passive. That is, the rate charged the member banks for rediscounts went up and down in response to changes in market interest rates. In general, the Reserve held its rate between the market rates on commercial paper and on bankers' acceptances. The reasons for this are not entirely clear. There is no general market and hence no market rate on the type of loan that the Reserve was rediscounting. Apparently the Federal Reserve did not want to use discount rate changes actively to affect the quantity of credit extended to the member banks. This, of course, is consistent with the commercial loan theory that matters such as the volume of credit should be allowed to take care of themselves.

For some time the Reserve did not recognize that it was inadvertently affecting the monetary and credit conditions of the country, and thereby even market rates of interest. Nor had the framers of the Federal Reserve Act or the Congress realized the potential significance, when undertaken by the Reserve, of a "normal" banking operation. The Federal Reserve banks were, of course, permitted to invest in United States government securities. At first the individual Reserve banks acted just like any bank would, treating government securities as earning assets to be bought or sold on the basis of general portfolio considerations. It was doubtless thought desirable to have the Federal Reserve able to support government credit upon occasion, as it indeed had occasion to do in its earliest years during World War I. Subsequently the Treasury itself found independent action by the twelve Reserve banks had a rather unpredictable net effect on the government securities market. The Reserve banks began to realize too that they affected the market and, moreover, had an influence on general credit conditions. They set up a joint committee to study the matter in 1922; the committee was soon advising the System on the timeliness or untimeliness of open-market purchases or sales of government securities. Open-market operations came to be coordinated through this committee, and the committee's recommendation began to be used upon occasion to ease money-market conditions or to tighten credit conditions. A quantitative criterion thus began to creep into Federal Reserve policy.

One of the earliest instances of this is in connection with seasonal variations in credit conditions, due in part at least to the way government fiscal operations worked. Before the income tax was put on a "pay as you go basis" (in World War II) with much of the tax withheld as income is paid, the federal tax was due March 15, and Treasury deposits at the Federal Reserve increased about that time. This reduced bank reserves and the public's money supply until such time as the government expenditures drew down the Treasury's balances again. There was no reason for this seasonal influence on credit—no reason why it should be more difficult to get a loan in March than in September. The Federal Reserve could even out credit conditions by the simple process of buying government securities in the open market to offset the effect on bank reserves and money supply of the Treasury tax collection and by selling off the securities again slowly as the Treasury's balance at the Reserve fell.

The Federal Reserve did not move rapidly, however, to a modern central banking policy. It continued to adhere to the idea that for the most part its job should be rather narrowly conceived and its role should be essentially passive. It was not until its Annual Report for 1923 that the Board of Governors gave official recognition to the idea that its credit policy could appropriately pay attention to the general state of business. And even this statement conceived of credit policy primarily in terms of changing the cost of credit to member banks and seemed to imply that all would be well if credit were confined to "productive" rather than "speculative" use. No test was indicated, however, to determine whether, say, inventory accumulation was the one or the other. The fact is that there were sharp differences of opinion within the Federal Reserve System as to the appropriate guides for credit policy. Even Governor Benjamin Strong of the New York Federal Reserve Bank, the most influential figure in the Federal Reserve until his death in late 1928, never gave a clear statement on the matter. He evidently believed that there was no single guide to credit policy, but he never reconciled satisfactorily the potential conflict among the different factors that he discussed nor did he indicate the priorities among them in different circumstances. Needless to say, then, no consistent policy was followed, and in retrospect it is not clear how various guides were weighted

It is worthwhile to examine the development of Federal Reserve policy. Let us first look at policy changes from 1923–1927. The first important use of open-market operations to affect general credit conditions may have been the sale of government securities by the Federal Reserve System in early 1923; the discount rate was also raised then. It is presumed that this was the response primarily to a boom and an increase in the domestic price level. The recession of June, 1923–July, 1924, brought a drop in Federal Reserve discount rates in early 1924, followed in the latter part of the year by some open-market purchases. But market rates fell, partly due to gold inflow easing the market, and it is not certain what would have happened had gold not come in to the market. Some Board of Governors members and Reserve Bank Governors continued to express doubts all through the 1920's and into the 1930's about the wisdom or effectiveness of such action when it was not merely "following the market" (that is, market interest rate changes). Similarly ambiguous changes in Federal Reserve action occurred in the 1925–1926 revival and in the 1927 recession.

The worst dilemma for the Federal Reserve System came in the late 1920's. Both stock market prices and loans to brokers were, at the end of 1927, approximately double what they had been four years earlier. There was a feeling that easy money had encouraged this. Although the Federal Reserve did not want to be put in the position of being responsible for the level of stock market prices or of regulating speculation in securities, it could not feel comfortable in ignoring the fact that bank credit seemed to be feeding the speculative orgy in the stock market. It became obvious from the experience that there was something wrong with the old theory that if the Reserve rediscounted only paper used to finance productive enterprises, other things would take care of themselves. Here was an unhealthy development to which the Federal Reserve was an unwilling and unwitting partner. Rediscount rates were increased in early 1928, and this checked an outflow of gold. The increased rates were reinforced by open-market sales by the Reserve, which forced member banks to rediscount. Call money rates (the rates on loans to brokers, repayable on demand or in practice callable on the following day) rose still further, but, bank loans to brokers continued to rise, as did security prices on the stock market. It was apparent that the rise in the Federal Reserve's discount rate had not been an effective brake upon bank credit flowing into the stock market.

The question was, would a further increase in the rate be effective in checking the flow, and even if so, could the general business situation stand it? The general price level had been fairly stable after reaching a peak in 1925; therefore, it could not be contended that a rate increase was required to check inflation. There did not appear to be excessive inventory accumulation either. Although it had become popular to talk as though the boom would last forever, there were signs that the boom was no longer very vigorous. Construction fell off after 1928, and some other signs of business decline began to appear. This was not generally regarded as cause for alarm, but it was ground for concern lest tight money have an adverse effect on business in general. It was also possible that Europe might be adversely affected, for high interest rates here might result in draining off gold from Europe. In these circumstances some members of the Federal Reserve Board of Governors were in favor of "direct action," that is, they wanted the Reserve banks to require member banks to reduce their loans to brokers and other security loans. It was argued that the whole intent of the Federal Reserve Act was that credit be extended only to finance increases in production and that funds from the Federal Reserve must not be permitted to be diverted to speculation on the stock market. The New York Federal Reserve Bank, which would have to enforce such a policy, opposed it. In addition to believing it was not the responsibility of the Federal Reserve to try to stop the diversion of credit, the New York Federal Reserve Bank argued that there were serious practical difficulties in carrying out such a policy. It was pointed out that the Federal Reserve credit to a member bank was not for a specific loan whose character could then be examined, but rather it was to cover a reserve shortage due to its total operations. To the suggestion that credit could be refused to banks whose security loans were increasing, the New York Bank replied that it could not supervise all the member banks in the area that closely and distinguish speculative loans from others that also pledged securities as collateral. The Board of Governors did attempt early in 1929 to exercise "moral suasion," as it came to be called, to discourage banks from increasing their call loans to brokers. The New York Federal Bank did not, however, use its leverage over rediscounts to enforce the policy. The member banks appear to have been affected by the message, nonetheless. But by that time brokers were able to increase their borrowings by tapping funds of lenders other than banks, attracted as these were by call loan rates that ranged from 10 percent to 20 percent. The prices of securities in the market continued to rise until the peak was reached on October 23, 1929. The subsequent stock market crash, and the inability to do anything to halt the decline of security prices when the speculative bubble burst, is probably the most familiar story of modern economic history.

The depression of the 1930's that ensued was blamed by many upon the stock market crash, and though other factors are now generally held to have been more basic, it is doubtless true that the crash had a very serious adverse effect upon the whole economy and made the depression more severe.

impact of the great depression

With the depression came changes in the thinking about the functions of our central bank, both within and outside the System. Although the policies of the Federal Reserve did not conform at once to what was needed, there was some gain. The structure of the System was itself changed in a number of respects to enable the Federal Reserve to operate more like a central bank. In the end the notion that we had an automatic or self-correcting monetary system died a belated death. It had been shown that neither a gold standard nor a qualitative guide to policy such as had been provided by the commercial loan theory of banking would suffice.

The failure of the Federal Reserve to pursue a vigorous easy-money policy from the onset of the depression may be explained partly in terms of the hangover of the old ideas and partly as due to the restrictions imposed in the law. To be sure, rediscount rates were reduced after the crash, and for a time the Federal Reserve purchased in the open market. But the Board of Governors, instead of providing leadership in initiating and continuing a vigorous easy-money policy, was drawn almost reluctantly into it by the New York Federal Reserve Bank. The action taken did not go far enough to bring down long-term interest rates very much. Then came the reversal of policy, the increase in discount rates and the sales by the Federal Reserve in the open market in the fall of 1931, with very serious adverse consequences for business generally. This policy move was the unfortunate result of the requirements placed upon the Federal Reserve, which proved unsuitable for the conditions. Bank failures here and abroad led to hoarding; so gold flowed out of the country, and more Federal Reserve notes had to be issued. The Federal Reserve's holdings of eligible paper looked as though they might not be sufficient for the 60 percent collateral for the expanding issue of Federal Reserve notes, and gold might have to be used instead. The actual reserve ratio of the Federal Reserve was falling, however, with the gold exports. Tight money was the result. The action taken was obviously inappropriate, given depressed business conditions. In this situation the Glass Steagal Act was passed (on February 27, 1932) permitting government securities to be used as collateral for Federal Reserve notes in place of eligible paper. This was another blow at the commercial loan doctrine, for now the volume of Federal Reserve notes was divorced from the volume of eligible paper.

Even though an easy-money policy was restored, there was still not complete understanding within the Federal Reserve System of the role the central bank needed to play. Its open-market purchases were concentrated largely on short-term securities, despite the need to bring down long-term interest rates. The idea seems to have been that the Federal Reserve must keep itself in a more liquid position by avoiding long-term bonds. This was in line with the thinking of an individual commercial bank, but it represents a failure to understand the different role played by a central bank. It is the function of a central bank to provide additional liquidity to a banking system when a crisis arises. The liquidity of a central bank must lie in the excess reserves that give it power to extend credit to commercial banks. A central bank's liquidity does not come by shifting assets to the public or letting short-term securities "run off" (that is, be paid off at maturity and not replaced), for such a tactic reduces rather than increases the liquidity of the public.

With bank loans turning sour, portfolios declining in value, and public hoarding of cash as a result of distrust of banks, bank failures continued to mount. Many states resorted to restrictions on the withdrawal of bank deposits, and on March 6, 1933, the national bank holiday was proclaimed. The reopening of banks depended upon their condition, but confidence returned as many were reopened shortly after the bank holiday. The Federal Reserve was not given additional power to deal with the "supply side" of the liquidity problem at this time, but within three months Congress passed legislation that dealt with the "demand side." Changes were made in banking to reduce the need for liquidity by the banks. Most important of these changes was the introduction of deposit insurance. For a small fee banks could (and member banks were required to) insure each deposit account fully up to $5000. This reduced the danger that small depositors would drain off a bank's reserves whenever they became fearful of the safety of their deposits. This single factor may have done more than any other single factor in reducing the danger of, or the seriousness of, any future liquidity crisis. Thus, not only was the general public protected, but the banks themselves were protected against unwarranted alarm.

In the last half of 1933 the Federal Reserve resumed an easy-money policy, and by the end of the year the reserve position of the banks was no longer tight. Open-market purchases by the Federal Reserve provided reserves that enabled the member banks to pay off rediscounts and thus get out of debt to the Reserve. The devaluation of the dollar in 1933 subsequently resulted in the growth of bank reserves. The higher price of gold and the de facto stabilization of the dollar brought about a "golden avalanche" or substantial inflow of gold to this country. By the time Congress got around to passing the Banking Act of 1935, the monetary and banking emergency was over, and the more permanent changes desired in the country's financial structure could be considered.

There had been considerable pressure on the government, and to some extent on the Federal Reserve, as soon as the depression had become serious to "do something": something to promote recovery and something to prevent such troubles from recurring. If the Reserve had not conceived its role as that of a central bank with responsibility to control credit to influence the general level of business activity, others came to view that as its function. For the public at large the doctrine of automaticity was killed by the Great Depression.

The Banking Act of 1935 made further changes in Federal

Reserve structure to agree with the changes in our conception of central banking. The close tie between commercial loans and the ability of the member banks to avail themselves of Federal Reserve credit if needed was cut. Although eligibility of paper for rediscount was not formally changed, in effect the old principle was abandoned as the Federal Reserve was authorized to lend to member banks upon any asset the Federal Reserve considered acceptable. The Board's dominant role in the System was more clearly recognized along with the central importance of the Open-Market Committee and open-market operations in effecting monetary policy, by contrast with the earlier emphasis on the strength of the twelve regional banks. The Federal Reserve was henceforth required to give an annual report of its policy decisions and the reasons for them. To deal with the depression itself, the Federal Reserve was empowered in addition to make credit available directly to business, upon recommendation of local committees of three to five businessmen appointed by the Federal Reserve Bank. This reflected the feeling that banking facilities were inadequate in some regions since the banking holiday and that bankers generally were unwilling to accommodate business to the degree necessary for recovery. In fact, direct lending by the Federal Reserve never became important. The demand for bank credit was not as large as was implied, and the government effort to meet credit needs came more largely through other agencies such as the Reconstruction Finance Corporation (RFC).

Some of the changes made in the 1930's in the financial structure added new dimensions to monetary policy and put the Federal Reserve in a position to deal more effectively than before with certain types of situations. The problem presented by the stock market boom was approached from the side of the borrower of funds. Brokers were prohibited from borrowing except from member banks, and the Federal Reserve was empowered to fix the margin to be required of their customers. These provisions of the Securities and Exchange Act of 1934 have been the basis of several subsequent changes by the Federal Reserve in the margin requirements. The Federal Reserve thus sought to influence the volume of bank credit flowing into purchases on margin in the securities markets. The Banking Act of 1935 gave the Federal Reserve the power to vary required reserve ratios for member banks between the original 7, 10, and 13 percent for different classes of banks, and twice those percentages. This constitutes a very powerful new tool of credit control. It enables the Reserve to lock up excess reserves, if requirements are not at their maxima, in order to forestall an inflationary expansion of credit. It also enables them to provide the banking system much additional reserve by lowering reserve requirements, if they are not already at the minimum, when easier credit conditions are desirable. The new power was first used in July, 1936, when reserve requirements were increased by 50 percent. Presumably this was not an attempt to halt the recovery, which was by no means complete, but to "lock up" some of the excess reserves of the banking system (which had grown partly because of the "golden avalanche" already referred to) so that control over the rate of credit expansion could become more effective. When no untoward effects followed this move, the Federal Reserve decided in January, 1937, to increase requirements to the maximum in two steps in March and May. This time many banks found themselves short of reserves, even though some excess remained in the system, and their sales of government securities to meet the higher requirements pushed up interest rates at an inopportune time. A sudden change in the federal government budget had a strong deflationary impact in 1937, and wage rates rose sharply. These were all factors in the recession of 1937–1938. The Federal Reserve took until April, 1938, to reduce required reserve ratios again. The power to vary the requirements, though an important one, clearly must be used with more perception of the impact on the situation. The power has been used relatively infrequently.

limitations of central bank policy

From time to time since its inception the Federal Reserve has faced the threat of new legislation requiring it to achieve some specified economic goal. Usually the goal has been stabilization of the general price level, though in the Great Depression it was to restore a more normal price level and to raise the level of employment. The proponents of such measures usually assumed that if the price level were stabilized, the economy as a whole would be stabilized. This was a hangover from the days when the business cycle was viewed primarily as a price-level phenomenon rather than as a change in the level of employment and output. The Federal Reserve officials have opposed all such efforts to make it mandatory for them to achieve some specified goal. This would be understandable in any case, for it reduces their freedom. But the arguments put forth against the proposals merit attention. Some arguments claimed that if the nation's monetary system is properly structured, the proper degree of stabilization automatically results. Many have contended that by restricting Federal Reserve credit and Federal Reserve note liabilities in the manner provided in the Federal Reserve Act, credit would be used only for productive purposes and would be neither too much nor too little to serve business needs. To some people a requirement that the Federal Reserve stabilize the economy by its own decisions on credit policy smacked of "managed money," and to many managed money would lead to all sorts of evils rather than to stabilization. The latter would be much better assured by maintaining our gold standard, it was claimed. On the other hand, the Reserve itself repeatedly has stressed its belief that it was unable, whatever it did, to guarantee price stability since it did not have complete control over the price level.

The fact was that the Federal Reserve did not clearly identify itself with the goals of monetary policy outlined at the beginning of this chapter, let alone resolve the relationships among them. And it did not act vigorously or consistently like a central bank in pursuit of the objectives. The stabilization bills might be regarded as efforts from the outside to enlarge the Reserve's role so that there would be a modern central bank instead of an institution that often failed to grasp fully the effect its own actions inevitably had upon the economy. It is probably better that the law did not impose a price-stabilization requirement upon the Federal Reserve. But the eventual outcome was the full-employment act passed at the end of World War II, in which the federal government committed itself to a more basic policy objective, namely the promotion of high levels of production and employment. The Federal Reserve was implicitly involved in that commitment. If the Federal Reserve officials do not always sound as though the battle for modern central banking has been completely won, there is little question but what the issues have been much clarified, and for the most part the Federal Reserve can be expected to do better than in its early history.

The failure of monetary policy to contribute more to recovery from the Great Depression, to sum up, was due partly to the Federal Reserve's inadequate conception of its own role, although the depression itself changed this to a major degree, and partly due to mistakes in Federal Reserve policy and to inadequacies in the structure of the System. In addition, it must be added that monetary policy faces certain inherent limitations in fighting a depression. The figure of speech often used here is that easy money, trying to increase bank lending, which is certainly the monetary policy appropriate to a depression, is like pushing on a string. One cannot produce an increase in borrowing from banks and spending for investment just by lowering interest rates and making banks liquid if conditions in the markets for goods are not favorable to new investment. The fact is that the banks did have more than adequate lending power by the mid-thirties, but the economy did not pull out of the Great Depression fully until the impact of war made itself felt upon the economy. This experience, coupled with the Keynesian General Theory, led to a downgrading of the possibilities of monetary policy. This occurred just about the time that the Federal Reserve was largely freed from the incubus of the erroneous theories on which it was founded and from some of the restrictions imposed upon its activity as a central bank. Indeed, the Keynesian revolution must be given some of the credit for destroying the old notion that automatic mechanisms in the economy assured that the economy would normally work satisfactorily and be stabilized automatically if anything did go wrong. But the Keynesians downgraded monetary policy too far at the same time that they placed their emphasis on the possibilities of fiscal policy for economic stabilization. The student can easily get the impression that because monetary policy could in some circumstances not cure depression, it was worthless. Perhaps the appropriate analogy here would be with a stalled car. Monetary policy may be likened to the brake on the car; it is needed at times to prevent the car from racing ahead too fast; and when the car is stalled, although it is no substitute for a motor to get the car started, the starting force will be much more successful if the brake is off than if it is on. An easy-money policy is not going to cure more than a mild setback in the economy, but even in a serious depression it will be much easier for other forces to produce a recovery if the tight-money brake is taken off in favor of an easy-money policy.

war finance

When the depression was over, the Federal Reserve was not able to deal with the inflation problem. Generally, a central bank can expect to be more successful in putting the brakes on the economy than in taking them off, for it can limit the lending power of the banking system and thus limit the growth of the money supply. However, World War II created monetary problems on a scale not suitably handled simply by a tight-money policy. One critical decision in effect prevented normal monetary policy not only for the duration of the war, but also into the postwar period. That decision was one to support the prices of government securities. The prospect of a major war presents problems of government finance. Military expenditures are certain to rise, and although taxes can also be increased, they are unlikely to be increased enough to avoid all deficit spending. Even economists were not sure during World War II that they could devise a tax structure that could avoid all deficit spending and yet not hamper production by dampening incentives or otherwise. Government deficits also face the danger that new issues of securities may be offered the public faster than they wish to absorb them. In such circumstances the price of securities drops. Each new government issue must then carry higher interest rates to make the new securities attractive. Since they have to sell in competition with old issues, they must yield as much. The drop in the market price of the old issues makes them yield an increased rate of return to new purchasers, since the interest payment on them is of fixed magnitude. Thus each drop in prices of old issues requires that new issues carry an interest rate high enough to match current market yields on old issues.

Furthermore, the danger that the price obtainable when securities are resold will be lower than when initially bought is a deterrent to their purchase in the first place. People may not wish to risk such a capital loss. And there may be a tendency to postpone purchase in hopes of obtaining a higher yield later for those who are willing to invest. Thus the decision to put a floor under government security prices was calculated to ease the problem of war finance; bond drives could be expected to be more successful, and the interest cost to the Treasury could be held down. In practice what was involved was having the Federal Reserve support the market for government securities whenever it sagged below predetermined levels. This is usually spoken of as "pegging" interest rates on governments. That is, the affective yield of government securities was prevented from rising. The pegs were maintained not only for long-term bonds but also for the entire range of government securities of different maturities.

While such a policy facilitated war financing, it deprived the Federal Reserve of its usual credit control technique. It could no longer use open-market sales of governments to put the brakes on credit expansion. Indeed, at times when the Federal Reserve had to buy government securities in order to support the market and hold down interest rates, it was adding to bank reserves and to the money supply. Yet, the fundamental problem of war finance is to minimize inflationary pressures. The problem is not to assure that the government obtains the money to buy the war supplies but that the government reduces the purchasing power in public hands so as to reduce inflation. Government can create money for financing war material if need be, and so in war it certainly will not be slowed up in procurement of supplies by failure of its citizens to turn over enough money to pay for them. Price controls were adopted to prevent inflation and its undesired effects on the distribution of income and wealth, but a price control system is in greater danger of breakdown the larger the excess purchasing power in public hands. The temptation to evade price controls increases as people have more money; those who can do so then become anxious to get the goods they want at any price that they may have to pay in the black market. So the mere existence of a price control scheme does not render unnecessary an effort to hold down the money supply.

The Federal Reserve also had power to raise required reserve ratios, locking up excess reserves and lowering the deposit expansion multiple for the System. It used this power as far as it could by raising the requirement to the legal maximum as early as September 23, 1941, during the armament boom and before the United States was a combatant. Thereafter there was no more power here. A grant of more power would not have resolved the problem satisfactorily as long as the interest rate pegs might be maintained by open-market operations and insofar as excess reserves were not evenly distributed throughout the banking system. The rediscount rate also became ineffective, for the Federal Reserve maintained a very low interest rate on the ninety-day Treasury bills in which banks invested as secondary reserve. When a bank needed reserves, it could easily obtain them at low cost by selling off some of its holdings of Treasury bills without any restraint from a high rediscount rate.

Thus the only way to reduce inflationary pressures generated by the war was to raise taxes and beyond that to sell such government securities as could cover the other government expenditures. But it was important that these be sold to the public instead of to the banking system or directly to the Federal Reserve itself. Hence, every argument that could draw on people's patriotism was used to get people to buy the government securities in the effort to reduce their spending (or at least their spending power). They were usually told that they had to do their part in furnishing the money or the boys would not get the guns. Although this was not true since the real bottlenecks were in production, not in creating or obtaining money, the sales propaganda probably sold more securities than would the truth that the sales of securities to the public were to reduce the danger of inflation. In the end, of the total United States government war expenditures of about $380 billion, approximately 40 percent was raised by taxes, about 35 percent from security purchases by individuals and businesses other than banks, and about 25 percent came from purchases by banks and the Federal Reserve.

postwar monetary policy

When the war ended, the economy was more liquid than ever before; total money supply and total liquid assets were each nearly three times prewar levels. The reconversion from wartime to peacetime production occurred more smoothly and more quickly than most people had thought possible, though of course it did take time before the flow of goods could match the pent-up demand, especially for consumer durables. Consequently, the problem continued to be that of inflation. But the public was tired of controls, and business interests in particular put pressure on Congress for their elimination. Although some rent controls remained for some time, general price controls were soon abolished. The Federal Reserve's power to control the expansion of consumer credit expired on November 1, 1947. (It was restored temporarily for the period of September 20, 1948, to June 30, 1949.) This had been a wartime power given the Federal Reserve to enable it to slow down the rate at which credit was being expanded for the purchase of consumer goods. With both these controls gone, the price level rose more in the early postwar period than it had during the war. This may be seen in the accompanying Table 13.1 and Figure 13.1. The consumer price index, which had fallen during the depression, rose from 59.4 in 1939 to 62.9 in 1941, a rise of 3.5 points before the United States was directly involved in the war. The index rose another 14 points, to 76.9 by the end of the war in 1945. Three years later, in 1948, it had risen to 102.8, a postwar rise of approximately 26 points. These index numbers are figured on a 1947–1949 base. The price level actually reached its peak in the initial postwar inflation after the middle of 1948 and then declined a little before the Korean war inaugurated a new period of inflation.

The Federal Reserve was still powerless in the initial postwar inflation to check the expansion of credit as long as it maintained the interest pegs on government securities. Of course, the inflation could not have been checked merely by halting the expansion of the money supply because there was already enough money available to generate inflation. But there was reason to avoid adding fuel to the fire. There were various proposals to give the Federal Reserve additional powers to cope with the situation, but these came to naught. The discussion in this period centered chiefly over the policy relative to government securities.

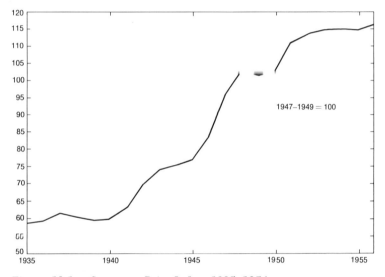

Figure 13.1. Consumer Price Index, 1935–1956
Source: Table 13.1.

The reasons for opposition to the Federal Reserve's dropping its policy of supporting the market for governments were various. Some people argued that it was not fair to sell people government securities and then allow the securities to fall in value; some even contended that the government was obligated to maintain their value. But no securities, even government securities, are sold with a guarantee of their market value from the time of sale to their time of maturity and payment. Therefore, there was no commitment by the government that people buying the securities it sold would always be able to resell them for as much or more than they paid for them. The fact that market values were supported for a time did not create any

Table 13.1 Consumer Price Index, 1935–1956
Averages of Monthly Figures, 1947–1949=100

1935	58.7	1946	83.4
1936	59.3	1947	95.5
1937	61.4	1948	102.8
1938	60.3	1949	101.8
1939	59.4	1950	102.8
1940	59.9	1951	111.0
1941	62.9	1952	113.5
1942	69.7	1953	114.4
1943	74.0	1954	114.8
1944	75.2	1955	114.5
1945	76.9	1956	116.2

source: U. S. Department of Commerce, Office of Business Economics, *Business Statistics: A Supplement to the Survey of Current Business* (Washington, D. C., 1957 Biennial Edition), p. 26. This is the Consumer Price Index compiled by the Bureau of Labor Statistics.

presumption that they would be supported forever, and people who did not understand that even government security markets fluctuate could not be considered very well-informed buyers.

More important was the fear in many quarters that our financial structure might be weakened by withdrawing market support, especially if the withdrawal was followed by a very substantial drop in the prices of government securities. Most of our financial institutions held rather large amounts of government securities after the war. About half of the assets of commercial banks were governments, for example. As the discussion about the withdrawal of support wore on, more people became convinced that a drop in value of these assets would not harm our financial institutions. They did not need to depend upon sale of the securities for liquidity; if liquidity needs did arise, they could be taken care of in other ways. In particular, the Federal Reserve could always make loans to member banks that had temporary need of additional reserves. Thus the banks would not need to sustain losses by selling governments that had dropped in price. Nonmember banks could borrow from correspondent member banks if need be. The liquidity needs of other financial institutions tend to be less pressing than that of the banks, which have so many demand liabilities, so that the impact on the former could not be as serious.

Consequently, the Federal Reserve began after a time to allow the interest rates to rise a little on short-term government securities, while continuing the pegs for longer issues. But when the Federal Reserve was ready to allow longer issues to seek their market level also, the Treasury objected, and there developed a long hassle between officials of the Treasury and the Federal Reserve over the matter. The President himself was brought into the controversy, but the issue was not resolved until March, 1951, when a so-called "accord" between the Federal Reserve and the Treasury was reached. The Federal Reserve had won. The policy of pegging the interest rates was changed, and the market allowed slowly to adjust.

This restored to the Federal Reserve, some time after the market had adjusted enough to make open-market operations by the Federal Reserve possible again, its normal credit control powers. It should be said, however, that the Federal Reserve, like other central banks, can be assumed to exercise some responsibility for what are called "orderly conditions" in government securities markets. The knowledge that this is so is itself enough to give some increased stability to the markets.

This sketch of the philosophy and policy of the Federal Reserve over the years since it was founded shows that it has been only since about 1952 that the Federal Reserve has had an opportunity to show what monetary policy can do in normal times. In its earlier years the Federal Reserve was hampered by a narrow conception of its role and by a structure that was not adapted to its playing the role of a modern central bank. The Great Depression changed both the conception and the structure to an important degree, but it also showed us that there were limits to what monetary policy could do to promote recovery. The war presented even more abnormal conditions and requirements, and for some years after the war the Federal Reserve's hands were tied by the policy with respect to government securities. Since 1952 the Federal Reserve has been free to act like a central bank to further the objectives discussed at the beginning of this chapter. If it has not compiled a brilliant record in that time, neither has it been a dismal failure. Its powers and its responsibilities are better understood both within the System and outside it now than ever before, though perhaps not yet as completely as might be hoped. In general, the policy of the Federal Reserve has been in recent years to employ a tight-money policy when the Board of Governors judges there is danger of inflation and an easy-money policy when it feels it is necessary to deal with deflation.

This has not ended the controversies over monetary policy. Indeed, they seem to have gained new life in the last few years. The Federal Reserve's record has been attacked, and there has been argument over the appropriate guides to credit policy. Various proposals have even been made to change the structure or powers of the Federal Reserve.

questions

1. *In what circumstances can you envisage conflicts arising between different objectives of monetary policy?*
2. *What was wrong with relying on the commercial loan theory of banking as a guide to central bank structure and policy?*
3. *What were the main changes in Federal Reserve structure and policy as a consequence of the Great Depression?*
4. *What were the relevant considerations for evaluating Federal Reserve policy regarding government securities during the 1940's?*

FOURTEEN

monetary policy

problems

THE IMPORTANCE OF CONTROLLING THE MONEY supply and the evolution of central banking policy in this country for the purpose of monetary control have been discussed in the previous chapters. We shall now examine some of the remaining issues of monetary policy.[1] It will be useful to review how such policy works. This can be done without repeating in detail the mechanics set forth in Chapter Six if we generalize about the effects of using the various credit control tools of the Federal Reserve System.

how policy works

Let us consider first tight-money policy. This is the appropriate policy to deal with inflation, where total spending is expanding so

[1] The full range of such issues is discussed systematically in a supplementary volume in this series: Thomas Mayer, *Elements of Monetary Policy* (New York: Random House, to be published in 1968).

rapidly that the general price level rises. When the Federal Reserve deems it desirable to dampen the rate of increase in spending, it employs a tight-money policy aiming to restrain the rate of growth of the money supply and to increase the cost and decrease the availability of credit. How much restraint to employ is a matter of judgment and varies with the amount of inflationary pressure being generated in the monetary sphere. The Federal Reserve may exert a restraining influence through techniques that have both direct and indirect effects. The growth of the money supply may be restrained by open-market sales of government securities by the Federal Reserve. Such sales directly reduce the money stock in the hands of the public as the public gives up deposits to buy the securities. The indirect effect is the reduction in the lending power of the banking system, which comes about as the Federal Reserve collects the checks drawn upon banks. The banks must honor these checks, whether written by themselves or their depositors to buy securities from the Federal Reserve, by paying the Federal Reserve out of their reserves. The significance of the indirect effect on the money supply is that it mops up excess reserves that might later become the basis of much additional credit expansion by the banks. But the indirect effect may go beyond that. If free reserves were low to start with, the open-market sales may be pushed hard enough to halt or even reverse the growth of the money supply. The availability of credit is thus decreased.

How is the cost of credit—the rate of interest—affected? The Reserve can set directly only the cost of obtaining money from the Federal Reserve itself. If a tight-money policy is pushed very far, the rediscount rates of the Federal Reserve banks are raised, perhaps more than once during a period of inflation. The rates are not likely to be pushed so high that the banks are unable to make loans at higher rates, but the rates can, if desired, be pushed up to the point where it is cheaper for the banks to seek added reserves through the sale of their own holdings of government securities rather than through rediscounting at the Federal Reserve. In any case, the rise in rediscount rates serves as a signal to the banks of the decreased availability of Federal Reserve credit and the desirability of more restrained credit policies on the part of the banks. Together the Federal Reserve's open-market sales and increase in rediscount rates in the context of heavy demands for bank credit may result in an increase in the discount rates of the member banks. If the banks do not raise their rates, they may "ration" their credit more tightly, making loans less readily available to potential borrowers. Other indirect effects are to be found in the money market and capital market. The Federal Reserve's open-market sales of government securities make their price lower than it otherwise would be and thus raise yields to the buyer of the securities. This tends to attract those who otherwise would have purchased various private securities, since the government issues are now relatively more attractive than they were before. Yields on other securities, therefore, tend to rise a little. This increases the cost of borrowing through issuance of securities.

In these circumstances the Reserve may try to enhance the indirect effect of its tight-money policy upon the banks by what is termed "moral suasion." It may, through private or public statements aimed at member bankers, try to persuade them to "hold the line" and be less liberal in the amount of credit that they extend. In its most developed form the Federal Reserve may even try to enlist banks in publicized "voluntary credit restraint programs." A much more powerful tool to restrain credit expansion by banks reduces the excess reserves on the basis of which expansion could take place. Especially if the volume of such reserves were considered dangerously large, the Federal Reserve might resort to increasing required reserve ratios rather than relying entirely on open-market operations, to reduce potential bank lending power. In addition to "locking up" some of the reserves of the banking system, this reduces the deposit expansion and contraction multiple applicable to each dollar of change in the reserve base.

Selective credit controls may be employed, especially if there is fear that an excessive amount of credit is being employed in certain lines. The Federal Reserve may raise margin requirements on loans for purchasing or carrying securities listed on national exchanges, thus limiting the rate at which bank credit might be drawn upon to finance speculative purchases of securities. If it were desired to place special restraint on the expansion of consumer credit, the Federal Reserve could again be given the power to do so, though it presently lacks that power.

Can a tight-money policy, using some combination of these controls in a coordinated fashion, do the job intended and bring inflation under control? No doubt the money supply and the cost and availability of credit can be affected to various degrees, depending upon how tough a policy is pursued. In the short run its effects may be somewhat offset by an increase in the velocity of the circulation of money. The high demand for funds can be met partly by tapping idle balances of individuals and business firms through inducing the purchase of the securities of those wanting more loans. A similar result on velocity follows as people try to buy some things before prices rise more. But there are limits to how far people are willing to reduce their average cash balances, unless inflation gets completely out of hand. These offsetting velocity changes thus affect only how hard or how long tight-money policies must be pursued to secure a desired effect. Applied vigorously enough and long enough, tight money can certainly check monetary expansion, reducing the availability of credit and raising its cost. That there may sometimes be reluctance to apply the brakes to the degree needed to halt inflation may be due in substantial measure to two factors. On the one hand there is room at times for the fear that too much pressure may overdo matters and result in a sharp reversal of the economy and consequent deflation. On the other hand there may be considerations arising from recognition of the political pressures that might be generated from beneficiaries of inflation or potential sufferers from deflation. Another complication that enters the picture in recent years will be discussed later in the chapter.

Let us consider the opposite set of circumstances—where deflation is to be offset. Deflation involves a declining volume of spending in the economy. As a result unemployment increases, and if the deflation is severe and prolonged enough, the general price level declines. Clearly, this calls for an easy-money policy by the monetary authorities. The real objective is to increase spending, hence sales and, in turn, production and employment. The Federal Reserve's efforts in this direction involve the use of its powers to achieve certain effects, direct and indirect, on the money supply, interest rates, and the availability of credit. Again the principal tool is open-market operations. When the Federal Reserve buys government securities, it directly increases the amount of money in the hands of the selling public. The indirect effect on the money supply comes from the fact that the same operation increases the lending power of the banking system by a multiple of the reserves provided when the Federal Rserve pays for the securities. The Federal Reserve's added demand for the securities tends to make their market prices higher than they otherwise would be and thus is a factor making for lower effective rates of return on them. The indirect effect on other interest rates is also downward. The Federal Reserve's rediscount rates may be lowered, and, although banks are not likely to be desirous of borrowing more at the time, this may be taken as an indication of easier money conditions. As banks begin to feel the own reserves are adequate, they may lower their own discount rates, or at least become a little more liberal in the volume of loans they grant. If this does not come about soon enough through continued open-market operations and a progressive lowering of rediscount rates, the required reserve ratios may be lowered, giving banks additional lending power. Any selective controls in use may also be relaxed, at least somewhat.

How successful can these measures be in arresting deflation? We saw earlier that monetary policies seemed relatively ineffective in depression. Yet it can be argued that easy money was not pursued with sufficient vigor. To be sure, there are factors that absorb the impact of an easy-money policy during deflation and thereby seem to rob it of its force. As economic conditions worsen, the demand for loans drops and interest rates drop. Banks reduce their own borrowings from the Federal Reserve as soon as they can, offsetting open-market purchases by the Federal Reserve to some degree. In the face of worsened economic conditions, banks come to feel that they need to be more liquid than normal and accumulate excess reserves as they are able. There may be no positive response by banks to easy money, then, until the bankers become sufficiently optimistic about economic trends in general and the prospects of their own loan applicants in particular. Until that time arrives, it appears as though easy money is about as effective as "pushing on a string." A good analogy would be that an easy-money policy is like taking off the brakes on the economic machine. Taking off brakes cannot be expected to be equivalent to stepping on the accelerator of a car, but it would be a lot harder to get the car moving again if the brake were left on. So banks must be made sufficiently liquid, their lending power increased, and the cost and availability of credit generally improved if recovery is to occur. A declining money supply, high interest rates, and low availability of credit would first aggravate deflation and then nip recovery in the bud. What easy money can do is not spectacular, but it can perform the valuable service of removing adverse monetary factors and replacing them with a favorable monetary setting.

In our review of the operation of tight-money and easy-money policies, we have seen some difficulties that attend their use. But we have still not gone substantially beyond suggesting that monetary policy is essentially the application of easy-money or tight-money policy to conditions of deflation or inflation. The matter is not quite that simple, however; therefore, we must consider some of the less simple problems of monetary policy. To do this attention will be focussed on the various objectives of monetary policy: full employ-

ment and growth, price stability and balance-of-payments equilibrium. This will lead us to consider the relation of monetary policy
to other policies in attaining these objectives.

business cycles and growth

The fact that the level of economic activity does not grow smoothly
but fluctuates, in the past in a rather irregular cycle, is the dominant feature in the setting for much of our monetary policy determination and execution. There would be general agreement on the
objective of trying to maintain a stable rate of growth.

To achieve economic growth, generated out of population growth
and increasing productivity, without generating potential instability
from the monetary sphere, requires the money supply to grow at approximately the same rate as output. The qualification arises from possible changes in the public's demand for currency or demand for
money balances in general and hence changes in the velocity of circulation of money. There is no likelihood that, aside from central bank
action, the sources and uses of reserve funds would behave in such
manner as to generate the appropriate rate of growth in reserve funds
and bank reserves. The Federal Reserve thus finds it necessary to add
to its holdings of government securities at a rate that provides the
indicated growth in bank reserves. The size of the government debt at
least presents no obstacle in this respect. However, this is not all there
is to the matter of growth, for the influence of monetary policy upon
interest rates may affect the rate of real investment and hence the
rate of economic growth. In general, the lower the level of interest
rates the higher the rate of real investment is likely to be, other
things being equal. Then how low should the level of interest rates
be kept on the average? Or, if we grant that the central bank is only
one factor influencing interest rates rather than being the chief
determinant of them, how much should it attempt to influence the
rates? Who should determine what rate of economic growth to try
to achieve? And how shall the possible effects of different average
levels of interest on the distribution of income be taken into account in making such a decision? These are questions that show one
of the bases for possible public disagreement over the general course
of central bank policy. There would be general agreement, however,
that the Federal Reserve should not undertake to hold interest rates
so low as to involve itself in a highly inflationary expansion of the

money supply. The memory of the preaccord pegging of rates by the Federal Reserve is still with us.

What has just been said does not, however, provide any support for those who want central bank policy to maintain easy money continuously or for those who want high interest rates all the time. With the type of economic fluctuations that the economy has experienced in the past, if economic stabilization is an objective, what is needed is a monetary policy that changes appropriately with economic conditions, sometimes toward tightness and sometimes toward ease. Therefore, it is necessary to examine variations in policy, not the level around which the policy tries to vary interest rates.

The problem is to vary policy appropriately. The first difficulty is to recognize soon enough the changes in the economic situation that call for changing responses by the monetary authorities. It is sometimes not very difficult in retrospect to tell when such changes occurred, but when one is in the midst of the process, one can never be sure that one is correctly interpreting the situation. Even the immediate future sometimes brings surprises, and what people come to expect may itself alter the course of events. The Federal Reserve Board of Governors and the Open-Market Committee provide themselves with a very substantial body of information on the state of monetary and general economic affairs throughout the country as a basis for their deliberations and actions. There is no single guide upon which they rely exclusively. When all the evidence points in one direction, the problem is simple, but all too commonly, at least around turning points of business cycles, the indications are mixed.

After a conclusion has been reached on a course of action and the action undertaken, the effects are not immediate. It takes time for the main effects of policy on money supply or interest rates to occur. And it takes still longer for these to have the bulk of their effect on spending, and thence on output, employment, and prices. Policy may even have to be altered before the effects of previous policy have worked themselves out fully.

If it is difficult for the authorities to decide just when to alter policy and by how much, it is also difficult for the public to tell the policy implications of Federal Reserve actions. For example, it is not safe to conclude because the Federal Reserve is buying in the open market that it is pursuing an easy-money policy. Ease and tightness are not opposites between which the Federal Reserve oscillates by big jumps; there are all degrees of ease or tightness, and how one characterizes a changing degree of either can involve purely semantic confusions. The further difficulty lies in the fact that some of the Reserve's actions are purely defensive. That is, the Federal Reserve may be buying in the open market not to pursue an easy-money policy of actively increasing total bank reserves but in order to offset other forces reducing bank reserves. Or a given purchase may be partly to offset other forces and partly to increase reserves. The precise target of the managers of the open-market account of the Federal Reserve is not known. And the general directives given by the Federal Reserve Board to the account managers, although worded with great care, are not such as to lead to straightforward and unambiguous interpretation by outsiders of the precise policy intent or the degree of policy change.

balance of payments

How to maintain or restore equilibrium in a country's balance of payments is a common concern of monetary authorities in many countries. The United States was lucky enough not to have had to face problems in this area until recently. If a country pegs the foreign exchange value of its currency, then it finds it necessary to avoid an inflationary monetary policy, under penalty of having to face a consequent deficit in its balance of payments. Even if monetary policy were not at fault for a balance-of-payments deficit developing, a situation that many sorts of economic change could bring about, it may be a useful tool to help deal with the disequilibrium. If the trouble is not too serious or too prolonged, monetary policy may be all that is needed, for the monetary authorities, by a policy that increases interest rates in the deficit country, may be able to attract foreign funds into the deficit country's money market. This inflow of funds may tide a country over the period of trouble. With more serious and prolonged disequilibrium a dilemma may arise. If correction in the balance of payments is undertaken by a monetary policy that produces a deflation of prices and incomes, in an effort to make exports more competitive and imports less so, the consequence is likely to be a decline in production and employment. With exchange rates pegged in the face of economic change, the conflict between international equilibrium, on the one hand and full employment, on the other hand, is apt to be resolved eventually by most countries by sacrificing the exchange rate pegs and favoring full-employment monetary policies. First every effort is made to postpone the final outcome or to buy time in the hope of bringing about other economic changes to solve the problem in the interim. The United States dollar is a key currency in the international monetary mechanism. Other currencies are pegged to it, and the dollar is held widely as a form of foreign exchange reserve by other countries. Consequently, we do not have the same freedom as others to devalue our currency as a way of eliminating the balance-of-payments deficit.

Monetary policy cannot in this situation solve the whole problem. Several courses of action have been taken in the United States to allay the situation. The deficit position was worsened by a tendency for short-term capital to flow abroad in response to higher rates of return in European money markets. With somewhat less than full employment in the United States there was reluctance to try to push up interest rates here lest such a policy would have an adverse effect on real investment and increase unemployment further. Accordingly, the monetary authorities attempted to alter the interest rate structure; they sought to raise short-term rates to stop the outflow of short-term funds, while trying to check any rise in long-term interest rates in the hope that this would make it possible to promote a higher rate of real investment. Subsequently an effort was made to restrain banks from expanding their foreign loans and to reduce the rate at which business firms were making longer-term foreign investments. This was an administration effort rather than an attempt by the Federal Reserve.

It is characteristic of a deficit position in the balance of payments of a country that its currency is subject to speculative international trading at times that threatens the ability of the country to maintain its exchange rate stability. Both England and the United States have experienced such speculation in the past decade. The Federal Reserve as well as the United States Treasury have taken action to deal with this. Both have begun to operate in foreign exchange markets, with the Federal Reserve actually handling most of the purchases and sales of foreign exchange. A much more novel development is the set of "swap" agreements entered into by the Federal Reserve and some foreign central banks whereby each is assured of the availability of certain credits from the others if needed to stem an adverse speculative move against their currency. Thus our monetary policies have been adapted to deal with our balance-of-payments problem to a degree.

inflation dilemma

We have already discussed the standard monetary medicine for inflation—a tight-money policy. The prescription is well designed to deal with what might be called the "classic" case of inflation, that characterized by the current term "demand-pull inflation." But recent years have made us aware of the possibility that the price level could rise as a result of other factors, and it is not obvious whether or not tight money is good medicine for them also.

A second type of inflation may be described as "cost-push" inflation. This sort of inflation could arise if labor unions were to succeed in pushing up wage rates faster than productivity could be increased and if, in turn, this increase in average costs of production is used as a basis for management to increase prices rather than permit any alteration in the distribution of income. A third type of inflation is commonly referred to as "administered-price" inflation and refers to the possibility of prices being increased by firms possessing substantial market power.

These factors obviously would have to be fairly widespread, not just confined to isolated instances, if the general price level is to be affected to any substantial degree. But what would be the outcome of a tight-money policy applied to either of these types of inflation? The way tight money works is by restraining spending. Where an increase in spending is the cause of the trouble, this gets at the cause directly. But if spending is reduced when prices are raised, due not to greater demand but to higher costs or to the exercise of market power, then the most likely consequence is a reduction of sales and thence of production and employment. It is sometimes argued that this may be the only way to check the exercise of power to raise wages and prices by powerful labor or business interests. This is not the place to discuss the full range of issues involved. Here we must confine ourselves to the possible roles that monetary policy might play in connection with these types of inflation; however, one more alternative for policy to take should be pointed out. These three types of inflation may be related in practice. It is when there is already excessive aggregate demand that unions can raise production costs without meeting as much opposition and with less danger of affecting employment adversely—and similarly that is when firms may raise prices with less danger of serious loss of sales. In short, the amount of cost-push and administered-price inflation probably varies directly with the amount of demand-pull pressure on the price level. If this is so, a tight-money policy can play a constructive role. If tight money is pushed just far enough to remove the demand-pull inflationary pressure, it will change the environment so as to be less favorable to the other inflationary pressures. How much further to press monetary policy is the question that must be left open. In practice, however, it is difficult to ascertain where to draw the indicated line when the several factors interact to produce a cumulative inflationary spiral, with prices and costs chasing each other upward and interacting upon one another.

There were times in the past decade when the price level was rising, but it did not appear that any one of these three factors was sufficiently widespread and general to explain the phenomenon. Analysis of the situation led us to recognize yet another possible type of inflation due to the operation of one or another of the above three factors upon certain key sectors of the economy. When prices rise in key sectors, this causes prices to rise elsewhere in the economy. This may be because the product of the key industry is widely used as an ingredient by other industries, for example, steel. Or it may be that the union in the key industry sets the "pattern" for wage demands elsewhere. It is difficult to find a role for monetary policy here that is comparable to the roles already discussed.

To form any judgment about how far to carry any course of action, the monetary authorities must know a great deal about the nature of the inflation. It is not a simple matter of continuing tight money as long as prices rise and switching to easy money when prices fall or unemployment rises. Such a simple formula produces a complete quandary when the authorities find themselves facing "too high" a level of unemployment and a rising price level at the same time. Nor is this a completely unlikely situation. Whenever the economy pushes ever closer to the full-employment mark, more and more bottlenecks appear in different sectors of the economy, and some increase in the price level results. The closer full employment is, the more of a threat arises from cost-push or administered-price factors. Some people are convinced that we cannot have simultaneously full employment, price stability, and all of our present economic freedoms. Again we have bumped into an issue too big and too complex for analysis here. Suffice it to say that it is not certain that the dilemma as stated is indeed inescapable. But it is clear that since the famous Treasury-Federal Reserve Accord the Reserve has faced decisions where its relative concern with inflation and unemployment was inevitably tied into its decisions, along with its estimates of their interrelation in various situations. The Federal Reserve's critics charge that it displays greater fear of inflation than concern for persistent unemployment.

coordination of monetary and fiscal policies

Monetary factors are affected significantly by various actions of the government as well as by the Federal Reserve. When the federal government deliberately varies its taxing and spending and borrowing and lending in order to achieve such objectives as full employment or economic stability, we refer to such policies as "fiscal policies." What is the relation between monetary policies and fiscal policies?

Both impinge upon some of the same variables (money supply, interest rates, credit, and ultimately spending) and may share common objectives. Obviously, they need to be coordinated lest they work at cross purposes, to their mutual frustration. And a coordinated attack on problems should indeed yield more fruit than either working at the task alone. If demand-pull inflation is to be controlled, the most effective attack should involve both a tight-money policy pursued by the Federal Reserve and a federal government budget surplus, the latter to withdraw more funds from the income stream than tight money alone can withdraw. Similarly, to combat a recession, an easy-money policy to increase the liquidity of the economy can be powerfully supplemented by government deficit spending that can directly increase income, spending, and hence, business sales.

There is the further relation between monetary policy and fiscal policy involved in the financing of a government deficit and the handling of a budget surplus. If a deficit-financing fiscal policy is adopted in order to promote recovery from a recession, the effect will vary in part according to who buys the government securities issued to cover the deficit. If the monetary authorities do nothing, the securities may be bought by the public with funds that they might otherwise have spent or invested in private issues of securities, thus offsetting to a substantial degree the effect of the government deficit. If banks buy the securities, it reduces the funds that they have available for lending. On the other hand, the Federal Reserve can buy enough securities in the open market to offset these effects if it will, thus permitting the government deficit to have its full effect in stimulating private spending. In circumstances where the government is spending less than it taxes, open-market operations of the Federal Reserve can help to adjust the net impact to the economic circumstances. Too much should not be expected of monetary policy, however, since it does not directly alter the income and spending stream as does fiscal policy.

When the government borrows new funds or when it refinances part of the public debt, selling new securities to pay off those falling due, it has a choice of issuing short-term bills or long-term bonds or anything in between. How liquid the public feels itself to be is affected by what the Treasury does and the consequent maturity structure of the public debt. The interest rate structure is also affected, although the Treasury obviously cannot ignore market interest rates in setting the nominal rates on its new issues if it wants to sell them in competition with outstanding securities. A government debt-management policy to contribute to economic stability would increase the average maturity of the government debt in a boom and reduce it during a recession.

While government expenditures and taxes are determined by Congress, the President has the initiative in proposals he puts before the Congress and has a certain degree of flexibility in the execution of Congressional decisions through varying the rate of expenditure of funds appropriated. If monetary and fiscal policies are to be coordinated, therefore, which is certainly desirable, it might be done most simply by altering the present separation of the Federal Reserve from the executive branch of the government. Proposals to this effect have been made from time to time, only to be met by a stout defense of the independence of the Federal Reserve. What is the nature of the defense? It is argued that a central bank that is beyond the immediate control of the government can exercise a healthy restraining influence upon what might otherwise be unsound monetary policies. It is implied that government officials tend to bow more readily to public pressures for such unsound policies than a board composed of persons of special competence in monetary policy and removed from immediate political pressures by long-term appointments. While this may be so, the fact is also that a central bank board that undertook to thwart a democratically determined government policy would be doomed, for Congress could alter the basic law establishing the central bank and ensure cooperation. If there is a case for the actual "semi-independence" of the Federal Reserve, it lies in the possibility that there is apt to be better opportunity for public debate over monetary-fiscal policy when differences of viewpoint between two responsible authorities are necessarily out in the open than when they are bottled up inside a single government agency. The scrap that led to the famous Treasury-Federal Reserve Accord of 1951 is a dispute that illustrates the point.

We have been speaking of the need for coordination of monetary and fiscal policies, for it, obviously, does not make sense for them to work at cross purposes. However, there is room for different combinations of monetary and fiscal policies to achieve a given end, without involving any fundamental conflict or mutual frustration. Indeed, to achieve some combinations of purposes, it is necessary to use monetary-fiscal combinations that might appear superficially to represent poor coordination if not conflict. Ordinarily one would expect that coordination would imply that a tight-money policy should go with a "tight" fiscal policy (a budget surplus), while easy money and a government deficit should go together. But it need not always be that simple.

The United States was recently faced with the need to stimulate spending in order to push the economy closer to full employment; at the same time the balance-of-payments deficit called for efforts to check an outflow of short-term capital. To achieve such a combination of objectives, we tried to stimulate spending through a tax cut and the maintenance of low long-term interest rates while raising short-term interest rates to check the outflow of short-term funds. If in another situation the country wants to increase its growth rate while checking inflation, the policy combination might well be one of easy money (low interest rates to stimulate investment) along with a tight fiscal policy to hold total spending within noninflationary bounds. It is sometimes contended, perhaps somewhat too optimistically, that full employment can be achieved by a wide range of policy mixes, at one end relying very heavily on monetary policy and very lightly on fiscal policy and at the other end relying very heavily on fiscal policy and only very lightly on monetary policy. The choice of monetary-fiscal policy mix might then be made in terms of their other differences, as for example different effects on the rate of economic growth. Similarly, different mixes to deal with inflation might be employed, with the decision based, for example, upon how people evaluated the alleged discriminatory impact of tight-monetary policy upon housing, or school construction, or small business. A recent example of an alteration in the monetary-fiscal policy mix was the proposal of President Johnson at the beginning of 1967 for easier money and lower interest rates to be accompanied by a tax increase (the surtax proposal). This followed substantial criticism of the impact of tight money on the mortgage market and hence on housing, along with continued concern over an increased rate of price inflation.

There will always be room for some differences of opinion over the proper choice of the monetary-fiscal policy mix, as well as over matters of timing and degree of application of monetary and fiscal policies. Economic analysis and experience can, of course, provide some policy guidance and can help avoid policies that would defeat the objectives they were intended to serve.

questions

1. *Summarize the direct and indirect effects achievable by use of the main tools of monetary policy.*

2. *What is meant by "defensive" open-market operations?*

3. *Compare the relative effectiveness of tight-money and easy-money policies.*

4. *Consider at some length why reliance solely upon a tight-money policy might not always be the best possible answer to any inflation.*

5. *Discuss the possible relations between monetary and fiscal policies.*

FIFTEEN

monetary reform

DISCUSSIONS OF MONETARY POLICY USUALLY RE-
fer to the actions of central banks in a given monetary and financial
structure; monetary reform usually refers to changes in that structure. Our present monetary and financial structure is the result of
many "reforms" over the years as well as of more gradual processes
of change that may be referred to as "evolution." Sometimes the evo-
lutionary changes have themselves so altered the character of our
monetary problems that they have themselves generated the need for
reforms. In any event, our economy has had problems in the monetary and financial sphere that could not have been dealt with satisfactorily except by changes in the structure of the system that are
entitled to be called "reforms."

There is no reason to expect that our system has today reached
the pinnacle of perfection, nor are we warranted in thinking that
future historical evolution of the system could not create new problems that might make further monetary reforms desirable. Indeed we

have just recently had the most extensive study of our monetary and financial structure since the establishment of the Federal Reserve; this study was undertaken by a privately organized group called the Commission on Money and Credit. Its published report runs to 282 pages, and the studies prepared for the Commission have been published in eighteen volumes. We will need to take a look at the extent of monetary reform called for by the Commission.

While we need to keep our minds open to the possibilities of useful reforms in the future or even the necessity for reforms we cannot now foresee, we need also to evaluate proposed reforms carefully. We need to make sure that they really do hold promise of effecting desired improvements and that they can do so without adverse side effects. Monetary reform is a field that has been populated with many crackpot schemes in the past, and will probably continue to sprout weeds as well as flowers. The trick is to be able to analyze the plants closely enough to be able to distinguish between them. Our problem may increase, instead of being solved, either by a bias against change or by too great a readiness to embrace anything that proposes improvement, whether or not its chances of delivering improvement are well founded.

Monetary reform proposals are of various types, differing according to what the proponent finds wrong or what objective he seeks to achieve as well as to the technique chosen to achieve it. It may be well to look at examples of several different sorts of reform proposals that have been important in the past, some of which may reappear.

monetary inflationists

One of the most persistent types of monetary reform proposal is that designed to inflate the money supply. The monetary inflationist is certain to raise his voice whenever there is a sharp decline in the price level and also in any serious depression with a substantial rise in unemployment. His diagnosis usually is that such conditions are the result of a decline in the money supply. In any case, the remedy is alleged to be an increase in the money supply. The historical record gives some basis for this view of the matter, for depressions often involved a contraction of bank credit, and, along with business failures, produced the phenomenon of "frozen credits" and loss of circular liquidity in the system. Many monetary schemes are not much more than devices to expand the money supply, although some have obvious advantages to special interests—for example, the silver-buying program launched by the Silver Purchase Act of 1934. Indeed, a number of arguments were made for the silver purchase program, but the heart of the matter seemed to be an effort to promote recovery from the depression by expanding the monetary base. The presumption was that this would mean an expansion in the money supply also. The act set as a goal a silver stock that would be one-fourth of the total monetary gold and silver stock. The silver interests subsequently benefited by the government's purchases at a good price. The Treasury issued silver certificates against the new silver to pay for it, thus temporarily increasing currency in circulation. But the public carries only such of its money supply in its pockets as it cares to. If paid additional currency, the public deposits it in banks, where it increases bank reserves. By 1934, when the act was passed, the money supply was not held down by the lack of bank reserves or by the lack of monetary stocks (gold and silver) in the hands of the United States Treasury. There were unused excess reserves of both, and the silver purchase program thus did not get at the reason why bank credit did not expand. As it turned out, it had international effects that were different from those its proponents sought. It helped force China off the silver standard, and it reduced the use of silver as a monetary metal by Mexico also. Instead of helping those countries, it created a problem of monetary stabilization for them. It is difficult to make an economic case today for United States silver policies since 1934 because in operation they did not cure the troubles that they allegedly would cure.[1] Interestingly enough, the market for silver has changed so much in recent years that the government now finds private interests buying its silver to such an extent that it is necessary to replace silver certificates with Federal Reserve notes and to reduce the silver content of coins lest they be melted down as the market value of the silver in them comes to exceed the face value of the coins.

There have been numerous other schemes to inflate the money supply; indeed, many a monetary reform seems to have an inflationary element in it. Whether there is danger of too much expansion of the money supply is something that must be ascertained in each given circumstance. It is, of course, true that in some circumstances an expansion of the money supply may be needed. However, in such cases it will likely be found that what is really important is that there be an increase in money flows. An increase in the stock of money

[1] For a fuller account of United States silver policies in this period see Ray B. Westerfield, *Money, Credit and Banking* (New York: Ronald, 1947), p. 816 ff.

may be brought about in ways that ensure an increase in the money-flow stream, while other measures might add to the stock of money but have little influence on the rate of money flow. If money income and real income are to rise, there must be an increase in spending, that is, an increase in buying, someplace in the economy, not offset elsewhere. Schemes that are well designed to induce such money flows are apt to have more merit than those that simply increase the money stock. At the present time it is not necessary to devise new monetary schemes or devices to expand the money stock or to expand spending when such a result is desired. The Federal Reserve can, if it wishes, always expand the money supply by buying government securities from the public and giving them dollars in return. But these may remain as idle deposits in the sellers' hands in some circumstances. Spending is more certain to be increased in general by increasing people's income directly rather than by merely increasing the public's liquidity by the difference between government securities and bank deposits. Experience has provided ample evidence that an increase in the flow of income to people increases their spending substantially. This is why government fiscal policy can readily be more potent than monetary policy.

In the past there was inadequate realization of the potential of modern monetary and fiscal techniques to increase the rate of spending by the public. Consequently, various schemes were proposed to try to stimulate spending when it was felt there was a need for such action. Not every method of trying to induce an increase in the flow of money had merit. In the 1930's various proposals were made to reduce hoarding of money. Some of the hoarding was a direct result of bank failures and the resultant fear of the unsoundness of banks. People took their money out of banks and simply held onto it. This made the situation worse. The banks were put under serious pressure by such tactics, and the deflationary pressure on the economy worsened the depression.

Some of the schemes proposed to correct hoarding in the past involve some form of tax upon money to be paid periodically (for example, each month). This makes it more costly to hold money for longer than for shorter periods of time and presumably would induce people to spend rather than hoard. Schemes of this type create problems of their own. For example, if spending is to be stimulated, allowing deposits to remain idle in a bank would require correction as well as allowing currency to remain idle. Indeed the purchase of money substitutes instead of goods and services might lower bank holdings of such assets and reduce the money supply, thus partially offsetting the desired result. The mechanical problems of taxing different forms of money are enough to give one pause, even if taxation could improve people's handling of their income. In addition, if it can be shown that such taxes induce people to handle their own finances in a way that in some respects is detrimental to them, then a better way of accomplishing the social objectives needs to be sought.[2] The guarantee of bank deposits undoubtedly did much to reduce the tendency to withdraw money from the bank and hold it in currency form. And if people judge that they need to be more liquid at times, making it possible for the system to be liquid enough may be preferable to penalizing liquidity by taxing it. To get people to spend more, modern fiscal policy expands the stream of disposable income. This is done either by reducing taxes or by increasing government expenditures, in either case the deficit is covered by new money creation (usually indirectly through open-market purchases by the central bank). A beneficial increase in spending is produced much more simply by thus increasing disposable income than by a direct penalty for hoarding. The point to be stressed is that when there is a need, a variety of schemes come forth purporting to meet the need. The questions to be asked of these proposals are "Will a proposed scheme do the job at all?" and "Is there a better way of doing it?"

reserves as stabilizers

Various schemes have been developed from time to time to provide improved stability for the economy. Some people have thought, for example, that a better way could be found to stabilize the value of the dollar. They have suggested tying it to a different type of reserve. Commodity reserve schemes used to be widely discussed. The essence of these is that the government, instead of buying and selling gold at a fixed price, as on a gold standard, would buy and sell a group of commodities in fixed proportions. This preselected bundle of commodities (in fixed proportions) would constitute the monetary

[2] A brief but sophisticated analysis of several schemes to tax hoarding is given by Albert Gailord Hart, *Money, Debt and Economic Activity*, 2nd ed. (Englewood Cliffs, N.J.: Prentice-Hall, 1953), Chapter 26.

The same chapter gives a good review and evaluation of a number of other monetary reform schemes.

reserve. The commodities selected for the purpose would have to be storable, and the government would have to have a considerable stock-pile of the bundles of commodities on hand the first time it tried to deal with inflation. The stabilizing effect of such a commodity reserve would come from the government selling bundles of the reserve in inflation and buying such bundles during deflation. Presumably there would be some spread between buying and selling prices so that the government operations would not have to be continuous. They would come into play only if a persistent price-level movement was felt. Inflation, if too persistent, is more apt to wreck such a scheme than deflation, for the size of the reserve and hence the amount at which the government can hold down the price of the bundle of reserve commodities by selling from the reserve will always be limited. Their relative cheapness during inflation will indeed move demand toward them and accelerate the drain on government re serves.[3] There is no such limit to the amount that the government may buy during deflation; the cost is met by the issuance of currency against the reserves acquired. To hold a floor under one set of prices may result in other prices falling less, as claimed for this scheme, especially since purchase of reserve bundles also helps maintain the incomes of their sellers. But unlike downward rigidity of wage rates, which exerts a general, if not exactly uniform, effect throughout all lines of production, keeping one set of prices rigid while deflationary pressure against the rest continue may produce serious price maladjustments and thus add further complications rather than effectively offsetting the deflation. This scheme, like many others, tries to cure the disease by treating the symptoms—price fluctuations. If changes in income and expenditure flows were dealt with directly, and in a manner that did not create maladjustment of relative prices, the only reason for concern with monetary reserves or the money supply itself would be to make sure that monetary reserves were not insufficient to finance the policy adequately. This is ultimately a matter of using central bank credit, unhampered by illogical minimum reserve ratio requirements upon the central bank itself.

Another monetary reform proposal, which has been advocated by a number of prominent economists, would deal not with the nation's monetary reserve stock but with the reserve required of commercial banks. It aims not to cure directly any ills arising outside the monetary system but to prevent the banking system from itself causing or aggravating our economic instability. This is often re-

[3] Hart, *op. cit.*, p. 445.

ferred to as "100 percent money," but it might more accurately be called "100 percent banking" for the proposal is simply to eliminate our fractional reserve banking system and require banks to hold 100 percent reserve behind demand deposits. Its proponents claim that the ups and downs of our economy have been aggravated by the "perverse elasticity of credit." This stems, in turn, from the ability of the banking system to expand credit by a multiple of new reserves in a boom, and from the necessity of contracting by such a multiple when liquidity needs rise during a depression. Both overexpansion and overcontraction can be eliminated by the 100 percent reserve proposal.

Although this proposal has usually been treated by its critics as unworkable, or destructive of private banking, it is nothing of the kind. Of course, it should not be inaugurated simply by raising the reserve requirements from present levels to 100 percent, leaving the banking system to fend for itself in the effort to meet the new requirements. Under those circumstances it could only contract its credit very sharply, and this probably would wreck the banking system as well as give the economy a depression. The economists who have proposed 100 percent reserves certainly were not proposing this, however they may have differed in the precise nature of what they proposed. Disregarding differences among proponents, we may visualize one way in which the reform might work out. When the reserve requirement was increased, the Federal Reserve could simply lend or give the banks enough additional reserves to enable them to meet the requirement at once, without any contraction. To be sure, thereafter the 100 percent requirement would apply to all new demand deposits; consequently, attracting new demand deposit accounts would not enable banks to expand their earning assets. Notice, however, that bank earnings would not be reduced by the introduction of the higher requirement. Banks could relend or reinvest as loans and investments fell due. Banks could no longer change the money supply in the manner that they now do, but the allocation of loanable funds would remain a function of private banking. Banks would be more like other financial intermediaries then and would depend upon attracting savings through raising more capital or otherwise in order to increase their earning assets. The money supply need not remain fixed under the system, for the Federal Reserve could then determine exactly how much money creation would take place. It could still use open-market purchases to create money, though in this case the banks would have no role. Or it could lend reserves to the banks, or perhaps pay them "interest" at a certain percentage of their reserves, which the banks could then invest in earning assets. To take care of the need for slow growth in the money stock, the idea of having the Federal Reserve pay interest on the bank reserves it holds has merit in the framework of a 100 percent reserve scheme. Bank earnings would then grow and not be frozen at existent levels.

The scheme is then quite workable and would increase effectiveness of the Federal Reserve's control of the money supply. It would avoid the bank failures attendant upon the banks being caught in the middle in a liquidity crisis. But, it does not follow that it is the easiest or best way to accomplish the objectives. Although modern banks evolved from the operations of the London goldsmiths, initially a safekeeping operation and only slowly developing into a fractional reserve operation, it would be a rather large change to return now to 100 percent reserves. It may not be necessary to change things so radically if the Federal Reserve will use its present powers more vigorously. It appears that the Federal Reserve today can put the brakes sufficiently on credit expansion if it chooses to do so. It can certainly provide abundant reserves to deal with a liquidity crisis if we do away with the anomalous reserve requirement on the Federal Reserve itself. The FDIC has already reduced the magnitude of the problem compared to that at which the 100 percent scheme was first directed.

Where we need to rethink the reserve problem then is at the central bank level. The recent balance-of-payments difficulties have induced some rethinking here, although it was not until the excess gold reserves were quite low that Congress acted to remove the reserve requirement behind the deposit liabilities of the Federal Reserve. There is no real basis for distinction between the treatment of deposit liabilities and note liabilities, however; and, both for domestic and international purposes, the minimum ratio requirement can do no good and at times can hamper desirable policies.

rules versus authorities

While the above reforms have been suggested as ways of giving the monetary authorities more control, there are reformers who would strip the authorities of much of their present power. The concept of an automatic system still lures them, and they think they can design one that will make fewer mistakes than will men who are free to use their discretion since human judgment is inherently fallible. It might be thought that it would require almost superhuman foresight to anticipate all possible situations and to design in advance a system that would meet all situations better than men could when they were actually in the situations and able to get a fuller view of the situations and take everything into account. But the contemporary proponents of removing discretionary powers from the hands of monetary authorities contend that the solution is the essence of simplicity. Merely require the monetary authorities to expand the money supply by a fixed percentage (3 or 4 percent) a year, they say. While the result may not be ideal, they allege it will be better than the record that monetary authorities have compiled in the past. We have given, in this volume, some reasons to think that the record up until 1952 in this country was not as good as it could have been if the problem had been conceived as it is now by modern central banking. So a claim for superiority over much of the past record is a very weak claim indeed, and essentially irrelevant. Since the United States has barely started in the development of an adequately conceived monetary policy, the record of its infancy is not to be expected to provide the best forecast of its record in the future. More to the point than a historical comparison is an analysis of the reasons for expecting the inherent difficulties of discretionary monetary policy to hamper it more than an arbitrary and rigid rule about the rate of expansion of the money supply. Will the lag between changes in the economic situation and recognition of these changes, plus the lag between recognition and action, plus the lag between action and its effects on the economy generally, be of such magnitude that the effects will come at inappropriate times and aggravate rather than offset the conditions that the authorities aimed to cure?

This sort of question, to which no definitive answer can yet be given, is crucial in evaluating the reform under discussion. It should be noticed, however, that the proposal does not eliminate all use of judgment by the authorities. It eliminates only judgment as to what the monetary expansion goal should be. Given the changing monetary environment, the authorities must in any case constantly estimate the degree of effort that they need to make. That is, they must estimate the volume of reserves that they need to supply or withdraw from the market in order to offset the other forces at work so that the net result will be the required or desired percentage change in the money supply. The best that they can be expected to do is to hover around the target so that the average for a period looks pretty good. The rule being discussed would also require that, if by mistakes or biases the money growth is more rapid than it is supposed to be over a period, the authorities must subsequently err in the other direction equally if they can. It is not clear that this will be better than aiming always toward the target rate without correcting the average. Nor is it obvious that the goals of modern monetary policy can be achieved better by any constant money growth guide than by a more complex set of considerations that allows for varying the rate of monetary expansion. This reform shares with the monetary inflationist schemes the assumption that a direct attack on the quantity of money is the best way to make the economy behave the way that we want it to. Clearly, the money supply cannot be ignored, but perhaps the role of the monetary factor is not so much that of a leading character as this suggests. Perhaps the important thing is to see to it that we design more basic policies to deal with our economic ills and to achieve our economic goals and to see to it that the monetary factors do not complicate the problems on their own. They should be handled in such a way as to facilitate the execution of the more basic economic policies.

other big or little changes

Banking is a business, and the men interested in the business are properly concerned with the opportunities in the field and with the framework of governmental supervision. The structure of our banking system, has been and still is the subject of animated debates within the banking community. Because our system has evolved from a federally chartered system added to a system chartered by the several states, there is substantial lack of uniformity in requirements for banks. It was thought that the establishment of the Federal Reserve would result in all banks joining the System; instead many of the state banks (some large, but mostly relatively small) remained outside. These nonmember banks enjoy some of the benefits of the Federal Reserve System by correspondent relationships with member banks. They also reap other benefits just from the general effects of the Federal Reserve on the economy. From time to time it is suggested that our dual banking system be replaced by a unified system. Nothing is more certain than such a proposal to unite the state bankers and their supporters to defend their position. There are several issues here. One concerns whether monetary policy is seriously hampered by the existence of diverse requirements on banks in different jurisdictions. It is not clear in this connection what further pressures the Federal Reserve could and would properly put upon member banks if the latter did not have the option of withdrawing from the System. Of course, open-market operations are not confined in their effect on member banks; all banks are affected. The power to change reserve requirements applies only to member banks, however, and its use may be affected some by the generally lower reserve requirements for nonmember banks.

It has long been obvious to students of money and banking that our system of many independent banks has necessarily been more vulnerable than a system of branch banking would have been. Some bankers have wanted to have the opportunity to do more branching than the laws have thus far permitted, but they have been effectively opposed by other bankers. It appears that the amount of branching permitted will continue to be a subject of heated debate. Since the soundness of the system does not now require branching, the debate centers around other issues.

The report of the privately sponsored Commission on Money and Credit in 1961 was something of a disappointment to those who expected that a far-reaching study of our monetary and financial structure and policies would result in proposals for substantial reforms in the system. The commission's report covers 282 pages. In addition to monetary policy in the narrow sense of central bank policy, it examines the public debt, fiscal policy, federal credit programs, the private financial institutions, international monetary relations, and the coordination of policies with respect to all of these. The report embodies a description of the monetary and credit side of the economy, summarizes current thinking with respect to numerous issues, and includes throughout recommendations on numerous specific aspects of policy. The title of the report itself suggests the orientation of the commission: *Money and Credit, Their Influence on Jobs, Prices, and Growth.* In all this there are no proposals for monetary reforms comparable in nature to those discussed previously in this chapter. There are no recommendations to alter very substantially any aspect of our monetary and financial structure. The reader of the report may ask himself whether this is due to the conservative nature of the commission, or to its finding that no problems are serious enough to call for more radical remedies, or to its finding that no "radical" remedies for our problems can pass the necessary tests. It is not clear whether the commission did or did not confine its inquiry to minor tinkering within the existing structure. There are some instances where specific changes in the handling of some matters were considered and rejected. For example, the commission considered and rejected the proposal to extend direct Federal Reserve controls to the nonbank financial institutions. The commission admitted it was unable to resolve the division among its own members over the desirability of giving the Federal Reserve, on a standby basis, the power to regulate consumer credit in peacetime as it did in wartime.

Perhaps the most far-reaching recommendation of the commission within the area of central bank powers, structure, and policy was the recommendation to require federally insured banks to become members of the Federal Reserve System. The report discussed briefly the alternatives, then made this recommendation, with no indication of why this solution of the problem was considered superior to the alternatives. The report itself does not go into the question of whether this requirement might result in fewer insured banks rather than more member banks. Nor does it probe why it would not be preferable, as one member suggested, to require all commercial banks to be members. An adequate explanation of the reasons for making the choices involved in the recommendations is too often lacking in the report. Nonetheless, it provides a significant set of recommendations to improve, through a number of minor changes, the operation of our monetary and financial system. It constitutes by and large a vote of confidence in our ability to manage the present system well.

We have come to the end of our task now. We have examined the fundamental features of our money and banking system. We have seen how they developed and how they operate. Such an understanding of the essentials is basic to any further study in the area and will enable us to judge better the claims and counter-claims made in debates over monetary issues that seem to be a permanent feature of the American political landscape.

questions

1. *Cite various popular movements that had an inflationist element in them with which you are familiar from the study of American history.*

2. *How do the proponents of "100 percent money" answer the usual arguments against them?*

3. *Summarize the arguments for and against "discretionary monetary policy."*

4. *Are the bankers in your community all in agreement with respect to the "dual banking" and "branch banking" issues?*

5. *In what respects, if any, do you now think, with this brief introduction to money and banking, that our monetary and financial structure might be capable of further improvement?*

index